The
Internationalisation of Capital Markets

and the
Regulatory Response

The
Internationalisation
of Capital Markets
and the
Regulatory Response

edited by
John Fingleton
Department of Economics
Trinity College

assisted by
Dirk Schoenmaker
Financial Markets Group
London School of Economics

Graham & Trotman
A member of Wolters Kluwer Academic Publishers
LONDON/DORDRECHT/BOSTON

Graham & Trotman Limited
Sterling House
66 Wilton Road
London SW1V 1DE
UK

Kluwer Academic Publishers Group
101 Philip Drive
Assinippi Park
Norwell, MA 02061
USA

ISBN 1 85333 767 6
© Graham & Trotman Ltd, 1992

British Library and Library of Congress Cataloguing-in-Publication Data is available upon request.
First published 1992

Computer typeset in Times by Tradespools Ltd., Frome, Somerset
Printed and bound in Great Britain by Hartnolls Ltd, Bodmin, Cornwall

The Financial Markets Group

The LSE Financial Markets Group was launched in January 1987. Its principal objective is to pursue basic theoretical and empirical research into the functioning of financial markets and their interaction with the real economy. The Group also has a keen interest in the regulation of these markets.

Professors Charles Goodhart and Mervyn King co-directed the original Group, and day to day management is handled by Professor David Webb. The members of the Group are drawn from staff and graduate students of the LSE Economics Department, together with associates from related departments. Great importance is placed on interaction with visitors from universities in the United States, Europe and elsewhere, of whom there is a regular flow carrying out joint research and providing stimulus to the intellectual life of the Group.

The Group's research spans a broad range of subjects including volatility of stock and foreign exchange markets, the micro structure and regulation of these markets, financial aspects of growth and fluctuations, and a growing interest in the structure of corporate finance and the market for corporate control. In each of these areas new problems worthy of academic attention are constantly being generated, but long-standing questions remain the subject of academic debate and need to be answered. Quality research into these questions is, for both intellectual and practical policy reasons, of fundamental importance.

The work of the Group is supported by donations from a number of British, European, American and Japanese institutions. The Economic and Social Research Council (ESRC) funds, as part of its Functioning of Markets Initiative, a major research project on the efficiency and regulation of financial markets. The Suntory-Toyota International Centre for Economic and Related Disciplines (STICERD) provides additional funding for several seminars.

The research output of the Group is published in the Discussion Paper Series, which is generally technical in nature. The Group also publishes Special Papers which deal with more topical matters. Both series illustrate the breadth of the Group's interests. In addition to its papers, from time to time the Group produces books which are of topical interest. The opinions expressed in this volume are those of the authors and not necessarily those of the Financial Markets Group or the institutions with which the authors are associated.

Steering Committee

Chairman: Sir David Walker,
Securities and Investments Board

Dr. John Ashworth
LSE

Mr. Michael von Brentano
Deutsche Bank

Mr. Paul Collins
Citibank

Mr. John Flemming
EBRD

Professor Charles Goodhart
LSE

Mr. Walter A. Gubert
J P Morgan

Professor Mervyn King
Bank of England

Mr. John Lake
Deutsche Bank Capital Markets

Mr. Ewen Macpherson
3*i*

Mr. Charles McVeigh III
Salomon Brothers

Mr. Tomonori Naruse
Bank of Tokyo

Mr. Robert Norbury
County NatWest

Dr. Andreas Prindl
Nomura Bank International

Sir Adam Ridley
Hambros

Mr. Miles Rivett-Carnac
Barings

Mr. Hans-Joerg Rudloff
Credit Suisse First Boston

Mr. John Trueman
S.G. Warburg

Financial Markets Group
London School of Economics and Political Science
Houghton Street, London, WC2A 2AE
Tel: 071-955 7002 Fax: 071-242 1006

Foreword

J. A. Fingleton

Twenty years ago, almost all activity on capital markets was domestic, and regulation was extremely restrictive and differed widely across national boundaries. In general, different activities such as banking and securities trading were clearly separate, the range of available financial instruments was relatively narrow, and many markets did not exist. Today the picture is vastly different. A relatively high proportion of all trades is cross-border. Domestic traders have gained access to products in other countries and new products have been developed within many countries so that the total range of products and markets available has escalated considerably (for example, trade in futures). At the same time, the long-standing distinction between banking and securities activities has been blurred. In the face of these and other developments, regulators have responded both by changing national regulation (often with the result of increasing internationalisation) and by increased international coordination of regulation.

As a result, one of the major issues facing regulators is the optimal response to the process of internationalisation. For instance, how are the objectives of regulators different in an international context than in the national case? What type of regulations will best achieve these objectives? How are such regulations to be achieved in practice? Is there a trade-off between the promotion of the financial services industry in one's own country and the coordination of regulation at the international level? Will competition between national regulators lead to an excess of laxity?

Ideally, the responses to these and similar questions should be based to some extent on rigorous analysis of the issues. Academics, in particular, have a role to play in (a) setting out a conceptual framework for the analysis of policy issues, (b) introducing recent theoretical developments to regulators and suggesting how these might be relevant, and (c) in performing empirical analysis on the (likely) effects of regulation or its absence. This volume acts as a conduit through which recent academic developments may be presented to the regulatory profession in particular, and to the financial services industry more generally. It is hoped that this communication will be two-way — that academics may learn about the major issues facing practitioners, and direct their research accordingly. Thus this volume includes contributions from both leading regulatory practitioners and distinguished academics working in the field.

The book is divided into five parts. Part I, the introduction, consists of contributions from two of the leading players in the international regulatory field, Sir David Walker of the UK Securities and Investments Board and Richard Breeden of the US Securities and Exchange Commission. Both consider the principle issues which regulators face as a result of the internationalisation of capital markets. Walker outlines those considerations which are germane to the analysis of issues such as the determination of the responsibility for authorisation across countries and the appropriate regulation of cross-border trading systems. Breeden reminds us of practical constraints: complete harmonisation is impossible due to fundamental difference in markets across countries; the complexity of the problems suggests that solutions will be complex. Both authors stress the important role to be played by academics in analysing these issues and assessing alternative potential solutions.

Part II is devoted to conceptual issues in the regulation of international banking. Sydney Key and Hal Scott propose the 'banking matrix', a framework for analysing the principles which should govern the regulation of international banking. They argue that careful consideration of the nature of each type of international relationship (e.g., cross-border, branch, or subsidiary) leads to different recommendations regarding the type of rules (e.g., home-country, host-country, or harmonised) which are appropriate. In addition, they assess various international fora such as the GATT and the BIS in terms of their suitability for implementing the regulation proposed. The second paper in this section, by Joseph Bisignano, investigates the consequences for international regulation of the differences in the structure of banking across countries, with particular emphasis on the mix between markets and institutional intermediation. In the process, he provides a very thorough review of recent relevant developments in economic theory and cites supporting evidence from a wide variety of countries. Bisignano argues that Central Banks should be involved in an increasing range of activities as a response to the movement of banking business to the non-bank sector in recent years. This section concludes with a discussion of both papers by Charles Goodhart.

Part III is broadly concerned with regulation as it operates in practice. First, Richard Dale investigates the securities activities of banks. He highlights the dichotomy between the widespread acceptance of banks involving themselves in securities activities on the one hand and the absence, on the other hand, of any widespread consensus about how this should be regulated. Various alternative policy choices are discussed in detail, including statutory separation, universal banking, risk segregation through firewalls, and narrow banks. In addition, a comprehensive survey of national practice is provided. Dale concludes that the increase in banks' securities activities at an international level requires a careful analysis of whether and how risks should be segregated and what should be the role of the lender of last resort. The second paper by Doreen McBarnet and Christopher Whelan focuses on how the reaction of the regulated players may be creative — that is, compliance with regulation in form but not in substance. Such 'creative compliance' renders regulation the raw material for the creation of competitive advantage by firms. They propose that regulation should concentrate more on flexible principles rather than on highly specific rules as they often do at present. Anthony Hopwood discusses the implications of the arguments in both papers for the practice of regulation.

In the first paper of Part IV, Stephen Schaefer argues that the theory of finance has important implications for the design of regulation. Specifically, he outlines and considers the rationale for capital adequacy regulation, and devotes particular attention to the manner in which risk is assessed for this purpose. Portfolio theory, which is now widely understood and accepted, offers a theoretically appealing and feasible approach to the assessment of risk. Yet, the BIS has recently instituted a linear risk-weighted system which Schaefer suggests is part of an '*ad-hoc* approach' to capital market regulation and is inferior to one founded in rigorous analysis. Schaefer argues that, as a result, regulators themselves do not follow the 'best practice', and that, in consequence, more accidents are likely. The second paper by Ailsa Röell analyses the detailed nature of competition between securities markets by considering the London and French markets in French equities. The Paris Market is seen to be more liquid for smaller transactions and the London market more liquid for larger ones. Thus, different market organisations may give rise to market segmentation. One possible implication of this is that regulatory differences across countries which affect the organisation of the market may lead to market segmentation across countries rather than to excessive competition between exchanges. The paper also has implications for the optimal design of certain regulations governing trading rules (e.g. transparency, which is now a contentious policy issue). This section concludes with a detailed discussion of this paper by Joel Hasbrouck.

In Part V, Caroline Bradley examines competition between investment exchanges and how this will be affected by increased harmonisation of international regulation — thereby focusing attention on the effect of the regulatory response. Bradley argues that international regulation should permit the efficiency gains which accompany the increased competition made possible by technological and other factors underlying internationalisation, while at the same time ensuring that excessive competition does not reduce the protection of investors unduly. Bradley points out that the national interests of regulators may not be consistent with achieving this objective so that international regulatory coordination may not have the effect of protecting investors. In the second paper George Benston also questions whether investor protection is enhanced by international regulation. He considers how the standard arguments for regulation in an international context differ from those in a national context. Benston suggests that international regulatory coordination has a role in dealing with (a) the safety and soundness of branches of foreign banks, (b) tax avoidance/evasion by banks, and (c) illegal activities, but not in any other area. So, for example he argues that there is no role for coordination to prevent systemic collapse, to protect the payments system collapse, or to increase consumer welfare. The discussion by Alfred Steinherr focuses on Benston's paper and suggests that market imperfections may provide theoretical support for regulatory intervention at both a national and an international level.

Dublin, June 1992

Authors

George J. Benston   John H. Harland Professor of Finance, Accounting and Economics, Emory University, Atlanta

Joseph Bisignano   Economist, Bank for International Settlements, Basle

Caroline Bradley   Lecturer in Law, London School of Economics

Richard C. Breeden   Chairman, Securities and Exchange Commission, USA

Richard Dale   Coopers Deloitte Professor of International Banking and Financial Institutions, Southampton University

Charles A.E. Goodhart   Norman Sosnow Professor of Economics, London School of Economics; Member of the LSE Financial Markets Group

Joel Hasbrouck   Associate Professor of Finance, Stern School, New York University; Visiting Research Economist, New York Stock Exchange

Anthony G. Hopwood   Ernst and Young Professor of International Accounting and Financial Management, London School of Economics

Sydney J. Key   Economist, Division of International Finance, Board of Governors of the Federal Reserve System, Washington DC

Doreen McBarnet   Senior Research Fellow in Sociology, Centre for Socio-Legal Studies, University of Oxford

Ailsa Röell   Lecturer in Economics, London School of Economics; Member of the LSE Financial Markets Group

Stephen M. Schaefer   Esmée Fairbairn Professor of Finance, London Business School; Director, Institute of Finance and Accounting

Hal S. Scott   Nomura Professor of International Financial Systems, Harvard Law School

Alfred Steinherr   Head of Financial Research Department, European Investment Bank, Luxembourg

Sir David Walker   Chairman, Securities and Investments Board, UK

Christopher Whelan   Senior Lecturer, School of Law, University of Warwick

Contents

List of Tables

List of Figures

Chapter Eight

List of Abbreviations

AFBD	Association of Futures Brokers and Dealers
AIBD	Association of International Bond Dealers
BCCI	Bank of Credit and Commerce International
BIS	Bank for International Settlements
CAC	Cotation Assistée en Continu
CHIPS	Clearing House Interbank Payment System
DTI	Department of Trade and Industry
EAF	Elektronische Abrechnung mit Filetransfer
EC	European Community
EEIG	European Economic Interest Grouping
FHC	Financial Holding Company
FSA	Financial Services Act
FSHC	Financial Services Holding Company
GAAP	General Accepted Accounting Principles
GATT	General Agreement on Tariffs and Trade
GEMM	Gilt Edged Market Maker
IASC	International Accounting Standards Committee
IOSCO	International Organisation of Securities Commissions
LIFFE	London International Financial Futures Exchange
LTOM	London Traded Options Market
MOU	Memorandum Of Understanding
NASDAQ	National Association of Securities Dealers Automated Quotations
NMS	Normal Market Size
OBSF	Off-Balance Sheet Financing
OECD	Organisation for Economic Co-operation and Development
PLOE	Public Limit Order Exposure
SBTS	Screen-Based Trading Systems
SEAQ	Stock Exchange Automated Quotations
SEC	Securities and Exchange Commission
SEM	Single European Market
SFA	Securities and Futures Authority
SIB	Securities and Investments Board
TSA	The Securities Association
UCITS	Undertakings for Collective Investment in Transferable Securities

Acknowledgements

The papers contained in this volume are based on those presented at a conference on *The Internationalisation of Capital Markets and the Regulatory Response*, held at the Barbican Centre, London on November 8th, 1991. The conference was organised by the Financial Markets Group at the London School of Economics as part of a major ongoing research project on the efficiency and regulation of financial markets. Financial support for this project from the ESRC is gratefully acknowledged.

The conference, and this collection of proceedings, owe much to the efforts of a number of people. Alison Brower, Charles Goodhart, Dirk Schoenmaker, and David Webb were closely involved in the organisation and running of the conference, while Caroline Bradley, Anthony Hopwood and David Walker provided invaluable advice and assistance at many stages of the venture. I should also like to thank Peter Cooke, Mervyn King and Charles Goodhart for chairing the sessions of the conference, and all of the contributors for their cooperation at every stage.

Dirk Schoenmaker and Alison Brower deserve special mention for the huge amount of time and effort they devoted to the administrative and other aspects of the conference and for their work on this publication. I should like to express my gratitude to them both.

Finally, I should like to acknowledge the permission of The Group of Thirty to include Sydney Key's and Hal Scott's paper which was presented by Sydney Key at the conference. The joint paper of Doreen McBarnet and Christopher Whelan was presented by Doreen McBarnet.

J.A. Fingleton

Part I

Introduction

Chapter One

Major Issues Relevant for Regulatory Response to the Internationalisation of Capital Markets

SIR DAVID WALKER

My approach to regulatory issues is predicated on the view that the process of internationalisation, in which national barriers are transcended by technology, competition and unrestricted capital flows, is basically healthy. This is because it promotes the allocation of capital by competitive merit, through the intermediation of markets and firms that are the most efficient, and provides effective means for managing risk.

The risk of the regulator in an international centre is to find ways of accommodating the process of internationalisation while ensuring proper protections for depositors and investors; minimising systemic risk; and achieving as level as possible a regulatory playing field so that regulatory considerations do not obtrude unduly in decision-taking about the geographical location and corporate structure for the transaction of financial service business.

Whatever degree of regulation is regarded as appropriate — and there is plainly scope for difference here — the achievement of these objectives calls for international co-operation in regulation to match the internationalisation of business itself. Of course, this process tends to start with understandings among regulators to co-operate in investigating wrongdoing (for which the possibilities are, also, increased by internationalisation) and catching wrong-doers. But important as such understandings are, I do not propose to discuss them further here: the need is obvious, and with the publication of the International Organisation of Securities Commissions (IOSCO) principles, I expect that such bilateral MOUs (memoranda of understanding) will come to take an increasingly standard form. Nor do I propose to touch here on improved mechanisms for clearing and settlement: the need for them, though very great, has an obviousness that does not apply to other issues.

There is, by contrast, scope for much greater debate about appropriate regulatory approaches to a whole array of issues relevant for the normal conduct and regulatory oversight of international financial service business. In these introductory remarks, I want to list some major issues on which regulators are currently more or less engaged, and in most of which there is an important need for analytical input. Let me identify five broad categories:

(a) *Allocation of responsibility* for authorisation prudential supervision and for conduct of business regulation in respect of international groups;

(b) *Harmonisation* of capital and other regulatory standards;

(c) *Methods of supervision* of international financial service groups;

(d) *Appropriate regulation of cross border trading systems*;

(e) Concerns about *international market linkages*.

My remarks on each of these will necessarily be brief, but I hope that they will whet appetites for the more substantive treatment that is given to many of them in the following chapters.

Allocation of responsibility

The UK has developed a system of bilateral understandings under which we have authorised overseas institutions with a UK branch to carry on investment business, provided we can rely on the financial supervision of the institution's home state supervisor and provided that supervisor enters into an information sharing agreement with us. For the rest, we have insisted on subsidiarisation. This is fully consistent with the Bank of England's reliance on home state financial supervision of overseas banks with UK branches and with the EC approach to the passport and, I believe, sets a model for a *mutual recognition* approach on a global basis.

But note that, in the securities area at least, we have a long way to go. Many countries, in practice if not formally, require subsidiarisation from the outset. It is significant that while the EC is moving substantially in the mutual recognition direction, via the passport, neither the USA nor Japan has yet been ready to do so. I should add that the mutual recognition approach which we so strongly favour, and is an early prospect in the EC, leaves responsibility for regulation of the conduct of business to the host country. I will touch in a moment on the need for harmonisation in capital requirements, but I see no comparable need for harmonisation of local conduct of business requirements — save perhaps in a few key areas like the segregation of client monies.

I should add in this context that it has been the conduct of their business rather than capital deficiency that originally posed such difficulty for international financial service groups — such as the Japanese securities houses, Salomons and BCCI — in the past 6 months.

Harmonisation of capital requirements

Much work is in train: the objects are to establish broadly common pruden-tial standards for similar business done by securities firms and as between securities firms and banks. These are two particular points to be noted.

First, because securities regulators require daily marking to market, and because market prices reflect the credit risk of issuers and general market risks in a comprehensive way, securities regulators approach capital require-ments on the basis of a comprehensive approach to risk. Bank supervisors in contrast focus on credit risk and other risks in a more specific or disaggregated way. So the first hurdle to be overcome is whether a practical means can be found of achieving reasonable convergence between the build-ing block approach of bank supervisors and the comprehensive approach used by securities regulators.

Second, it is important to be clear that the principles governing the prudential regulation of banks and securities firms are quite different. Traditionally, a bank balance sheet incorporates relatively long-term and unmarketable assets, which is why bank supervisors place such emphasis on sufficient long-term or permanent capital. By contrast, securities-trading businesses hold assets that are highly realisable and whose market value fluctuates, hence the insistence of securities regulators on tough net liquid assets requirements and regular marking to market as well as their readiness to allow short-term subordinated debt to serve as capital. I emphasise this fundamental difference because it is essential for regulators to continue to assign the highest priority to prudence, with concerns about competitive equality necessarily taking second place.

Let me give a specific example. There is a concern on the part of some bank supervisors that for a securities firm to draw capital from an unregu-lated group (or non-group) source effectively involves double leverage since there is no regulator to haircut the balance sheet of the source of the capital. This has led to some suggestion that the access of securities firms to capital from unregulated sources should be rationed. But such a restriction would check the amount of external capital that is available to the securities indus-try, hardly an acceptable proposition for any securities regulator concerned with adequate prudential standards. And there is an at least equally strong argument in the opposite direction, some would say much stronger, that banks have a significant advantage by virtue of their ability to use insured deposits in the funding of their securities business, a lower cost of capital than securities firms by virtue of their access to central banks for liquidity support, and access to wholesale funds at a finer rate than non-banks.

Methods of supervision

The debate centres on the problems that financial institutions, whether banks, securities or futures firms, depend to some degree on short-term market funding and on the need for trading counterparties, and are vulnerable to the risk of contagion from problems in one part of the group to others. Regulators thus need to be aware of developments in the wider group to which the regulated entity belongs and to assess, on a continuing basis, the risks that other parts of the group may pose. All this arises domestically and is addressed within the UK by the so-called college arrangements among regulators under which information is shared about regulated entities and the risks being carried in unregulated entities.

But the problems are of course similar in kind internationally, and regulators then have to fit together a cross-border jigsaw.

It is extremely difficult for any one regulator to assess adequately the risk of an international group, particularly when most of its operations are conducted in other jurisdictions and may include financial or other activities away from the mainstream of one regulator's competence. The question is whether the supervision should be done on a 'DIY' basis, at one end of the spectrum, or, at the other end, in a way that involves collegial arrangements for regular non-crisis and preventive medicine information-sharing among regulators? In my view, the task ahead for regulators is to develop effective channels internationally and for cooperation that enhances supervision without unnecessarily increasing the regulatory burden on financial institutions. To achieve the second will require the development of much greater mutual confidence than currently exists.

Appropriate regulation of trading systems

Among the more important criteria for assessment of the quality of a market or exchange are liquidity and transparency. But the demands of liquidity and transparency do not always point in the same direction, and different countries have resolved what may in practice be a trade-off between liquidity and transparency in different ways, as well as the balance between the interest of professional and retail investors.

Advances in technology have made the internationalisation of capital markets possible. But they have also brought into being Screen-Based Trading Systems which perform many of the same functions as stock exchanges and so compete directly with them. Such systems have customers, not members, and do not take on the regulatory role that stock exchanges have traditionally fulfilled. At one level, the development of Screen-Based Trading Systems (SBTS) introduces a welcome element of competition where stock exchanges have hitherto enjoyed a monopoly position. But such systems also pose regulatory challenges. Who should regulate them, particularly when they operate cross-border, and what is the appropriate form of regulation? If stock exchanges are in direct competition with operators which are not burdened with regulatory responsibilities, should they be relieved of these obligations to allow them to compete freely? And if so, are the regulators of market intermediaries equipped to take on this aspect of the conduct of business regulation?

However, the internationalisation of equity markets means that individual markets no longer operate in isolation and that the trading structure in one market has implications for other markets in terms of encouraging or discouraging the flow of business from one market to another. The answer does not necessarily lie in the development of identical trading structures, because these properly reflect cultural and historical factors and the different clientele that local markets serve. But over time there will need to be a greater meeting of minds as to what characteristics are essential for a fair and efficient market and how these characteristics interrelate, particularly where there may appear to be some mutual incompatibility between them, as is the case, to some degree, with transparency and liquidity.

Market linkages

The internationalisation of capital markets also has major implications for another topical issue in regulatory circles, the nature and extent of linkages between equity and index-based derivative markets. While the growth of these derivative markets in the USA and Japan has been little short of phenomenal, there has also been a significant increase in the volume of index-based derivatives traded in financial centres such as London. The relationship between the two markets has been an on-going issue in both the USA and Japan, with concerns that the scale and nature of trading in their derivative markets has increased volatility in the equities market. These concerns have led some to favour regulatory action in the shape of measures such as circuit-breakers, the restriction of trading hours, the raising of margin requirements on derivatives and tighter regulatory control on both derivative product design and the introduction of new derivative contracts.

The issue of course has a major international dimension, because derivatives contracts based on an index of equities traded primarily in one jurisdiction are now increasingly being introduced in other jurisdictions. Regulatory measures aimed at dampening down the perceived impact of derivatives trading on the underlying cash market will not wholly succeed unless similar regulatory action is also taken in these other jurisdictions.

Calls for international regulatory cooperation in this area make it important to establish with much greater confidence than is now available the nature and extent of the linkages between these two markets. There is, in fact little clear-cut evidence that index-based derivatives have increased the long run volatility of equities, although there is some evidence that derivatives trading may for short periods of time induce a small increase in share price volatility. This is an area where regulators need the help of academics to clarify the relationship between the two markets and the consequences of any regulatory measures which may be contemplated.

In this country, regulators have so far taken the view that the relationship between the markets has not caused problems in the UK and that we see no reason to deviate from our traditionally liberal approach to the free development of markets. But to ensure that our instinctive approach is the right one, and to be sure that we are alert to any symptoms of the concerns identified in the USA and Japan, we have commissioned academic work on the relative levels of price and volume volatilities in the two markets and any causal link there may or may not be.

Tailpiece

But I have said enough by way of introduction. I made the normative point at the beginning that the internationalisation of capital markets is a basically healthy process. I want to end with the positive point that, whether or not my value judgment is shared, the process is continuing, may be accelerating, and has no obvious stopping place. This means that the issues I have mentioned summarily will not go away and will have to be faced.

Chapter Two

Reconciling National and International Concerns in the Regulation of Global Capital Markets

RICHARD C. BREEDEN

The regulation of world capital markets is a timely and important subject, as it does not require any significant feat of intellect to notice that the world's major capital markets have 'gone global'.

The evidence of that fact is literally all around us:

— one out of every seven equity trades worldwide involves a foreign party on one side or the other;

— the gross value of purchases and sales of securities of foreign issuers by American investors now averages around $4 billion every day, an increase of about 1/3 in only the last two years;

— more than 350 mutual funds in the USA (investment trusts), with combined assets of approximately $66 billion, invest mainly in foreign securities;

— an estimated 10% of all trading in US equities takes place outside the USA;

— in the past decade British pensions funds have increased their international investments from an average of 7% to 18% of their portfolio, and Japanese pension funds have gone from 1% to 16% in the same period;

— 'BCCI' is as much a household word in the USA as it is in Britain, and financial scandals or failures such as Drexel, BCCI, Salomon, Nomura and others have the direct potential for disrupting markets all over the world;

— between 1984 through 1990, Japanese investors increased their holdings of foreign securities by 30% per year, German investors increased theirs by 18% per year, UK investors by over 17% per year, and US investors by 14% per year;

— during the same period, 1984 to 1990, gross cross-border equity flows have increased from about $300 billion per year to about $1.7 trillion per year.

This 'globalisation' of trading and investing patterns has powerfully shaped the development of today's financial markets. It has also enhanced the capital-raising capabilities of businesses around the world. Once rare, multinational offerings of securities in ever huge amounts — like the $2 billion raised worldwide by Teléfonos de Mexico ('Telemex') — and many similar transactions have demonstrated that businesses now[1] have the option of raising large sums of primary capital in foreign markets irrespective of the ability of the issuer's domestic market to absorb a particular size or type of financing.

Despite the significance of international developments, many of the most powerful forces influencing the size, dynamics and evolution of our securities markets are domestic rather than international in nature. These 'domestic' qualities reflect sharply differing patterns of investor demographics, market participation, commercial traditions, tax laws, history and many other factors.

In the USA, our securities market remains overwhelmingly characterised by the widespread participation of public, or 'retail' investors. According to the latest survey by the New York Stock Exchange, there are now more than 50 million individuals who own US equity securities directly or through stock mutual funds. Here in the UK, there are now 11 million individual shareholders, up from only 3 million in 1980, in large part because of the widespread retail distribution in the recent privatisations. As a result of dramatic growth in the size of holdings of institutional investors like pension funds (a process occurring in many other nations), the percentage of the equity market owned by individuals in the USA has declined from 72% in 1970 to a little less than 50% today. Individual ownership of US public corporations is therefore more than three times greater than is the case in Germany (16% of the German market owned by individuals), and more than two times greater than in the UK (21%) or Japan (22%).

The USA also has a far-flung market in terms of the number and variety of issues traded. About 8000 different securities are listed on securities exchanges or traded in NASDAQ in the USA. Another 8000 securities are traded in an over-the-counter market we know as the 'pink sheets'. The UK

---

[1] Other recent global offerings include: Attwoods PLC, a UK company which has a worldwide offering for $142 million in progress; Elf Aquitaine, which offered $183 million worldwide in mid-1991; New Zealand Telecom, which offered $819 million worldwide in mid-1991; and Tubos de Acero of Mexico, which is in the middle of a global offering of $65.6 million. Other UK global offerings include: the British water companies, which were sold for a total of $8 billion in late 1989, and British Airways, which raised $508 million through a rights offering at about the same time.

and Japan, by contrast, each has about 2000 listed domestic companies, and Germany has only about 700 listed domestic companies.

The US market, like that of Japan, also differs sharply from markets in other countries in terms of the nature of the intermediaries. Though the prohibitions of the Glass-Steagall Act have been eroded considerably over the last decade through regulatory actions and judicial decisions, there are still significant barriers to bank participation in the market as an intermediary. In addition, the number and variety of foreign participants in any market, and the number of domestic firms with extensive foreign offices, varies quite widely.

Establishing sensible regulations for the protection of investors, inspection and supervision of securities firms, minimum capital levels, disclosure and accounting standards and other issues inherently requires balancing the steps that would appear most appropriate solely to meet domestic market needs and those that appear best suited to accommodate the realities of international competition. For example, as a practical matter it is simply not possible to rely solely on foreign regulators for reviewing the condition and practices of a large multinational firm. National regulators differ greatly in their analytic capabilities, level of inspection resources, independence from regulated firms and other critical factors. This is a problem that we have faced in our banking sector, where some of our states that serve as chartering authorities have as few as three or four bank examiners. Here federal agencies must duplicate the examinations of such state agencies in order to produce reliable results.

Candidly, the same problem exists internationally. There is an obvious efficiency to utilising the supervisory process in various foreign countries to develop a picture of the condition of a multinational group of companies, rather than each country trying to examine every affiliated company in every country around the world. On the other hand, some of the local authorities may not be capable of detecting the growth of even a very serious problem. Others might detect a problem, but for various reasons might determine not to take any corrective action.

Pure reliance on foreign oversight is therefore not likely to prevent periodic large shocks, and protection of the home country market may require some level of review of supervisory information already submitted to one or more foreign agencies. Such duplication should ideally be minimised to the greatest possible extent to prevent excessive costs to either regulated firms or to national supervisory authorities. This issue of how to organise and conduct the supervision of a group of banks or securities firms operation in numerous countries is one very good example of a problem that requires difficult tradeoffs between domestic and foreign concerns. In most such issues, there is certainly not any clearly defined 'right answer'.

There are a great many common risks that regulators of securities markets around the world must face, each of which raises potentially significant issues of reconciling our respective approaches. Without even attempting a comprehensive list these challenges for regulators would include:

Fraud

The insider trading, market manipulation, parking and other forms of fraud engaged in by Michael Milken and Dennis Levine damaged numerous innocent market participants, and constituted an attack on the viability and credibility of public securities markets. Detecting and punishing 'penny stock' manipulations and financial reporting frauds of every imaginable permutation represent a constant ongoing challenge. Obviously the Salomon case shows the degree to which financial fraud can undercut the perceived fairness of an entire market.

Insolvency

As bad as market frauds can be for investors or creditors, the insolvency of a major firm is certainly capable of adversely affecting a huge number of 'innocent' depositors, counterparties and other market participants. The failure of the BCCI here in the UK, and the Bank of New England in the USA (the latter failure cost investors more than $2 billion) demonstrate the potential costs of insolvencies of firms. Here improvements in both the Basle Capital rule and that of securities markets, better financial disclosure and accounting, and improved analysis of overall risk portfolios — including derivatives positions — may all be important areas for future action.

Market Disturbances

The market crash in 1987, and its smaller cousin in 1989, demonstrated that a major market decline has the potential for producing failures among clearing member firms that could spread through the clearance and settlement system, as well as producing sharp reductions in investor participation. The failure of a clearance system, or of a major firm, coupled with a market disturbance could prove extremely damaging to financial markets and economic activity more broadly.

Rigged Markets

As long as markets exist, people will try to rig them. Markets that are driven by secret deals and planned concerted action rather than market forces will result in large losses to investors, such as the roughly $30 billion in market values suffered by investors in high yield securities when Milken's market shams were finally ended. Rigged markets undercut economic efficiency and create the risk of potentially far-reaching loss of public participation.

Uncompetitive markets

Barriers to competition can arise through very obvious structural restrictions like Glass-Steagall (and Article 65 in Japan) and interstate banking laws. Other restrictions may be equally damaging to competitive markets, yet less apparent on their face as protectionism. Italy's statutory requirements of a local office through which to book trades involving Italian nationals,

Germany's requirement that a multinational broker – dealer must have a data processing centre in Germany, Japan's structural requirements for conducting a mutual fund business and other similar provisions can sharply reduce the competitiveness of international firms.

Disclosure and Financial Reporting

Investors, analysts, rating agencies and others need to be able to obtain clear, reliable and accurate information concerning public companies. This information enables the market to work efficiently in valuing the shares of companies. The level of detail in required disclosure, and whether it is delivered through a prospectus used as a selling document, through periodic disclosures like our annual report 10-K or otherwise, can of course vary from country to country.

Sales practices

The practices of intermediaries in selling stock to retail customers are vulnerable to abuses that are generally addressed through governmental standards, self-regulatory body standards, or both. Rules against placing 'unsuitable' securities, 'churning' (or 'swapping') accounts excessively, making unauthorised trades, excessive markups on securities sold by a dealer from inventory and other practices are designed to meet standards of ethical conduct in the securities business. Though these rules vary somewhat in their specifics, most major markets have standards designed to address the conduct of sales personnel of banks or brokers in this area.

Each of the major markets must in its own way face each of these problems and more. The specific form of regulations to address these issues has to reflect the conditions in the local market. At the same time, the aggregate cost of regulation and the effect of particular regulations on the efficiency of cross-border transactions must be watched carefully. Here regulations must be framed to accomplish domestic needs in a manner that does not damage the efficiency or reduce the safety of the larger world trading markets.

Conclusion

This is obviously just a small sample of the international issues facing securities regulators in every market. Reconciling the complexity of laws and rules (both of government and Self Regulatory Organsations) in numerous countries is a daunting task. In addressing these issues we need to recognise several realities. First, the issues are difficult and complex, so the rules will also be somewhat complex no matter what level of coordination exists. Second, even with substantial international cooperation, fundamental differences among markets in terms of investors, issuers, intermediaries, government credit underwriting, volatility and many other factors justify differences in regulation. Therefore, 'common' global standards, if read to mean identical, is an illusory and unobtainable goal. However, seeking to achieve similar objectives and to address in an effective way similar problems is a realistic goal. Third, there are many issues where scholars and academics can make significant contributions in improving our understanding of the economic forces at work and the best ways to achieve our goals.

In the last decade our markets changed dramatically, and I do not expect that the next decade will prove any different. However, we made enormous strides in regulatory harmonisation in the last decade, and I also expect that to continue in the coming decade. Through direct bilateral discussions, groups like the 'Trilateral Talks' between the USA, UK and Japan, and multilateral groups ranging from the European Community to the International Organisation of Securities Commissions, we must continue to explore and redefine our national and international tools for dealing with a whole range of common problems. Ultimately our efforts will be critical to allowing continued growth and development of a world capital market that can help deliver the most efficient allocation of goods and services to a rapidly changing world community for the benefit of peoples all over the world.

Part II
International Banking Regulation

Chapter Three

International Trade
in Banking Services:
A Conceptual Framework*

SYDNEY J. KEY
HAL S. SCOTT

3.1 INTRODUCTION

The Uruguay Round of trade negotiations within the General Agreement on Tariffs and Trade (GATT) that has been under way since 1986 includes discussions on liberalization of trade in services in addition to trade in goods. The inclusion of services for the first time in GATT negotiations reflects their increasing importance in international trade, especially over the last decade. Financial services in general, and banking services in particular, are now a significant component of international trade in services, in part because of the growing interdependence of national financial markets.

Principles in Use

The search for principles to govern the provision of financial services by foreign firms, whether located inside or outside the national market of the customers, has taken place in a number of contexts in addition to the GATT

* The authors wish to thank Howell E. Jackson, Karen H. Johnson, James S. Keller, Robert W. Ley, Kathleen M. O'Day, Patrick J. Pearson, Fernando Perreau de Pinninck, William A. Ryback, and Alexander K. Swoboda for valuable comments and suggestions. The authors also wish to thank Mendelle T. Berenson for her work in editing the manuscript. The views expressed are those of the authors.

negotiations. These contexts have included unilateral national policies toward foreign providers of financial services, bilateral treaties such as the USA–Canada Free Trade Agreement, the supranational rules adopted by the European Community (EC), and the multilateral codes of the Organization for Economic Co-operation and Development (OECD). In the banking sector, the major industrial countries have negotiated informal guidelines covering prudential matters such as minimum capital requirements under the auspices of the Bank for International Settlements (BIS).

In this paper we focus on the principles for regulating the international provision of banking services because of the unique character of such services and because, despite the increasing internationalization of financial services and markets, national regulatory systems still differ substantially. The banking sector of a national economy is a particularly sensitive one. Reserves held by banks have traditionally been used as an instrument of monetary policy, and banks play a key role in the payment system and in financing the real economy by intermediating between savers and borrowers. The latter role depends in part on public confidence in the banking system. The failure of one bank can trigger imitative runs on other banks or a chain reaction of failures through the payment system or through default on interbank obligations. This phenomenon is often referred to as 'systemic risk'.

For international trade in banking services, the most generally accepted principle is national treatment, which seeks to ensure equality of competitive opportunity for domestic and foreign firms providing banking services in a host country. Under a policy of national treatment, foreign banks are treated as nearly as possible like domestic banks: they have the same opportunities for establishment that domestic banks have, they can exercise the same powers in the host country, and they are subject to the same obligations. But differences between regulatory and institutional structures in home and host countries can make it difficult to apply the principle of national treatment.[1]

Some of the most intractable problems stem from the lack of agreement among the major industrial countries regarding the permissible activities of banks. For example, the European Community finds it difficult to accept US restrictions separating commercial and investment banking in the USA when the Community does not apply such restrictions to the activities of EC banks. Problems also arise in trying to apply to foreign branches capital adequacy and other requirements developed for the domestic banks of a host country. Moreover, national treatment does not address the extent to which multinational cooperation and agreement are necessary to regulate and supervise financial activities conducted internationally.

---

[1] See Sydney J Key, 'Is National Treatment Still Viable? US Policy in Theory and Practice', *Journal of International Banking Law* vol 5, no. 9 (Winter 1990), pp. 365-381. An earlier version of this paper was presented at a *Conference on World Banking and Securities Markets after 1992*, International Center for Monetary and Banking Studies, Geneva, February 1990.

Other principles for governing international trade in financial services go beyond national treatment, that is, they presuppose national treatment and seek something more. These principles have been advanced as the basis for requirements imposed by national reciprocity policies or as obligations undertaken in connection with international agreements or supranational regulation. Although these principles, with labels such as mutual recognition and effective market access, are not always precisely defined, they involve explicit or implicit harmonization of national regulatory structures, with concomitant changes in the regulation of domestic as well as foreign banks.

The Banking Matrix

In this paper we develop a conceptual framework for analyzing the principles that should govern the provision of international banking services. To do so, we substitute for the conventional terminology more basic, albeit less colorful, terms. National treatment and the principles that go beyond it can be understood in terms of three basic components that can be applied separately or in combination: (1) host-country rules; (2) home-country rules; and (3) harmonized rules that apply in both countries. For example, national treatment requires the nondiscriminatory application of host-country rules to foreign banks. By contrast, mutual recognition, which is the basis of the EC internal market program, involves both harmonization of essential rules and, in the absence of harmonization, acceptance by host countries of home-country rules. Even if rules are harmonized, there is the question of who administers the rules — the host country, the home country, or a supranational entity. In the banking sector, this question is particularly important because harmonization does not by itself guarantee the quality of supervision.

The public policy question is what basic principle or combination of principles — host-country rules, home-country rules, or harmonized rules — should govern international trade in banking services. Our analysis suggests that no single rule is appropriate for the provision of all international banking services. The choice of a rule depends on the interaction between two factors: the manner in which the service is provided and the public policy goals underlying the regulation of banking services. A bank located in one country (the home country) can provide services to customers in another country (the host country) in three principal ways: across borders, that is, without establishing a presence in the host country; through branches established in the host country; or through subsidiaries, which must be separately incorporated in the host country. Countries generally have four principal policy objectives that affect their regulation of such services: promoting competitive markets, ensuring the safety and soundness of banks, protecting against systemic risk, and ensuring adequate protection of consumers.

In regulating the international provision of banking services, countries must choose from among the basic principles the ones most likely to promote these policy goals, given the forms in which banking services are provided. To help organize thinking about these choices, we have constructed a 'Banking Matrix,' which sets forth the combinations of public policy goals and forms of provision of banking services.

Policy goal	Method of providing banking services				
	Cross-border	Branches		Subsidiaries	
		Entry	Operation	Entry	Operation
Competitive markets	Home-country rules	Home-country rules and harmonized rules	Home-country rules and harmonized rules	Host-country rules and harmonized rules	Host-country rules and harmonized rules
Safety and soundness	Harmonized rules, home-country enforcement of rules	Harmonized rules, home-country enforcement of rules	Harmonized rules, home-country enforcement of rules	Host-country rules	Host-country rules
Avoidance of systemic risk	Home-country rules	Does not apply	Host-country rules with additional requirements for foreign banks	Does not apply	Host-country rules
Consumer protection: Deposit insurance	Home-country rules	Does not apply	Host-country rules with additional requirements for foreign banks, agreement on host-country bankruptcy jurisdiction	Does not apply	Host-country rules
Consumer protection: Disclosure	Host-country rules	Does not apply	Host-country rules	Does not apply	Host-country rules

Fig. 1. Banking Matrix — rules to govern international trade in banking services, for combinations of policy goals and methods of providing services.

The entries in the cells of the Banking Matrix summarize the results of our analysis. For example, the analysis suggests that the best way to govern the entry of foreign branches so as to promote safety and soundness would be to apply harmonized rules that the home country would enforce. Similarly, consumers would be protected best if subsidiaries of foreign banks operated under host-country rules. The matrix emphasizes a major theme of our analysis, namely, that different principles may be appropriate for different forms of provision of services or for different policy goals. Thus, the matrix indicates that, with some important exceptions, home-country rules should be applied to cross-border services, host-country rules to subsidiaries, and harmonized rules or special host-country rules to branches. It also indicates that harmonized rules are particularly important for the goals of promoting competitive markets and ensuring safety and soundness. Although reasonable people may differ over the particular principles we propose for each cell of the matrix, it is still valuable in relating policy goals to methods of providing services.

The Appropriate Forum

Our analysis suggests that a fully satisfactory international framework for trade in banking services would require countries to agree whether host, home, or harmonized rules should apply in particular situations, and on the specifics of harmonized rules when harmonization is the accepted principle. Since that effort would clearly go considerably beyond the one currently under way in the GATT's Uruguay Round, the paper also discusses the characteristics of a forum in which such agreements might be negotiated.

In principle, the forum would comprise primarily the most developed countries; it would have the participation of finance ministry officials and financial service regulators; and it would possess the authority to formulate proposals, monitor their implementation, and resolve disputes. No such forum exists at present. However, we suggest that the OECD or the GATT might, with some modifications to their current structure, serve as a broad forum for agreement on appropriate principles and could participate in or coordinate the efforts of other specialized fora, such as the BIS Committee on Banking Regulations and Supervisory Practices, in arriving at harmonized rules.

We begin our analysis by discussing the different, and sometimes conflicting, public policy goals that form the vertical dimension of the matrix. Next, for each of the different forms of international trade in banking services, the horizontal dimension of the matrix, we discuss which of the three basic principles, or combination thereof, best furthers each of the policy goals. We then summarize the results by providing generalizations about the appropriate rule for a particular form of provision of services or for a particular policy goal and identifying the areas in which such generalizations break down. Our analysis makes it clear that the provision of international banking services through branches presents the most difficult public policy choices. Finally, we discuss the forum issue, and draw some general conclusions.

3.2 COMPLEMENTARY AND CONFLICTING POLICY GOALS

In this section we review the goals countries generally pursue with respect to banking services and examine how these goals may complement or conflict with one another.

Promoting Competitive Markets

It is generally agreed that free trade results in competitive and efficient markets that maximize consumer welfare. To achieve free trade in banking services, then, what barriers must be removed? Clearly, national rules that *discriminate* between foreign and domestic providers of banking services constitute barriers to free trade. The principle of national treatment, which applies host-country rules to foreign and domestic firms on a nondiscriminatory basis, is meant to ensure equality of competitive opportunity by eliminating such discriminatory barriers. It is generally understood that national treatment must be applied *de facto* as well as *de jure*. For example, the OECD National Treatment Instrument defines national treatment as treatment under host-country 'laws, regulations and administrative practices — no less favourable than that accorded in like situations to domestic enterprises.' The expression 'no less favourable' acknowledges that exact national treatment cannot always be achieved and that any adjustment should favor the foreign firm.

But the appropriate market for achieving equality of competitive opportunity for multinational banking institutions may be broader than a single country. Because such banks compete on a global scale, barriers to international trade in banking services may also result from *nondiscriminatory* differences in national rules, that is, differences in national rules that do not discriminate between domestic and foreign firms. Fundamental differences in rules for permissible activities of banks or for the products they may offer can create significant barriers to trade. Even if they are nondiscriminatory, a country's rules may be so much more restrictive than those in other major countries that they create market distortions and inefficiencies. For example, in the view of the European Community, prohibitions on combining banking and securities activities in the USA and limitations on interest rates in Japan restrict the ability of EC banks to compete effectively in those markets.

Although market forces may foster regulatory convergence in the longer run, in the short term removing nondiscriminatory barriers among countries may be extremely difficult politically. However, within the European Community, where political agreement on goals for regulatory convergence has already been reached, the elimination of nondiscriminatory barriers to trade in banking services is a critical element of the internal market program.[2] This liberalization is being carried out in an environment of substantial coordination and of common obligations established through a supranational structure to which the member states have already transferred a significant degree of sovereignty. By contrast, the OECD Codes of Liberalization and National Treatment Instrument are concerned only with discriminatory barriers, a limitation that reflects the absence of a comparable political consensus or degree of integration among members of that organization. For this reason, a GATT agreement on trade in services would have even more difficulty in addressing nondiscriminatory barriers.

'Reverse discrimination' could occur if foreign banks were to receive treatment better than that granted to host-country banks — if, say, a German

---

[2] See Sydney J Key, 'Mutual Recognition: Integration of the Financial Sector in the European Community', *Federal Reserve Bulletin*, vol.75 (September 1989), pp.591-609.

bank were permitted to offer a service in France (even when French banks could not do so) on the grounds that Germany permitted the service to be offered. Under the EC internal market program, powers permitted in the home country (provided such activities are listed in the Second Banking Directive) will govern the provision of banking services across borders and through branches. However, the expectation — indeed, the overall EC strategy — is that any resulting competitive inequalities for a host country's banks will quickly force that country to conform its national rules to those of other member states. Within the Community, such reverse discrimination is essentially a strategy to produce harmonization and is predicated on political agreement on goals for convergence of national regulatory systems.

Another dimension of national policies to promote competitive markets involves adoption and enforcement of policies to prevent concentrations of market power ('antitrust policy' in the USA, 'competition policy' in the European Community). These policies generally support *de novo* entry by new competitors, and thus do not pose obstacles to foreign banks offering cross-border services or establishing branches or subsidiaries in host countries. They might prevent a foreign bank that already has a substantial presence in a host country from acquiring a bank of significant size in that country, but such restrictions would apply equally to domestic banks.

Other considerations may sometimes modify — or even overrule — the economic goal of promoting competitive and efficient markets. In particular, developing countries often restrict competition from foreign banks out of concern that those banks will dominate their less efficient domestic institutions. To such countries, the efficiency gains achievable through competition are outweighed by the loss in national control of the banking sector. In some cases, such countries gradually open up their markets as they become more confident about the ability of their local institutions to compete. Industrialized countries are not immune to similar considerations: France and Italy in effect protect some of their major banks from foreign ownership through state ownership of these institutions. The governor of the Bank of England has stated that in the UK, which is generally regarded as having an open and competitive banking market, 'it is of the highest importance that there should be a strong and continuing British presence in the banking system. . . '.[3]

Devising a policy to promote competition in the banking sector through the entry of foreign banks is complicated by the need to ensure the safety and soundness of banks and to protect consumers of banking services. Countries have often justified limits on competition, such as chartering restrictions, ceilings on deposit interest rates, and restrictions on permissible activities, on prudential grounds. Some have argued that less competition means fewer failures. In the international context, countries may fear unfair competition from banks of other countries that regulate their institutions less stringently.

[3] Robin Leigh-Pemberton, 'Ownership and control of UK banks', *Bank of England Quarterly Bulletin*, vol.27 (November 1987), p.526.

Lower home-country capital requirements, for example, may allow foreign banks to operate on narrower margins. Given the significance of financial services to consumers, national legislation to protect consumers is also an important factor. The line between legitimate host-country consumer protection and anticompetitive policies is often hard to draw, particularly when the service provider is foreign and thus may be beyond the reach of the local authorities.

Ensuring Safety and Soundness

Because of concerns about systemic risk and consumer protection countries seek to avoid bank failures through safety and soundness policies. If, for example, capital adequacy requirements provided a 100% guarantee that a bank would never fail, other measures to deal with systemic risk or depositor losses would be unnecessary. If a country has a deposit protection scheme, capital and other requirements to ensure the safety and soundness of banks protect the insurer, and possibly the taxpayer, not just the consumer of banking services. In this paper, we view deposit insurance schemes as related primarily to the goal of consumer protection. However, such schemes are usually justified also as ensuring the stability of the banking system. By providing safety for the funds of individual depositors, these schemes protect those who are relatively unsophisticated financially and also reduce the systemic risk resulting from withdrawal of depositors' funds not only from troubled institutions but also from other banks. Some might argue that to the extent a bank is experiencing difficulties solely because it lacks liquidity, a deposit insurance scheme contributes to its safety and soundness. But the US experience suggests that the moral hazard of an overly generous deposit insurance scheme can encourage excessive risk-taking by bank owners and managers and thereby, perversely, undermine the safety and soundness of individual banks.

National authorities impose a variety of rules to ensure the safety and soundness of banks. These include capital requirements, limitations on large exposures, liquidity requirements, restrictions on permissible activities, requirements for accounting that accurately reflect the bank's condition and help to prevent fraud, and requirements for reporting and examination for regulatory and supervisory purposes. Ensuring the safety and soundness of foreign banks providing services in its territory poses special problems for a host country because it does not directly regulate or supervise the foreign parent bank.

This issue frequently arises with regard to branches of foreign banks, whose capital is essentially that of the foreign institution and whose condition is monitored and supervised by home-country authorities. To address this situation, host countries often impose special quasi-capital or liquidity requirements on branches of foreign banks. However, these rules can unduly restrict competition. Unlike most countries, the UK does not impose such requirements and instead relies on procedures for screening of banks seeking to establish branches in its territory and regular monitoring of branch activities.

One promising approach to ensuring the safety and soundness of foreign banks operating in a host country is to reach international agreement on prudential rules, that is, the harmonization approach. In general, the internationalization of financial services and markets has both necessitated and facilitated international cooperation with regard to supervision and regulation. But the coordination and harmonization of rules have been accomplished by bank regulatory authorities in a relatively limited and informal way. For example, the 1988 Basle risk-based capital framework is an accord among the banking authorities of the major industrial countries rather than a formal international agreement or treaty. It was negotiated under the auspices of the BIS Committee on Banking Regulations and Supervisory Practices, a committee established in December 1974 as a mechanism for regular consultation among the banking authorities of the Group of Ten countries.[4] Two earlier accords had been negotiated in the same way: the 1975 Basle Concordat, which sets forth general principles regarding the relative roles of home- and host-country supervisors in an effort to ensure that all banking organizations operating in international markets are supervised institutions; and the revised Concordat, released in 1983, which incorporates the principle of supervision of multinational banking institutions on a consolidated worldwide basis.[5]

Protecting against Systemic Risk

The need to protect against systemic risk arises because prudential controls may be ineffective in preventing liquidity or solvency problems for a particular institution. In that event, the difficulties of one bank may be transmitted to others, and ultimately affect the banking system as a whole. For example, a failing bank may hold substantial interbank deposits, either as a result of placements or through furnishing correspondent payment services. This was a particular concern in the case of the near failure of Continental Illinois Bank in the mid-1980s. Moreover, if a bank that participates in a net settlement payment system, such as CHIPS in the USA or EAF in Germany, is unable to settle its position, other participating banks may incur losses.[6] A chain reaction could also occur through withdrawal of depositors' funds

---

[4] The Group of Ten, or G-10, actually consists of twelve countries: Belgium, Canada, France, Germany, Italy, Japan, Luxembourg, the Netherlands, Sweden, Switzerland, the UK, and the USA.

[5] The original 1975 Concordat is reproduced in International Monetary Fund, *International Capital Markets: Recent Developments and Short-Term Prospects, 1981*, Occasional Paper No.7 (August 1981), pp.29-32. The 1983 revised Concordat is reproduced in 22 *International Law Magazine* 901 (1983).

[6] See Hal S Scott, 'A Payment System Role for a European System of Central Banks,' in Committee for the Monetary Union of Europe, *For a Common Currency*, pp. 77-106 (The Committee, 1990). A modified version of this paper was published in *Payment Systems Worldwide*, vol.1, no.3 (Autumn 1990), pp.3-15.

from the troubled institution and from institutions that have claims on it or that are perceived to be exposed to the same risks.

Domestic regulations may limit the participation of foreign banks in inter-bank markets or national payment systems in order to minimize the possi-bility that a foreign bank failure could trigger a series of domestic bank failures. The BIS, through its Committee on Interbank Netting Schemes, has recently set out minimum standards for the design and operation of cross-border and multicurrency netting schemes, as well as principles for cooper-ative central bank oversight of such schemes.[7] The major purpose of such standards is to minimize the possibility of settlement failures and thereby to limit systemic risk.

Many countries seek to avoid systemic risk by rescuing failing banks. They employ a variety of techniques: extensions of credit by the central bank, injections of capital, arrangement of mergers with healthy institutions. Because such measures are designed to restore the solvency of failing banks, they can be viewed as another aspect of policies to promote safety and soundness. However, because they become necessary only when a bank is in danger of failing, it is useful to distinguish them from the normal prudential regulation and supervision that apply to all banks. In countries with a government-operated deposit insurance scheme, such as the USA, measures for dealing with failing banks may be part of that scheme because the insurer has an interest in the comparative costliness of alternative rescue measures. Nonetheless, rescue measures are widely employed by countries without deposit insurance schemes, and thus we consider such measures as furthering the policy goal of avoiding systemic risk.

Ensuring Adequate Consumer Protection

Consumer protection measures in the banking area generally fall into two broad categories. The first — primarily deposit insurance systems — con-sists of laws and regulations to limit losses of depositors. Host-country branches of foreign banks may be required to participate in such a system, particularly if they take domestic deposits in the host country.[8] The second category of consumer protection measures consists of disclosure rules. They typically apply to terms of credit, interest rates payable on deposits, charges for checks, and so on. Some countries go beyond simply requiring disclosure and mandate certain provisions in consumer contracts; some countries also try to protect the consumer against unwarranted disclosure of personal finan-cial information.

Consumer protection policies are often politically sensitive. In the Euro-

---

[7] The standards were part of the 'Lamfalussy Report', see Bank for International Settlements, *Report of the Committee on Interbank Netting Schemes of the Central Banks of the Group of Ten Countries* (BIS, November 1990).

[8] Another example of loss-limitation measures is the limitation on the amount a consumer may have to pay in charges on a lost bank card.

pean Community, where the basic approach to banking regulation consists of a combination of harmonized and home-country rules with home-country enforcement, consumer protection rules could still be adopted by the host country. However, if such rules create barriers to the provision of banking services by banks from other member states, the host country must be able to justify the restrictions as necessary to protect the 'public interest,' a stringent standard established by the European Court of Justice. The Court not only requires that host-state restrictions apply equally to foreign and domestic firms, but also prohibits such restrictions if the public interest is already protected by the rules of the home state or if less restrictive rules could achieve the same result.

Maintaining the Effectiveness of Monetary Policy

In the absence of a monetary union, domestic monetary policy is, of course, set and implemented by host countries. Although the provision of international banking services cannot change this basic fact, it does raise the question of whether such policy can be effective. In a world of economically interdependent nations, domestic monetary policy cannot be made in isolation. Over the past few decades, in several fora, the major industrial countries have sought to consult and cooperate with regard to the formulation of macroeconomic policies; during the last five years, among the Group of Seven countries, the process has become somewhat more formal.[9]

Theoretically, international banking activity should not interfere with the conduct of domestic monetary policy in a large open economy. Such activity would not render domestic monetary policy ineffective even though it might change the responsiveness of interest rates to a given change in the monetary base or modify the relationship between a change in interest rates and a change in nominal gross national product. The monetary authorities would still be able to achieve their targets; they would, in effect, adjust their decision making to take into account the effect of the offshore activity. Because the offshore activity could, over time, alter these relationships in unpredictable ways, the availability of data on such activity is helpful. Thus, some countries collect and share information: for example, Canada and the UK provide the USA with aggregate data on US dollar-denominated deposits of US residents at banking offices in those countries.

In any event, host-country rules, with some degree of international coordination and cooperation, govern the conduct of monetary policy. The use of host-country rules is not dependent on the way in which international banking services are provided, and monetary policy considerations thus should not affect our analysis.

---

[9] The Group of Seven, or G-7, consists of Canada, France, Germany, Italy, Japan, the UK, and the USA.

3.3 PRINCIPLES APPLICABLE TO DIFFERENT FORMS OF TRADE IN BANKING SERVICES

International trade in banking services, as we use the term, refers to provision of banking services by a bank whose principal place of business is in one country to customers in another country. Providing banking services to host-country residents from an office in another country — cross-border provision of services — is analogous to trade in goods. But providing banking services may also involve direct foreign investment if it takes place through a branch or subsidiary in the host country. Thus, rules regarding both the establishment and the operation of host-country offices of foreign banks play an important role in international trade in banking services. Because the different forms of providing banking services pose distinct issues in terms of the public policy goals discussed above, we consider each form separately.

Cross-border Provision of Services

Cross-border services are those offered by a bank located in one country to customers in another country without establishing an office in the customer's country, the host country. In general, the liberalization of cross-border services has concentrated on removing exchange controls. In recent years, however, increased attention has been given to barriers in such areas as portfolio management and investment advice; this shift has been particularly apparent within the OECD, where much of the multinational work on international trade in financial services has taken place. Examples of host-country rules that impede the cross-border provision of services include restrictions on particular products or instruments, prohibitions on the solicitation of business by foreign entities, and tax rules that favor transactions with domestic rather than foreign offices.

The OECD principles for treatment of foreign providers of cross-border services depend on whether the transaction takes place in the host country or abroad. In the first case, the transaction may be significantly regulated but only on a nondiscriminatory basis; in the second, only advertising in the host country may be regulated, but discrimination is not forbidden. Because they are intangible, however, locating the situs of banking services provided across borders is fraught with difficulties. This issue typically arises with respect to tax treatment of cross-border transactions and the choice of law governing a particular transaction. For example, lenders and borrowers can easily adapt to formalistic rules that make tax treatment turn on where a loan agreement is signed.

Competitive markets. In the interest of promoting competitive markets, host countries should allow cross-border provision of services under home-country rules without imposing any restrictions. This practice would permit host-country consumers access to a broader range of services and a larger number of service providers. On the other hand, broader powers, lower capital requirements, subsidies, and other advantages offered by foreign governments may make for 'unfair' competition in the context of cross-border services. As discussed below, the Basle risk-based capital accord partially addresses this concern by setting minimum capital requirements for banks in countries party to that agreement. However, if the only consideration were maximizing the welfare of host-country consumers (but not producers), it might be preferable to allow them to benefit from, for example, more favorable pricing by foreign banks, even in the absence of additional harmonization. In any event, for large business customers, host country limitations on the provision of services would be largely ineffective since such customers have easy access to banking offices located abroad. Thus, we conclude that the goal of competitive markets can best be promoted by applying home-country rules, as the Banking Matrix indicates.

Safety and soundness. The host country has a concern with the safety and soundness of foreign banks offering cross-border deposit services to retail customers, who could be defined as those with deposits of, say, under $100,000. Other customers, it is presumed, can protect their own interests and, in any case, can more easily place funds in the Euromarkets. If a foreign bank taking such retail deposits were to fail, host-country customers would be at risk unless the deposit insurance scheme in the home country protected them. However, absent at least some international harmonization of deposit insurance schemes (which we discuss below), a host country could not rely on the adequacy of such a scheme in the home country, even if one existed.

In any event, prudential rules are the first line of defense against bank failures, and the international harmonization of these rules is the most promising approach for ensuring the safety and soundness of a foreign bank providing cross-border services. Harmonization could occur through adherence to the Basle accord by a broader group of countries or by the host-country conditioning acceptance of retail deposits on the home country's adherence to the accord. To further the goal of safety and soundness, we therefore envision international harmonization, as depicted in the Banking Matrix.

Since the service provider is located entirely abroad, only the home-country regulators could enforce the international standards. Ensuring some degree of uniformity in the enforcement of such standards would depend primarily on cooperation and consultation among supervisors. In this regard, it should be noted that the 'home-country' supervisors might include not only those from the place of incorporation or location of the entity providing the service but also those from the country in which the banking organization as a whole has its principal place of business. This would also be the case with respect to branches and subsidiaries, discussed below.

Avoiding systemic risk. A host country has minimal concern with systemic risk in the provision of cross-border services. The risk for individual domestic banks of holding deposits with foreign banks can be addressed by regulating such exposure directly rather than by imposing restraints on foreign banks. Cross-border services do not directly involve a foreign bank in the payment system of the host country, nor is the failure of a foreign bank likely to trigger imitative runs on domestic banks. If such runs were to occur, they would, in any case, have little relation to the foreign bank's provision of cross-border services. Thus, home-country rules should apply with respect to systemic risk, as noted in the matrix.

Consumer protection. For cross-border services, deposit insurance must necessarily be provided under the home country's scheme. The host country could, of course, best protect its consumers if basic elements of deposit insurance schemes were harmonized among nations. But achievement of this goal, although highly desirable, seems unlikely given the vast disparities in these schemes. Furthermore, the enormous effort that would be required to achieve harmonization does not seem justified by the host country's policy concern with insurance of its residents' deposits in foreign offices of foreign banks. Therefore, home-country rules, without any harmonization, should govern deposit insurance for cross-border provision of services.

By contrast, host-country rules can be used for disclosure requirements or mandatory contract terms. For example, host countries could require a foreign bank to disclose whether its deposits are insured and, if so, by whom and on what terms. If the deposit were denominated in a foreign currency, disclosure of the currency risk might also be required. Such rules would not impose extra requirements on foreign banks because they would be associated with the nature of the transaction, not with the nationality of the provider. Thus, domestic banks that offered foreign currency deposits would be subject to the same disclosure rules about exchange risk. In contrast to the OECD approach, determining the situs for provision of the service would not be important. If host countries were to impose overly burdensome disclosure requirements or mandatory contract terms, there might be a need to harmonize these measures to avoid an adverse impact on competition. However, for purposes of this paper, we assume such harmonization would not be necessary.

Branches

Traditionally, analyses of issues relating to international trade in banking services have distinguished between providing services across borders, on the one hand, and providing them through the establishment of subsidiaries or branches, on the other. But a further distinction is useful because, unlike a subsidiary, a branch is an integral part of the foreign bank and is not separately incorporated in the host country. Recently, the special characteristics of branches have been given increased attention in international fora such as the OECD. Moreover, the European Community has in effect drawn a line between financial services provided through subsidiaries (which are subject to nondiscriminatory host-country rules) and those provided through branches and cross-border services (which are governed by home-country rules and enforcement, based on harmonization of essential rules). Our analysis seeks to identify the rules that should be applicable to the establishment (entry) of branches and to their operation.

Entry

Only two of the policy goals we have identified seem relevant for the entry of branches of foreign banks: competition, and safety and soundness.

Competitive markets. Some countries limit or prohibit entry by branches of foreign banks by, for example, applying quotas or limitations on geographic location that do not apply to domestic banks. Developing countries often impose restrictions out of fear of foreign domination, although developed countries may also restrict branch entry. Canada, for example, prohibits the establishment of branches of foreign banks, although it would justify the prohibition on grounds of safety and soundness.

Because branches can operate on the basis of the consolidated capital of the foreign bank and are often a more efficient method of doing business than operating through subsidiaries, permitting branch entry is important in promoting competition among foreign and domestic banks in a host-country market. This consideration suggests that, for competitive purposes, branches should be allowed to enter under home-country rules; that is, if the home country authorizes a bank to establish a foreign branch, the host country would be required to accept that decision. Safety and soundness concerns would be addressed by harmonization of prudential standards (see discussion below).

A further problem arises with respect to nondiscriminatory restrictions imposed by a host country. For example, a host country such as the USA may restrict intranational branching of its own banks and, accordingly, also place geographic limitations on the establishment of branches of foreign banks. Even if they are nondiscriminatory, such limitations may be anticompetitive and create barriers to the provision of banking services, both on an *intra*national and international basis. This type of problem could be resolved through international harmonization of rules for intranational geographic expansion.

In view of these considerations, home-country and harmonized rules appear to be the best way to promote competitive markets with regard to the establishment of branches, as reflected in the Banking Matrix. Thus, home-country rules would be used to determine whether a foreign bank was permitted to establish branches in the host country. Harmonization of prudential standards would remove the safety and soundness justification for discriminatory host-country restrictions. Harmonization is included under the goal of competitive markets to deal with a different issue, namely, the elimination of nondiscriminatory barriers to branch entry.

Safety and soundness. Prudential concerns regarding entry of foreign branches cannot be allayed by the nondiscriminatory application of host-country law. Allowing entry by a foreign branch is inherently different from permitting a domestic bank to open a branch. Branching by a domestic bank is predicated on initial approval for the establishment of the bank itself, and establishment of a branch is merely incremental. Moreover, domestic banks are subject to domestic (host-country) regulation for safety and soundness, whereas a foreign bank establishing a branch is not. The host country therefore needs to assure itself on this point in permitting entry for a foreign branch.

When a country permits entry by a foreign branch, it is implicitly or explicitly accepting the adequacy of home-country regulation and supervision, including enforcement of those rules. But why should it accept the adequacy of regulation and supervision by all home countries? Some degree of harmonization of rules — say, by adherence to the Basle accord or other internationally agreed standards — might be required before permitting entry. Even if rules were harmonized, a host country might have reservations about the quality of enforcement in a particular home country; but conditioning entry on the quality of supervision would be extremely difficult unless home-country supervision was extraordinarily lax. The only answer may be sufficient cooperation and consultation among national supervisory authorities to establish an atmosphere of mutual trust.

The approach of harmonization with home-country enforcement is reflected in the Banking Matrix. By removing the safety and soundness justification for discriminatory restrictions on entry, international harmonization of prudential rules would enable nations to permit branches of foreign banks to enter under home-country rules, and would thereby promote competitive markets.

Operation.
In contrast to entry, the operation of branches raises issues for all four of the policy goals.

Competitive markets. Competition within a host-country market would be promoted by allowing branches of foreign banks to engage in the same activities permissible for domestic banks, that is, by a policy of national treatment. However, competition could be further promoted if branches of foreign banks were allowed to engage in any activities their home countries permitted. If home-country rules were the more liberal ones, host-country banks would suffer reverse discrimination that could be removed only by a change in the host-country rules. However, if home-country rules were more restrictive than host-country rules and the home country applied identical rules to its banks' foreign and domestic activities, branches of home-country banks would be at a competitive disadvantage in the host-country markets.

The European Community is using the home-country approach, but bases that approach on agreement among countries regarding convergence of national rules. Thus, the EC's Second Banking Directive involves both harmonization and home-country rules.[10] It sets forth a list of activities subject to mutual recognition; a host country is required to permit a bank from another member state to engage, through a branch or through the cross-border provision of services, in any activity on the list that the home country permits. Without implicit or explicit agreement on such a list, it would be politically impossible, either within or beyond the Community, to allow branches of foreign banks to operate under home-country rules for permissible activities.

Home-country rules combined with harmonization of basic rules for permissible activities would best promote competitive markets for operation of branches, and this is reflected in the Banking Matrix. Such harmonization could be explicit, as in the European Community, or it could occur *de facto* through unilateral changes in national rules to conform to the more liberal rules in other countries. However, a broader group of countries may find it difficult to agree on permissible activities, especially securities activities or insurance activities (the latter are not even included on the EC's list). Countries have different traditions and experience in this area. Some view expansion of bank powers as a positive promotion of competition; others have concerns about safety and soundness, potentially anticompetitive concentrations of power, or conflicts of interest.

At present, two major countries with restrictive rules for permissible activities — Japan and the USA — are considering proposals for change. However, adoption of these proposals would not produce the harmonization necessary to allow branches of foreign banks to operate under home-country rules for permissible activities. The reason is that the proposals envision that securities and insurance activities would be conducted in affiliates of the bank rather than in the bank itself. This approach contrasts with that of the European Community, discussed above, under which securities activities (though not insurance activities) could be conducted in the bank. As a result, a second-best alternative to the entry in the Banking Matrix — that is, home-country and harmonized rules for permissible activities of branches — would be host-country rules for permissible activities of branches combined with harmonized rules for permissible activities of bank affiliates. Such harmonization would, in effect, require implicit or explicit agreement on a list of permissible activities for bank affiliates. There would also need to be agreement that foreign banks could operate such affiliates in addition to branches in a host country.

Safety and soundness. The issue of safety and soundness with regard to operations of branches of foreign banks in a host country is similar to that with regard to entry. Once a branch was permitted to enter, its safety and

[10] Second Council Directive of 15 December 1989 on the coordination of laws, regulations and administrative provisions relating to the taking up and pursuit of the business of credit institutions and amending Directive 77/780/EEC (89/646/EEC), 32 *O.J. European Communities* (No.L386) 1 (1989).

soundness would continue to be determined largely by harmonized standards enforced by the home country. If, in the absence of a more widespread international agreement, adherence to the Basle standards by the parent bank had been a condition of entry, continued adherence should be included as part of the condition. As in the case of entry, the issue of adequate enforcement of harmonized standards could be dealt with through cooperation and consultation among national supervisors. In the extreme case, branch activities could be terminated by host-country authorities.

Systemic risk. Considerations of systemic risk are of particular significance for branches of foreign banks because the failure of a foreign bank necessarily means that its branches cannot continue to operate. The inability of a branch that played a significant role in host-country financial markets to meet its obligations could lead to a chain reaction of failures of other banks through the interbank market or payment and settlement systems or through imitative runs on branches of other foreign banks and on domestic banks. If a home country rescues a failing bank, systemic risk can be avoided; but host countries cannot count on such rescues. The decision of a country to rescue a failing bank depends on a variety of considerations, including the immediate financial cost and the longer-term potential for increasing moral hazard.

If necessary, the interbank market problem can be addressed by prudential regulation of domestic banks, for example, by limiting large exposures to less creditworthy banks, whether domestic or foreign. The risk to domestic banks from the failure of a foreign bank would generally not increase because funds were placed with a host-country branch of that bank rather than with the foreign bank in its home country or with a branch in a third country.

The payment and settlement system of a host country is subject to two risks from foreign branches. First, a foreign branch might default on a settlement position through failure to cover uncollateralized overdrafts on its clearing account with a central bank, incurred in connection with the use of a central bank payment system, such as FedWire in the USA. Such a failure might result in a loss for the central bank. Second, the failure of a foreign branch to meet its uncollateralized settlement obligations in a net settlement system, such as CHIPS in the USA, could expose other bank participants to losses.

Given that the ability of foreign branches to meet their settlement obligations depends ultimately on the solvency of the bank as a whole, which is regulated by the home country, host countries may be reluctant to allow foreign branches to participate in their payment systems on the same terms as domestic institutions. In addition, branches of foreign banks may have more difficulty than domestic institutions do in promptly covering settlement shortfalls: They may be less able to fund themselves quickly in host-country money markets, and home-country markets could be closed. The costs of settlement failure could be avoided if a central bank were to extend lender-of-last-resort facilities to the failing bank. But it is not clear whether any central bank would make these facilities available in such a situation. And then, which central bank would do so — that of the home country of the failing bank or that of the country in which the payment system operates?

The risks that participation by branches of foreign banks pose to a payment system could be controlled by a variety of measures. The BIS Report has formulated minimum standards for the G-10 countries that are designed to minimize the possibility of a settlement failure in net settlement systems. These standards would affect all participants in such systems, whether branches of foreign banks or domestic institutions. Although adoption of these standards will decrease the risk of settlement failure, it will not eliminate it. Moreover, the standards do not apply to use of central bank gross payment systems, such as FedWire, so that other policy measures will still be required.

One approach is to exclude branches of foreign banks from direct participation in the payment system by requiring them to clear payments through domestic participants. France, for example, permits only domestic banks to participate in Sagittaire, its net settlement system for cross-border payments. Alternatively, branches of foreign banks could be subject to special position limits or collateral requirements. Although such requirements could be viewed as discriminatory, they may be the only practical alternative to a system under which the host country's central bank may be forced to act as a lender of last resort for such branches. The Banking Matrix therefore indicates that host-country rules should apply with respect to systemic risk, with the qualification that the rules for branches of foreign banks may be different from those for domestic banks.

Harmonization might be used to avoid special requirements for branches. For example, the Federal Reserve Board in the USA now allows branches of foreign banks to participate in FedWire on terms closer to those afforded to domestic institutions, provided the home country of the foreign bank adheres to the Basle capital accord. Adherence to the accord would give host-country authorities greater confidence in the safety and soundness of the foreign bank. This approach, however, does not address the issue of systemic risk that arises when a foreign bank with a branch in the host country actually fails. Under our framework, capital requirements would already have been harmonized for purposes of safety and soundness for the entry and operation of branches. Extra measures would be needed to avoid systemic risk if this first line of defense proved inadequate.

Consumer protection. If a branch of a foreign bank accepts deposits of host-country residents, the host country has an interest in protecting the depositors against the possible failure of the foreign bank. To this end, a host country could require branches of foreign banks, or at least those that take 'retail' deposits, to participate in its deposit insurance system. The problem with this approach, that is, using host-country rules, is that the exposure of the host-country insurer is dependent on home-country regulation and supervision of the bank. Harmonization of rules for safety and soundness could make this situation more acceptable; but because such rules cannot provide a 100 percent guarantee against failure, the host country might still be required to pay for the ineffectiveness of the home country's supervisory policies.

One solution to the problem of potential losses by the host-country insurer is to permit the host country to require branches of foreign banks to pledge readily marketable assets as a condition for insurance. In addition, the host country might require that branches of foreign banks maintain total assets that exceed total liabilities and that the assets not be excessively risky, a quasi 'capital' requirement. In the event that a foreign bank failed, the pledged assets would be immediately available to host-country authorities to cover or reduce the losses of the insurer, or they would be available directly to uninsured local depositors. Although other branch assets would be subject to host-country liquidation, the 'capital' requirement would help to ensure that such assets were sufficient to cover the claims of branch creditors, including those of the insurer. However, special host-country requirements for branch assets might unduly constrain the ability of the bank as a whole to operate in an efficient manner and, given harmonized capital requirements, would be unnecessary to maintain the safety and soundness of the bank.

Moreover, the effectiveness of these measures assumes that the host-country authorities have the legal power to seize branch assets and control their disposition, either through realizing on the pledge or putting the branch into liquidation. This assumption is not free from doubt. It depends on whether a branch is treated as a separate entity in a liquidation (host-country jurisdiction) or there is unity of the bankruptcy (home-country jurisdiction). If the home-country receiver asserts a claim to the assets of the entire bank, including the assets of foreign branches, the host country may not be able to dispose of the assets of the branch without causing conflict with the home country.

In practice, host countries may try to liquidate a branch of a failing foreign bank as if it were a separate entity. For example, in the USA, state or federal authorities have seized assets (in one case a building, in another large local interbank deposits) and used them to pay off local depositors and creditors; in one instance, a surplus was sent to the home-country authorities. Nonetheless, the home-country receiver may well consider all of the assets of the failed bank — including those booked at its foreign branches — to be within the jurisdiction of the home country. In the case of the 1974 near failure of Franklin National Bank, US authorities persuaded the UK authorities to allow the US receiver to take control of the London branch of the USA bank.

There is no generally accepted international rule in this area. The Basle Concordat deals with supervisory issues (it assigns primary responsibility for solvency to the home country and liquidity to the host country) and does not address assignment of responsibilities in the event of bankruptcy. Financial institutions are not covered by a bankruptcy convention recently agreed upon in the Council of Europe or by a draft EC convention still in long-standing negotiations.

If the home country has the legal power to control the disposition of all of the assets of a failed bank, including those at its foreign branches, the pledge and quasi capital requirements of the host country would be rendered ineffective. In this situation, a host-country insurer would be fully exposed to the risk of inadequate supervision by the home country. To reduce this exposure, the host country would need to have jurisdiction over the disposition of the branch assets. Thus, the use of host-country rules for deposit insurance requires use of host-country rules for bankruptcy (that is, the separate entity approach).

There are, however, significant drawbacks to this approach. Home-country depositors, or their insurers, may be deprived of claims to assets booked at foreign branches, and it is far from clear why host-country claims to such assets should be superior. Since the bank as a whole has gone bankrupt, fairness suggests that claims should be resolved in one collective proceeding in which similarly situated creditors are treated alike. In addition, dismemberment of the bank through host-country liquidations of branch assets may effectively prevent the home country from restructuring or selling the bank, thus interfering with the preservation of the bank's overall value. Nonetheless, the fact remains that it would be exceedingly difficult to achieve an international agreement providing for exclusive home-country jurisdiction over bank bankruptcies.

As an alternative to host-country deposit insurance, deposits in a branch of a foreign bank could be covered under the deposit protection scheme of its home country. For host countries, this raises the question of what amount of protection provided by the home-country scheme would be acceptable; for example, the level of coverage, the degree of risk-sharing by depositors, the types of deposits covered, and the speed and convenience of payouts. This question is further complicated by the fact that the lack of uniformity in deposit protection schemes is not the only factor contributing to differences among countries in protecting depositors. Other factors that can be equally important to host countries include government ownership of banks and central bank lending to or government recapitalization of private banks.

The concerns of the host country about the adequacy of depositor protection afforded by the home country could be resolved only by harmonization of deposit protection schemes. Indeed, the EC Commission is now considering whether to propose the home-country approach for Community branches of EC banks and, if so, what harmonization such an approach might entail. Beyond the Community, whether sufficient harmonization of deposit protection schemes exists or could ever be agreed upon is far more uncertain.

If harmonized and home-country rules were used for deposit insurance, home-country rules could then be used for bankruptcy. Because host-country authorities would not be providing insurance for deposits at branches of foreign banks, the host country would no longer need to have jurisdiction over the liquidation of the branch. Thus, home-country deposit insurance would work in tandem with home-country bankruptcy jurisdiction and avoid the drawbacks of the separate entity approach to bankruptcy. Whether, and if so to what extent, acceptance of the principle of the unity of the bankruptcy would require harmonization among nations on priorities of creditors is beyond the scope of this paper. Within the European Community, the Commission has proposed a 'winding up' directive that would give home-country authorities exclusive responsibility for winding up branches of EC banks; this approach would work effectively with home-country deposit protection if that were to be proposed.

For deposit insurance, the Banking Matrix envisions a second-best solution: the application of host-country rules with special requirements for branches of foreign banks and agreement that, in the event of bankruptcy, the host country would have jurisdiction over the disposition of the assets of branches of foreign banks. Although this approach is theoretically inferior to the use of harmonized and home-country rules for deposit insurance and bankruptcy, we do not believe the alternative is realistically achievable in the foreseeable future. We would be happy to be proved wrong.

Subsidiaries

Unlike branches, subsidiaries are separately incorporated under the laws of host countries and are therefore similar to domestically owned banks. Subsidiaries of foreign banks have their own capital, which is within the regulatory and supervisory jurisdiction of host-country authorities. Because such subsidiaries are part of a multinational organization, however, a host country might still be concerned with the condition of a parent bank and the extent to which it might serve as a source of strength by standing ready to inject capital into its host-country subsidiary.

Entry
As with branches, the relevant policy goals for entry of subsidiaries are competition, and safety and soundness.

Competitive markets. Promoting competitive markets requires that foreign ownership of domestic banks not be prohibited. But two major competitive issues do arise with respect to the establishment of subsidiaries. The first is whether non-banking firms can establish banking subsidiaries in the host country. Some countries that limit the non-banking powers of banks also limit the ownership of banks by non-banking firms. The prohibition against non-bank ownership of banks has been justified on the grounds of either safety and soundness or competition. The arguments are that non-banking parents cannot serve as a source of strength for their subsidiaries as well as banking parents can, and that the prohibition of ownership by non-banks prevents concentrations of power and conflicts of interest. The issue of ownership of banks, like the question of non-discriminatory restrictions on branch entry, might best be addressed through international harmonization of rules.

The second competitive issue regarding entry for subsidiaries is whether foreign banks can establish subsidiaries at multiple locations within the host country when domestic banks are not free to do so. Such geographic restrictions, even if applied to foreign banks on a non-discriminatory basis, could be viewed as anticompetitive. This problem, like that which arises for branch entry, could be solved by international harmonization of intranational rules, for example, by prohibiting geographic restrictions.

When a country has a federal structure other difficulties appear. If it permits subnational governments, such as states or provinces, to define the scope of interstate banking, as the USA does for subsidiaries, certain problems may arise in dealing with foreign banks. Foreign banks may, for example, need to be 'domesticated' by being assigned to a home state or region for the purpose of the application of host-country rules. A more serious problem arises if subnational governments discriminate between foreign and domestic banks, for example, by permitting only domestic banking organizations to acquire banks within their jurisdiction. Such policies violate the principle of non-discriminatory treatment, and host countries with federal systems may have to resort to federal statutory or constitutional changes to resolve such problems.

Our approach to promoting competitive markets for the establishment of subsidiaries calls for host-country rules and harmonized rules, as indicated in the Banking Matrix. Harmonization may be necessary with respect to rules relating to ownership and geographic location. In other respects, application of nondiscriminatory host-country rules to the establishment of subsidiaries — in contrast to the establishment of branches — does not seem to compromise competition. Moreover, unlike the establishment of branches, the creation of host-country subsidiaries requires compliance with the corporate laws of the host country.

Safety and soundness. The goal of safety and soundness provides a justification for the host country to impose certain conditions on entry, such as capital requirements equivalent to those applied to domestic banks. If the source-of-strength doctrine is accepted, the host country's interest in the safety and soundness of the subsidiary's foreign parent is similar to its interest when the host-country entity is a branch. As a result, the host country may have an interest not only in the capitalization of the subsidiary but also in the capital adequacy of the parent banking institution. For example, the Federal Reserve Board requires foreign banks seeking to establish or acquire banking operations in the USA to meet 'the same general standards of strength, experience and reputation' as are required of domestic banking organizations and to serve on a continuing basis as a source of strength to their banking operations in the USA.[11] Application of the source-of-strength doctrine would be facilitated by more widespread international harmonization of capital standards.

The Basle accord, in conformity with the earlier BIS agreement on consolidated supervision, envisions that for supervisory purposes home countries will apply bank capital requirements on a consolidated basis. Such consolidation would complement, but not replace, the capital requirements applied to a subsidiary by the host country. The purpose of applying home-country capital requirements on a consolidated basis is to ensure that the group as a whole has adequate capital to support all of its activities; and these requirements may affect the activities of subsidiaries. But a host country would nonetheless want to ensure that the subsidiary itself had adequate capital to support its activities. This is consistent with the host country's interest in the safety and soundness of its own banks.

The Banking Matrix, therefore, reflects our view that, to ensure safety and soundness, host-country rules should apply to the establishment of subsidiaries. But because we have recommended international harmonization of captial standards for branch entry, most countries would already be adhering to the same standards.

Operation.
Both goals relevant to entry of subsidiaries — promoting competitive markets and ensuring safety and soundness — are, of course, also relevant to their operation. In general, the same considerations and rules apply.

Competitive markets. One additional issue arises with respect to permissible activities of subsidiaries. Competition in a host country would be promoted by permitting subsidiaries to engage in at least the same activities as domestic banks; but it would be even further enhanced by permitting subsidiaries to conduct the same activities they are permitted at home. As in the case of branches, basic rules for permissible activities would need to be harmonized to avoid competitive inequalities. These considerations suggest that the entry in the matrix could be the same as that for branches, that is, home-country rules and harmonization.

But even the European Community is using host-country rules — that is, a policy of national treatment — for subsidiaries. However, the national treatment policy for subsidiaries is somewhat misleading. The Community relies on home-country rules — subject to the constraint of an agreed list of activities — to determine the permissible activities for branches and banks providing cross-border services. This serves as a tool for regulatory

[11] See Board of Governors of the Federal Reserve System, 'Supervision and Regulation of Foreign-based Bank Holding Companies', Policy Statement, February 23, 1979, F.R.R.S. 4-835. See also Regualation Y, 12 C.F.R. §225.4(a)(1) and Board of Governors of the Federal Reserve System, 'Unsound Banking Practices — Failure to Act as Source of Strength to Subsidiary Banks,' Policy Statement, April 24, 1987, F.R.R.S. 4-878.

convergence. The almost inevitable harmonization of rules for permissible activities that will result from this process will also affect subsidiaries. Similarly, beyond the Community, if home-country and harmonized rules were used for branches, there would effectively be harmonized rules for subsidiaries.

The Banking Matrix reflects our choice of host-country and harmonized rules for operations of subsidiaries. We view harmonization as the critical element of this entry whether it occurs through *de facto* market pressures, through convergence resulting from negotiated harmonization only for branch activities, or through explicitly negotiated harmonization about the permissible activities of subsidiaries. We have entered host-country rather than home-country rules where harmonization has not occurred primarily on practical grounds because subsidiaries, unlike branches, are separately incorporated host-country entities.

Other policy goals. Because subsidiaries are separately incorporated in the host country, the remaining policy goals — avoiding systemic risk and consumer protection — can be furthered by treating the subsidiaries under host-country rules exactly like domestically owned banks. Measures to deal with systemic risk as well as consumer protection measures can be applied without regard to the ownership of a bank.

3.4 OVERVIEW OF THE MATRIX

Our analysis, whose conclusions are set out in the Banking Matrix, relates the choice of rules governing international trade in banking services both to the means by which such services are provided and to the policy goals countries seek to achieve. The most obvious conclusion is that no single rule can be applied to all the combinations of methods and goals. Moreover, with the exception of disclosure requirements, no single rule can support a particular policy goal for every method by which the banking service is provided. The analysis also demonstrates that of all the goals, promoting competitive markets and ensuring the safety and soundness of banks depend most heavily on harmonization.

With some important exceptions, our analysis suggests that home-country rules should be applied to cross-border services, host-country rules to subsidiaries, and harmonized rules or special host-country rules to branches. For cross-border services, in general, host-country regulation — that is, national treatment — is not appropriate. Those services should be governed by home-country rules: they enhance competition, the systemic risk is small, and only the home country can provide deposit insurance. However, even for cross-border services, home-country rules do not adequately address safety and soundness and the disclosure aspect of consumer protection. If foreign banks solicited retail deposits from host-country residents, the host country would have a concern with safety and soundness that could be addressed through international harmonization of prudential standards. However, if the home country provided, through its own deposit insurance system, protection to such depositors that the host country considered adequate, the host country's concern with the prudential standards applied to the foreign bank would be lessened. This consideration serves to highlight a more general point about the analysis: The choice of rules for one combination of goals and methods may affect the choice for another.

In contrast to the rules for cross-border services, host-country rules are generally appropriate for subsidiaries. The reason is that subsidiaries can, for the most part, be regulated just as their domestic counterparts are without raising any special concerns about safety and soundness, systemic risk, or consumer protection. Application of the source-of-strength doctrine would be facilitated, however, by more widespread international harmonization of capital standards. In any event, as the matrix indicates, international harmonization of rules may be necessary to promote competitive markets with respect to both entry and operation of subsidiaries. Harmonization seems the most useful solution to the competitive problems raised by host-country restrictions on the ownership of subsidiaries conducting a banking business, on the geographic locations at which they can be initially established or subsequently operated, and on the services that they can provide. But harmonization would not be easy to accomplish: For example, it could require the USA to remove its restrictions on interstate banking, and it could require Japan and the USA to permit banks to offer securities services.

The treatment of foreign branches raises the most complicated questions. These arise because branches, though located and doing business in a host country, are an integral part of banks located in the home country. Thus, by their very nature, branches are subject to conflicting regulatory regimes that can be reconciled for the most part only through harmonized rules.

Our analysis suggests that ensuring safety and soundness and competitive markets when services are provided by branches of foreign banks requires harmonized rules, home-country rules where harmonization is not deemed necessary, and home-country enforcement. This is the EC approach under the Second Banking Directive. Competition, particularly with regard to geographic location and permissible activities, would be enhanced by this approach. The goal of safety and soundness requires harmonization of prudential regulations, but such regulations ultimately must be enforced by the home country. Harmonization of prudential rules is also important because it permits greater use of home-country rules to promote competitive markets. Once the goal of safety and soundness is assured, the main rationale for discriminatory restrictions on competition is removed. This is another example of the interdependence among the rules selected for the various combinations of methods and goals.

Our analysis further suggests that host countries might justifiably apply different rules to branches of foreign banks than to domestic banks for purposes of avoiding systemic risk and protecting depositors. Arguably, such policies might not be truly 'discriminatory' because domestic banks and the branches of foreign banks might not be in 'like situations,' at least for these purposes. In any event, special treatment may be necessary to avoid the potential risk arising from participation by branches in host-country payment systems. Requiring branches to pledge or maintain marketable assets might also be justified to cover potential losses of host-country depositors or insurers. But such rules would be ineffective without host-country jurisdiction over the disposition of branch assets in the event of bank bankruptcies. Application of special host-country rules to protect host-country depositors could be avoided through harmonization of deposit insurance schemes and application of the home-country scheme to deposits in host-country branches; in that event, home-country rules should also be used for bankruptcy. Although this alternative is theoretically preferable, we did not adopt it in the matrix because of the considerable practical difficulties in achieving harmonization of deposit insurance schemes and in reaching an agreement providing for exclusive home-country jurisdiction over bank bankruptcies.

We can also analyze the way in which international banking services are provided from the perspective of each of the policy goals. For example, for systemic risk and deposit insurance, the matrix shows that quite different rules may be required for different forms of operation. Systemic risk is of minimal concern for cross-border services. For subsidiaries, systemic risk can be handled by the rules applicable to domestic banks because the subsidiaries are regulated for safety and soundness by the host country. In the case of branches, the host country must apply special rules.

With respect to deposit insurance, for cross-border services, home-country rules must govern because the foreign bank has no presence in the host country. Although the host country can require that domestic deposits at branches of foreign banks be insured, it then has an interest in ensuring that the branch has sufficient assets to cover potential payouts to depositors. As discussed above, these interests could be addressed by an agreement on host-country jurisdiction over branches in the event of bankruptcy. For separately incorporated subsidiaries, host-country rules for deposit insurance can readily be applied.

Harmonization of rules is important with regard to the policy goals of safety and soundness and competitive markets. Harmonized prudential rules help protect depositors or insurers against bank failures. The Basle accord indicates that this approach is feasible, but harmonized capital requirements are only a first step. Other aspects of prudential supervision, such as examination and reporting requirements, are also important. Harmonized rules with respect to the powers of banks and the geographic locations at which they can operate would clearly promote competitive markets. This is true both for subsidiaries and branches of foreign banks. In theory, one could allow subsidiaries to be governed by host-country rules; but as a practical matter, harmonizing rules that govern competition for branches will necessarily result in the same rules for subsidiaries if competitive equality between domestic banks and branches of foreign banks is to be maintained.

In stressing the need for harmonized rules for competition, we do not mean to prejudge the content of such rules. In other words, we are not using harmonization as a code word for deregulation. With regard to entry, however, harmonization for competitive purposes should involve removal of restrictive measures that limit market access. With regard to branch operations, efforts to harmonize competition rules might result in agreement to permit the same powers to banks as now specified by the EC's Second Banking Directive. If so, the result would be liberalization of existing rules in the USA and Japan. Although broadening powers would generally enhance competition if safety and soundness concerns were addressed, it might not always be possible politically. Nevertheless, without convergence of rules for powers of banks, problems in this area may continue to arise, with the risk of retaliatory actions that could curtail competition.[12] In the case of safety and soundness, harmonization could involve reregulation, such as strengthening capital requirements.

3.5 THE APPROPRIATE FORUM

Our analysis suggests that an international framework for the provision of international banking services would require agreement both on basic principles — that is, whether host, home, or harmonized rules should apply in particular situations — and on the specifics of harmonized rules when that is the accepted principle. Achievement of such a framework, which goes considerably beyond the effort currently under way in the Uruguay Round, would, of course, require an international forum. In this section, we consider the ideal characteristics of such a forum and the extent to which existing international fora — the General Agreement on Tariffs and Trade, the Organization for Economic Co-operation and Development, and the Bank for International Settlements — meet these criteria.

Characteristics of a Forum

An appropriate forum might (1) include only countries whose levels of development were sufficiently alike that they had similar interests in the liberalization of banking services; (2) include the relevant financial service regulators and finance ministry officials from such countries; and (3) have authority to formulate proposals, monitor their implementation, and resolve disputes. These characteristics flow directly from our previous analysis.

---

[12] See Hal S Scott, 'La notion de réciprocité dans la proposition de deuxième directive de coordination bancaire,' *Révue du Marché Commun*, no. 323 (January 1989), pp.45-56.

The appropriate group of countries. As our analysis shows, competition and safety and soundness considerations are important in establishing a conceptual framework for international banking. Thus, at the outset, the forum should perhaps consist primarily of developed countries that have a common interest in the extent to which their home-country banks can operate in each other's markets. It may be extremely difficult to get more than a few developing countries to accept the same competitive principles as developed countries, particularly with respect to the entry of foreign banks. Many of these countries are quite concerned with foreign domination, and they see little to gain from liberalization of the terms of entry of their banks into developed countries. Moreover, developed countries may be particularly concerned with safety and soundness problems that could arise from entry by banks from developing countries.

The forum should nevertheless have sufficient flexibility to accommodate a growing number of countries. For example, if a host country conditions entry for foreign banks on home-country acceptance and observance of certain internationally agreed supervisory standards, banks from countries not in the initial group but subsequently meeting such standards might be given the same rights of entry as those in the initial group.

Officials participating in the forum. The officials from the countries involved in devising an international framework would ideally include regulators of banking and other financial services (including central bankers) and finance ministry officials. Because of their expertise and previous experience in devising harmonization measures, such as those developed by the BIS Committee on Banking Regulations and Supervisory Practices, banking regulators are clearly essential to the development of the more extensive harmonization envisioned in our analysis. Moreover, with regard to the goal of safety and soundness, banking regulators are the officials who would implement any agreed-upon rules.

An important part of an effort to develop the international framework we envision would involve a determination of the powers that foreign banks may exercise in host countries. As we have indicated, this determination turns upon questions of competition as well as those of safety and soundness. If banks are to be permitted to offer a broad range of financial services, the expertise of non-banking regulators, such as securities and insurance regulators, will also be important in formulating international rules.

Moreover, in most countries, government officials other than regulators, such as those in finance ministries, deal with the formulation of policies regarding the basic structure of the financial system. To become effective, these policies often require legislative changes, and finance officials often take the lead in such a process. Although regulators clearly have an important role, their policy choices are frequently circumscribed by the broader legal framework for which the other government officials are responsible. Some of the harmonization issues that we have discussed, such as additional powers for banking organizations, would require legislative changes and would be highly political. These issues have the potential to affect the political and economic interests of the participating countries and thus require the involvement of finance ministry officials as well as financial service regulators.

Authority of the forum. Ideally, the forum would be more than a meeting place. It would be an international institution with delegated authority from participating countries that enabled it to reach decisions binding on participants and that permitted it to monitor implementation of its rules and resolve significant disputes about them. The supranational character of the European Community, as discussed above, has been important to the ability of the EC countries to harmonize certain features of their banking laws as part of the internal market program. Though the supranational structure of the Community goes far beyond what would be required for an international regulatory forum, any forum undertaking international harmonization would be strengthened to the extent it possessed some supranational authority.

As our analysis demonstrates, the forum would inevitably confront issues that go beyond banking, at least as narrowly conceived. It would have to deal with whether banks should have the power to offer securities and insurance services, and with the appropriate structure for regulating banks offering such services. These issues would necessarily overlap with other issues regarding such services — for example, disclosure requirements for cross-border securities offerings or capital requirements for non-bank securities firms. There would also be overlap with the macroeconomic measures required to realize the full benefits from developing an international framework for banking services — for example, liberalization of rules relating to capital movements.

The ideal international forum would have authority to deal with all issues involving financial services, but in practice it would be difficult to find one forum with such broad authority. Even on a national level, many countries have found it difficult to integrate different types of financial service regulation. A second-best, but more realistic alternative would be to have several fora whose efforts would be coordinated by a broader forum. For example, the BIS might deal with harmonization of capital requirements for securities activities of banks and coordinate with a broader forum that dealt with the powers of banks generally. Similarly, the International Monetary Fund or the OECD might serve as a specialized forum for rules governing capital movements. In principle, a specialized forum could also serve as the broader forum.

The Choice among Existing Fora

The creation of a new forum for developing an international framework for banking services along the lines we have suggested merits consideration. In the absence of a new institutional framework, the most likely fora for undertaking the effort are the GATT, the OECD, and the BIS. How well do these fora meet the ideal criteria?

The GATT. The GATT falls short of the ideal forum in several ways. One problem is that it comprises a large number of economically diverse countries, many of whom have little interest in liberalizing rules for financial services. In particular, few of the developing countries in the GATT are likely to agree to be bound by the same principles as developed countries. However, in accordance with an approach that has been suggested in the GATT negotiations on financial services, the developed countries and some of the more industrialized developing countries could try to reach agreement among themselves before trying to resolve their differences with other developing countries. Moreover, principles agreed to by a primary group of countries, in the GATT or elsewhere, might subsequently be applied to other countries whose banks are seeking to enter markets of countries in the original group. This broadening of application has already occurred in some instances with respect to the Basle accord.

Another problem with the GATT as a forum is that, for the most part, the participating officials are experts in trade in goods rather than in banking or other financial services. This emphasis was natural because, before the Uruguay Round, the GATT dealt solely with trade in goods. As this paper has suggested, liberalization of international trade in banking services raises complicated issues that are best handled by specialists. If the somewhat autonomous GATT Financial Services Body being discussed in the Uruguay Round negotiations were to be established, it could conceivably play a role in the development of an international framework for banking services of the sort suggested here.

The BIS. Though it is closer to the ideal forum for international trade in banking services than the GATT is, the BIS also has some drawbacks. The G-10 countries that are represented on the BIS Committee on Banking Regulations and Supervisory Practices have a common level of development; but the group may be too narrow because it excludes a number of developed countries with similar interests in international banking services. On the other hand, the BIS Committee includes banking regulators with substantial expertise and experience in harmonizing banking rules on an informal and nonbinding basis; they have negotiated the risk-based capital accord, the Concordats, and the minimum standards for interbank netting schemes. However, the BIS does not formally include other financial service regulators or finance ministry officials, whose participation would be necessary to reach government-to-government agreements as opposed to understandings among bank regulators.

The BIS could play an extremely useful role in the international regulatory framework we have described as a specialized forum for issues involving safety and soundness and systemic risk. Other countries could be brought into the discussions of these issues after the BIS had formulated preliminary proposals. The proposals of the expanded group of banking officials could then feed into a broader forum that included government officials more attuned to competition and consumer protection considerations. Similar input to the broader forum could also be made by other financial service regulators.

The OECD. The OECD has some advantages as a forum for the purposes discussed in this paper. Currently, it comprises twenty-four countries at relatively similar levels of development.[13] Also, most of the relevant government officials from the finance ministries, central banks, and supervisory authorities regularly attend meetings of its committees or the working groups established under its committees.

The OECD also has some experience with non-binding harmonization of national laws. In the 1970s, the Committee on Financial Markets issued recommendations that came close to harmonization of rules in the area of operation of unit trusts (mutual funds) and disclosures applicable to publicly offered securities. In addition, the Committee on Fiscal Affairs has developed a model tax convention to avoid double taxation. For the most part, however, the OECD has sought to establish the principle of nondiscriminatory application of host-country rules rather than dismantle nondiscriminatory barriers that could involve changes in the regulatory framework of a host country. Some of the latter work could be carried on by specialized fora such as the BIS. The OECD could thus be the broad forum that coordinated the efforts of other groups.

One problem with the OECD is that its members, unlike those in the European Community, have not surrendered any sovereignty to it. Decision making, as in the GATT, must be unanimous. Moreover, although its rules are legally binding, the OECD lacks a strong mechanism for settling disputes. If it were to play the role of the broad forum, its ability to resolve disputes would have to be greatly strengthened, a move that would involve a major change of style for the organization. The OECD would also need to find ways of including nonmember countries that meet certain criteria based, for example, on regulatory and supervisory standards as well as liberalization of access.

3.6 CONCLUSION

This paper sets forth a conceptual framework for analyzing international trade in banking services and uses it to suggest rules applicable to various forms of such trade. Determining the appropriate rules requires systematic

[13] Australia, Austria, Belgium, Canada, Denmark, Finland, France, Germany, Greece, Iceland, Ireland, Italy, Japan, Luxembourg, the Netherlands, New Zealand, Norway, Portugal, Spain, Sweden, Switzerland, Turkey, the UK, and the USA.

examination of the policy goals involved in the regulation of banks, as well as of the methods by which international banking services are provided. Our framework — with the principles of host-country, home-country, or harmonized rules — enables one to go beyond conventional verbal formulations, such as national treatment or effective market access, that often avoid or paper over underlying concerns and the complexities of the issues. Although reasonable people may differ over the details of our analysis and the solutions we propose for each combination of policy goals and methods of providing services, the systematic approach embodied in the matrix that relates the choice of rules to both the goals and the methods remains useful. Indeed, a similar approach could be used for other financial services, such as securities and insurance.

From the perspective of this paper, the establishment of an appropriate international regulatory framework for trade in banking services is an ongoing, long-term effort. The current efforts of the Uruguay Round could be viewed as an important beginning. Our analysis suggests that consideration should be given to continuing this work in the OECD or the GATT, either of which could serve as the forum for agreement on the appropriate principles and could participate in or coordinate the efforts of other specialized fora in arriving at harmonized rules where they are deemed necessary.

Chapter Four

Banking Competition, Regulation and the Philosophy of Financial Development: A Search for First Principles

JOSEPH BISIGNANO

4.1 INTRODUCTION

The financial structures of countries in many ways mirror a variety of non-financial economic preferences and behaviour. Comparing financial systems and understanding their evolution can be aided by looking behind institutional structures to some of the building blocks and first principles of financial contracting. This chapter attempts to draw out some of the linkages between the micro-economics of financial contracting and corporate financial structure, the structure of financial markets and intermediation, and lastly, the role of the central bank as a provider of liquidity to the financial system. An analysis of some of the elements of financial contracting may then help to understand the implications of the continuing shift in financial, especially banking, regulation from predominantly structural regulation (regulations concerning permissible activities of financial institutions, their prices and the quantities offered) to the greater use of prudential regulation (balance-sheet and off-balance-sheet requirements) aimed at ensuring the liquidity and solvency of financial institutions.

To motivate the attention to contracts and finance we start out by noting the similarities among countries between financial systems and legal structures. If we look at banking from a strategic bargaining vantage point, we see that in those countries where there are close ownership, control or long-run informal ties between non-financial firms and banks the litigation process is commonly a co-operative solution, meaning often out of court. Where the banking laws keep separate the ownership and control relations between banks and non-financial firms the legal process is frequently one of trial dominance, i.e. non-co-operative solutions. At the same time we see that in the former case credit contracts are more frequently long-term and relational and in the latter case discrete and short-term, often structured to facilitate their trading. The nature of contracts is argued to influence the structure of the financial system, the system of corporate governance and the forms of enterprise financing, as well as the need to resort to the courts to settle contract disputes.[1]

The paper is organised as follows. Section 2 briefly considers the nature of contracts, contract enforcement and the resolution of contract disputes as elements determining both enterprise financial structure (debt vs. equity) and the degree of financial intermediation in an economy. Section 3 looks at the manner in which central banks enter the financial system as providers of liquidity to financial intermediaries and the way in which they are exposed to credit risks in their support of the financial system. Section 4 analyses the shift from structural to prudential banking regulation and the ways in which the growth of non-intermediated sources of finance (capital markets) has fundamentally changed the 'insider' role of central banks as providers of liquidity, 'immediacy' and financial stability and increased the need for an 'outside' role of private markets, with greater public disclosure, to ensure the stability of the financial system. Section 5 looks at the industrial organisation concept of 'the nature of the bank' in the context of vertical integration. We conclude in Section 6 with some comments on bank capital and the safety net.

4.2 FINANCIAL STRUCTURE, CONTRACTS AND TRANSACTIONS

The nature of contracts, the manner in which they are enforced and the means by which contract disputes are resolved varies considerably between countries. Scholars of industrial organisation in recent years have emphasised the role of transaction costs in attempting to understand the structure of organisations (e.g. vertical integration). Attention has been given to the form of contracting between economic agents. Here distinction is made between formal contracting (classical contract law), where the emphasis is on 'legal rules, formal documents and self-liquidating transactions', less formal

---

[1] An interesting analysis of the economics of legal disputes, which provides a useful backdrop to the study of banking contracts, structure and regulation is Robert D Cooter and Daniel L Rubinfeld, 'Economic Analysis of Legal Dispute and Their Resolution', *Journal of Economic Literature*, September 1989.

long-term contracts written with knowledge of the uncertainty of contract settlement (neo-classical contract law) and so-called relational contracting, where the length and complexity of the relationship between the parties to the contract requires unprespecified renegotiations over the duration of the contract.[2]

The vantage point of contracting is useful in understanding differences in financial and legal structures between countries. The two structures are related since contract enforcement and the resolution of contract disputes will depend on the governance relations between parties to a contract. Financial markets and financial intermediaries are, roughly speaking, alternative ways of arranging and enforcing particular contracts between debtors and creditors, owners, creditors and managers of firms, and represent alternative ways of organising and governing enterprise behaviour via firms' needs for capital.

Scholars of the interrelationship between law and economics have emphasised that the so-called classical contracting paradigm is often impossible in practice because of the need at times to arrange for long-term contracts. Since future contingencies are both difficult to prespecify and costly to contract over, economic agents may wish to conduct transactions outside of the market place and within an organisation (internal contracting). The withdrawal from the market (spot markets) and towards internal, sequential contracting (within organisations, informal clubs or cartels) may minimise transactions costs and opportunistic behaviour of economic agents, particularly when the absence or underdevelopment of 'futures markets' does not permit firms or individuals to contract for certain events or to hedge their risk exposures to a potential future outcome ('state of the world'). In a sense, internal (organisational) contracting may be looked at as a result both of the non-existence of futures markets for certain transactions and the impossibility of establishing futures contracts for all possible contingencies.[3]

The structure of financial systems and their evolution is dependent on the types of contracting performed in an economy, in particular if the contracting is of a standardised, recurrent kind or whether it is of an idiosyncratic and less recurrent (e.g. long-term) variety. In the former case markets would tend to dominate and in the latter institutions. The nature of the financial system, for example 'intermediated' or 'market-based', also depends on the desirability and capacity for information transfer between contract agents, in particular between borrowers and lenders. Hence information property rights (disclosure requirements) are an issue in the formation of alternative financial systems. The financial structure further depends on the desire and

[2] See Oliver E Williamson, *The Economic Institutions of Capitalism*, The Free Press, 1985 and 'Transaction Cost Economics: The Governance of Contractual Relations', *Journal of Law and Economics*, October 1979.

[3] James Tobin looks at the inadequacy of modern options and futures contracts to achieve the Arrow-Debreu contract optimality in informally judging the efficiency of the financial system. See 'On the Efficiency of the Financial System', *Lloyds Bank Review*, 1984.

ability of lenders to protect their investment by exercising some form of control over the activities of borrowers (e.g. firm managers).

When information on enterprise activities can be easily and unambiguously transferred to an open market without jeopardising the status of the firm and where its quality can be reasonably evaluated, the firm may seek to obtain finance from open markets. The control of the firm will be influenced by the financial markets to the degree that the market's perception of the firm influences the firm's cost of capital. But where information is difficult to transfer to an open market (idiosyncratic) or revelation of information could undermine the firm's competitive position, it may seek a non-open market source of finance, financial intermediaries. This could occur with the case of long-term investment contracts where the enterprise has a need for non-standardised contract negotiation. In this case the financial intermediary may gain both an information and control advantage over the firm, which the firm would be unwilling to arrange with marketable debt or equity holders. That is, the firm's contract with an intermediary may involve the transfer of valuable private information which the firm would be reluctant to share with a wide group of creditors. Moreover, the credit contract involves an implicit residual right of control (implicit corporate governance) which may be more efficiently exercised by one intermediary than a multitude of individual bond holders. The long-term nature of the borrower firm/intermediary relationship may also represent an implicit equity-like relationship, loosely speaking, where the investment in the firm is particularly risky (i.e. the intermediary is putting itself at risk) and where the intermediary can exercise some direct or indirect management decision-making over the activities of the firm.

The view of financial intermediaries as the result of relational contracting is not unrelated to the popular term relationship banking. Non-standardised, non-self-liquidating and incomplete contracts create a demand by the firm for a financing source which efficiently permits future recontracting (renegotiation). This element of renegotiation also implies that the financial intermediary may engage in a risk-sharing relationship with the borrowing enterprise. (The bank may ease credit conditions when the firm temporarily runs into hard times.) The banks may indeed have a desire to structure industry in a manner which would reduce their exposure to 'excess competition'. In this light we can view the bank-aided cartelisation of German industry during the 19th century as attempts by banks to exercise control over their risk exposure.

To give some real world content to some of these issues, consider a related topic, bank ownership of equity in non-financial enterprises. Currently in Europe we observe strong differences of opinion over this issue. German and Spanish banks are sizable owners of shares. Italy and the UK, however, have for some time been strongly opposed to share ownership by banks, primarily for the market risks to which it may expose the banking system. But if financial intermediaries provide value added through their ability to develop relational contracts with borrowers and by their supposed superior ability to monitor the performance of firms, given a privileged information position, they may in a sense already be exercising what organisational theorists describe as a 'residual right of control'.[4]

The residual right of control arises from the fact that when contracts are incomplete, as they typically are, renegotiation of the contract over time directly implies that a financial intermediary can exercise residual control over the firm's activities when the firm wishes to renegotiate the loan contract. While the financial intermediary may not be a direct owner of the firm, it has nonetheless a residual form of control arising from the incompleteness of the original debt contract. Contrast this with, say, short-term commercial paper. In this case the debt contract is more complete compared with the bank loan and the only residual right of control would occur in the case of default. This illustration suggests that financial intermediation arises where incomplete (relational) financial contracts are desirable, while security markets prevail where more discrete, complete contracts are possible.

Incomplete financial contracts (e.g. loans) are likely to be less marketable than more complete financial contracts (commercial paper), as the former would be less standardised and the information held by the intermediary on the borrower more difficult to credibly transfer in an open market. Incomplete financial contract markets would thus likely be less liquid. Technology could alter the liquidity of some financial instruments by making it possible to group incomplete contracts which, when combined, form a more complete instrument which can be priced and marketed, creating a liquid market where none previously existed.

The above argument draws a relationship between the notions of financial contract completeness and the liquidity of financial markets. We now draw a thread through to the role of the central bank in indirectly providing liquidity to the market for certain incomplete financial assets, e.g. bank loans. Because bank loans represent more relational than classical contracts we can see a role for the central bank in ensuring the smooth functioning of an illiquid, incomplete contract market, the bank loan market. We can observe this currently in the USA, where the central bank is concerned with a bank credit crunch, ignoring somewhat the increased substitutability in recent years of bank and non-bank credit.

Because of its concern with the potential illiquidity of the banking system, the central bank attempts to bring greater completeness to particular types of relational financial contracts. By providing liquidity to the banking system it assures the absence of undesired interruptions of a particular type of credit, bank loans. In the process of ensuring the completeness of contracts, the central bank is exposed to two types of credit risk, one in operating the payments system (e.g. if it provides overdraft facilities) and another by ensuring the

    [4] See Oliver D Hart, 'Incomplete Contracts and the Theory of the Firm', *Journal of Law, Economics, and Organization*, Spring 1988.

liquidity of an incomplete contract market. (The levy of a reserve requirement on commercial banks can be viewed as the tax offset to the subsidy the
central bank provides the banking system in running the payments system
and standing by to provide short-term financing to banks to indirectly assure
the liquidity of the bank loan market through short-term financing facilities
and lender of last resort guarantees.)

These arguments illustrate a common theme in recent work in financial
theory that 'financial contracts and institutions are determined simultaneously with real variables'.[5] The need to finance French industrialisation
in the mid-nineteenth century gave rise to demands for close ties between
banks and industry, and the creation of a central bank for industry, leading to
the revolutionary Crédit Mobilier. The idea of close bank-industry links was
later exported to Germany and can be said to represent the roots of German
universal banking.[6]

In addition to the nature of financial contracting, national policy regarding
the ownership and control (corporate governance) of private enterprises also
has shaped the structure and regulation of financial markets and institutions
(e.g. anti-trust policy, the separation of banking and industry, government
ownership of banking and industry). In the context of the previous discussion, alternative forms of corporate finance (bonds, equity, bank loans,
commercial paper) contain different degrees of 'contract completeness' and
'residual rights of control' (i.e. influence) over the management of private
enterprise activities. For example, while legally equity holders are defined as
the owners of firms, there are few countries where individual equity holders
of large firms can be said to exercise significant control or influence over the
strategic activities of firms. In some countries the residual right of control
appears to have gone to major holders of incomplete financial contracts,
namely banks. The example is often given of Germany, where banks
dominate the external financing of many major private enterprises and there
is relatively modest use made by German firms of either equity or bond
markets. Although German banks have sizable equity holdings of some
major firms and exercise significant proxy voting rights, their influence also
derives from the management role played by bank executives as members of
boards of directors of German firms. (The role of banks on company boards
facilitates the renegotiation of the incomplete contracts and the selection of
company managers.) The dominant use of longer-term bank loans requiring
the transfer of proprietary information on the firm and the periodic renegotiation of lending terms and agreements imparts a degree of control rights to
banks which could in some sense be optimal given the nature of the contract
agreement between the firm and its creditors.

    [5] Mark Gertler, 'Financial Structure and Aggregate Economic Activity: An Overview', *Journal of Money, Credit and Banking*, August 1988, part 2, p.560.
    [6] See Rondo E Cameron, *France and the Economic Development of Europe*, Princeton University Press, 1961.

The USA, on the other hand, represents a case where the residual rights of control over enterprise assets and activities have gone largely to the managers of enterprises and not to equity holders or debt claimants. The disenfranchisement of equity holders has increased with the further concentration of equity with institutional investors, whose control rights are seriously circumscribed by law.[7] Regulation has limited the influence over enterprises that can be exercised by debt claimants. This is most notable in the US legal doctrine of equitable subordination. The origin of this doctrine, which limits the management role of creditors, lies partly in the legal distinction between debt and equity, the former defined as a fiduciary relationship between the enterprise and the shareholders and the latter as a voluntary contractual relationship between creditors and the firm. (A creditor may have his claim subordinated to other creditors, but not to equity holders, if it has been shown to exercise some influence over management which resulted in harm to other creditors. Specifically, 'the claimant's conduct must have resulted in harm to the other creditors or in an unfair advantage to the claimant'.[8] The issue is of some importance in the case of bank involvement in highly leveraged corporate financing.) Again the notion of contract completeness is useful. As argued by Scott, 'the law has historically assumed that debt contracts are discrete (complete contingent contracts). This is because the principal subject matter of the exchange was credit at a fixed price. ... Predictably, legal disputes have centred on whether the 'relational' obligations of good faith and best efforts should be applied to debt contracts. The issue, then, is not whether shareholders are owed fiduciary obligations and creditors contractual ones. The issue in these leveraging disputes is which legal default rule best suits the needs of most debtors and creditors'.[9]

Regulation has also severely constrained the ability of US shareholders to influence enterprise management. Although corporate governance in the USA is thought to take place via the market through equity price signalling and the exercise of voting rights by shareholders, in fact, as suggested by a former chairman of the Securities and Exchange Commission, 'managements want to retain the traditional legal doctrine that they are responsible only to shareholders while simultaneously constraining shareholders' ability to oversee management performance, and legislatures seem to agree'.[10] The

---

[7] For example, see Mark J Roe, 'Political and Legal Restraints on Ownership and Control of Public Companies', *Journal of Financial Economics*, 1990.

[8] See Andrew De Natale and Prudence B Abram, 'The doctrine of equitable subordination as applied to non-management creditors', *The Business Lawyer*, February 1985.

[9] Robert E Scott in *'Are the Distinctions Between Debt and Equity Disappearing?'*, by R W Kopcke and E S Rosengren (eds.), Federal Reserve Bank of Boston, October 1989. The fiduciary principle as applied to corporate management is discussed in Richard A Posner, *Economic Analysis of Law*, third edition, Little, Brown and Company, 1986.

[10] Joseph A Grundfest, 'Subordination of American capital', *Journal of Financial Economics*, 1990, p.92.

structure of US corporate finance and the governance of corporate behaviour
is further influenced by regulations which severely limit financial intermediaries from making large debt and equity investments in the same firm and in
exercising their ownership rights, unlike regulations in Germany and Japan.
The US philosophy of corporate governance is one of a separation of
creditors and equity investors.

The issues of contract completeness, corporate governance and financial
asset liquidity may appear somewhat removed from what is the subject of
this essay, bank competition and regulation. Yet all are related to two fundamental issues in theories of the firm and of financial intermediation: moral
hazard (hidden action) and adverse selection (hidden information).[11] The
combination of the illiquidity of (some) bank assets, liquid liabilities
(deposits), the residual rights of control of firms by banks and the role of
banks in the payments system makes banks, and the central bank, vulnerable
to the absence of full information on the behaviour of managers of firms
acting as agents for the owners.[12]

The ability of managers to hide actions and information is relevant to the
writing of (incomplete) debt contracts with banks. These informational
asymmetries give rise to contractual imperfections of bank loans.[13] Information asymmetries are in a sense part of the fabric of credit risk. The moral
hazard problem can in theory be reduced, for the firms as debtor and the bank
as creditor, by vertical integration, combining the production of goods
together with the closely related production of credit by a bank which can
influence the investment decisions of the firm and closely monitor the firm's
performance. Conceptually this is what the Société Générale de Crédit
Mobilier in France, a *banque d'affaires*, represented in the 1850s. It was a
mixed bank, accepting deposits on current account and capable of issuing
long-term bonds. 'It specialised in company promotion and provided general
financial services for the enterprises it patronised'.[14] Although the July 1984
French banking law removed the distinction between the three types of
banks (deposit banks, investment banks and long and medium-term credit
banks), recent activity of some French banks in taking major shareholder
interests in commercial and industrial firms again raises a fundamental
organisational issue in banking: how close ought to be the relationship
between banks and non-bank enterprises? The structure of financial
institutions is basically an industrial organisation issue.

One reason for the revival of interest of French banks in the purchase of
corporate shares is said to have been the October 1987 equity market crash,
which made equity investment attractive. A second reason was the request

---

[11] Kenneth J Arrow, 'Agency and the Market', in *Handbook of Mathematical Economics*, Vol.III, K J
Arrow and M D Intrilligator (eds.), 1986.

[12] Note that legally firm managers do not have a formal agency relationship with shareholders.

[13] See Hart, op. cit., p.135.

[14] Rondon Cameron, 'France, 1800-1870', in Rondon Cameron et al., *Banking in the Early Stages of
Industrialisation*, p. 108, Oxford University Press, 1967.

by firms for help from banks in reducing the risk of takeovers.[15] The re-emergence of *banque-industrie* ties in France illustrates both the importance of reducing moral hazard problems of banks as creditors and the desire of non-financial firms to seek control relationships with financial intermediaries who, practically as well as conceptually, already have some residual rights of control as a result of incomplete contracts.

Banks face a moral hazard problem in their role as borrowers as well as lenders. Depositors have limited information on banks' activities and thus can only imperfectly monitor them. Similarly, bank depositors have only a limited ability to refrain banks from engaging in activities which puts their deposits at greater risk than they believed they contracted for. The difficulty in altering the deposit contract (reflecting its incompleteness) is greater when there is no way in which the market can be used to signal a change in the borrower's perception of bank risk (e.g. marketable deposits), other than through deposit withdrawal. Moreover, the difficulty for the bank in conveying to depositors its underlying quality, since bank loans are not visible to outsiders, at times may cause depositors to exit their contract. A good deal of the bank's capital is hence reputational, particularly where banks do not have direct claims on the real capital of their clients.

The above arguments suggest that a possibly fruitful angle from which to view the evolving structure and regulation of banking is that of incomplete contracts, moral hazard and the residual right of control. Because of the strategic role of banks in the economy as deposit-taking financial intermediaries in most countries banks have been constrained by governments in reaching out for economies of organisation — both scale and scope. Governments have frequently restricted the size and competitiveness of banking institutions, the variety of services offered (the separation of commercial banking, investment banking and insurance), as well as regulating the prices of their services. Modern industrial organisational theory suggests we look at banking structure and regulation not simply from the objectives of regulation (stability of the financial system, depositor and borrower protection, control of monetary and credit flows, efficiency, and limiting the concentration of wealth) but attempt to search for some fundamental reasons why banking has typically been the most regulated of all financial activities. With this in mind we consider next the role of the central bank in financial markets and its relationship with deposit-taking financial intermediaries.

---

[15] This is said to have been the origin of the share purchase of the French communication firm Havas by Société Générale. See Madlyn Resener, 'Haus banks à la française', *Institutional Investor*, December 1990.

4.3 CENTRAL BANKS AND THE LIQUIDITY
OF FINANCIAL MARKETS

This section attempts to draw out some interrelationship between the completeness of (financial) contracts, the residual rights of control, liquidity and banking. Banking might be described as an activity involving incomplete financial contract formation (bank lending) by depository institutions, in which there is a reasonable probability that the contract will be revised at some point (renegotiation of terms, etc.) during its life. Moreover, the information the bank has on the borrower is often specialised and idiosyncratic, and thus difficult to credibly transfer to another party without (possibly) transferring confidential (proprietary) information on the borrower (e.g. the deposit history of the borrower). The incompleteness of the contract implies that the bank has some residual right of control over the activities of the borrower. The contract incompleteness implicitly passes to the lender an ability to influence the risk-taking (investment) behaviour of the borrower. These characteristics make bank loans relatively illiquid, particularly if the lender's legal rights of control are uncertain or circumscribed. Moreover, unlike marketable securities, a bank which attempts to sell a loan to another bank may be able to do so only by providing a guarantee to buy it back under certain conditions: the right of recourse, in which the seller of the loan retains some credit risk after having sold the loan.[16] The liquidity of the market for bank loans then is enhanced by a sharing of credit risk. The need for enhancement of incomplete financial contracts may result from the difficulty to credibly transfer information on the borrower or because of the superior knowledge and skill of the loan originator in analysing particular loan contracts and credit markets.

One can think of the liquidity role of the central bank as that of ensuring the stability of a market for certain incomplete financial contracts, bank loans. Because of their incompleteness, bank loans may be difficult to sell should the bank experience a temporary liquidity need. The central bank underwrites the liquidity of the banking market, and in some cases a particular bank, thereby facilitating the extension of relational, incomplete loan contracts. And by purchasing (discounting) bank loans (commercial bills or other private eligible paper) the central bank assumes some credit risk. (With the exception of the USA and the UK, in several countries the central bank conducts extensive domestic credit risk analysis to determine discountable paper and/or provides a pooling of credit information service for banks on large loans — a central risk office.) Even with more complete financial contracts, such as commercial paper, the central bank implicitly may be providing liquidity to a less than complete financial contract market.

---

[16] See Owen Carney and Ellen Starr, 'Reporting and Regulatory Treatment of Asset Sales with Recourse', *American Banker*, 8th June 1990.

Commercial paper, for example, is typically non-collateralised. Its marketability is enhanced by standby credit lines with commercial banks. The liquidity support of the central bank thus implicitly stands behind the liquidity of the commercial paper market. There is an implicit risk-spreading among the players in this chain of incomplete contracting. The recourse the commercial banks have to the liquidity of the central bank makes more liquid a financial asset which might otherwise be less transferable and enhances the development of a secondary market. This chain of liquidity support for private financial contracts was quite apparent in the USA when the central bank purchased bankers' acceptances. (In 1984 the Federal Reserve ceased to conduct repurchase agreements in bankers acceptances.) The lack of good substitutes for bank credit in some countries means that the stability and efficiency of the financial system is more dependent on the central bank's liquidity support and implicit risk-sharing and less on an endogenous creation of inside liquidity provided by private agents. This role of the central bank as residual market-maker may also explain why in some countries without well-developed capital markets the topic of lender of last resort is a very sensitive one, on which discussion is seldom encouraged by the central bank.

In financial systems dominated by incomplete financial contracts and poorly developed secondary markets in financial claims it is also likely that the ties between banks and non-financial enterprises are closer and more interdependent. Banks may hold large equity stakes in enterprises as well as exercise significant rights of control. This is most apparent in countries where industry and the ownership of firms are highly concentrated. The residual right of control falls more easily to banks since by their very nature the financial contracts (loans) are incomplete and relational. From this point of view it is not surprising, for example, that individual equity holders in Japan exercise very modest influence over corporations, that banks hold large portfolios of corporate equity and that several of the Japanese keiretsus,[17] informal industrial groupings, are centred on a large Japanese main bank.

An example of the vulnerability of incomplete financial contract markets is that of the recent fall of several Swedish finance companies and the associated weakness in some Swedish commercial banks. The growth of finance houses was in part the result of earlier restraints on banking activities. The banking sector was obliged over many years to purchase large portions of government paper and required to finance particular sectors, such as housing, in response to political priorities. These constraints gave rise to a

---

[17] Stephen D Prowse found that in 1984 Japanese commercial banks held over 20% of the outstanding stock of all Japanese corporations. Insurance companies (life and non-life) in Japan held over 17% of all outstanding shares, more than three times the amount held by US insurers. He found very little difference in the degree of ownership concentration between keiretsu and independent firms. See 'The Structure of Corporate Ownership in Japan', manuscript, Board of Governors of the Federal Reserve System, March 1991.

non-regulated sector, heavily involved in incomplete financial contracts. With the deregulation of the banking industry the large banks engaged in significant foreign lending, building up large loan portfolios denominated in foreign currencies. Foreign currency credits in mid-1991 were about as large as those in Swedish kronor.[18] Deregulation contributed to a major expansion in bank balance sheets, which more than doubled in the five years through 1990. Moreover, the lending by finance companies was bank-related, as one-third of total finance company lending in recent years has been by finance houses owned by banks.[19] The rapid growth of finance houses was also aided by commercial paper financing. Between 1985 and 1990 commercial paper had grown much more rapidly than bank certificates of deposit. With the bursting of the bubble in Swedish property prices the commercial paper market collapsed. And with the weakness in the commercial paper market, banks stepped in to support the finance houses. The fall of the finance houses then led to some major losses for Swedish banks, one of which was the largest ever experienced.[20]

The difficulties of Swedish finance houses in recent years provides an illustration of the argument that central banks are concerned with the vulnerability of the financial system from incomplete contract markets, and not simply those arising from bank loan contracts. In mid-1988 the Riksbank imposed a 4% cash ratio requirement on bank 'commitments' (deposits and other liabilities), in itself nothing of great note. What is interesting is that at the same time a cash reserve requirement was placed on all finance houses, in the form of a 4% cash requirement on borrowed funds, to be held in a non-interest-yielding account with the Riksbank. The cash reserve requirement was later cancelled in April 1991. It appears that the central bank was concerned with the rapid growth of non-bank lending and attempted to restrain its growth by placing a tax on a form of non-bank intermediation.

Central bank attention to important illiquid (incomplete contract) markets can be viewed as a concern with what financial theorists have called the demand for immediacy, the desire at any moment to sell an asset in lieu of holding it and waiting.[21] The sudden increase in the demand for immediacy in incomplete contract markets can give rise to a liquidity crisis, causing a sharp fall in price (e.g. the international equity price collapse in October 1987). Financial theorists argue that the market-maker essentially provides the 'immediacy' by standing ready to purchase the asset, thereby bearing the interim credit risk until the buy side of the market organises itself and is convinced of the underlying value of the asset. This residual market-maker role

[18] 'Profits in Commercial Banking', *Quarterly Review*, Sveriges Riksbank, No. 2, 1991.

[19] 'Sweden: Credit and Foreign Exchange', Sveriges Riksbank, 1990.

[20] 'Eroding Swedish property prices make banks seek firmer footing', *Wall Street Journal*, 1st October 1991.

[21] Sanford J Grossman and Merton H Miller, 'Liquidity and Market Structure', *Journal of Finance*, July 1988.

(the ability and offer to bear credit risk in periods of temporary market failure) can be said to be one of the roles of the central bank. This role, which may be reluctantly performed because of the potential moral hazard it can create, in theory is not restricted to any one particular type of asset market (e.g. government securities). An example is the support of the Japanese equity market in the mid-1960s and the related aid to a large securities firm. The satisfaction of the demand for immediacy by the central bank would appear to depend on the degree of departure of the asset price asset from its true present value, the ability of private participants to diversify price risk of the asset, and the exposure of financial institutions to the particular asset. The role of the central bank as supplier of immediacy (immediacy of payment and ability to bear credit risk) relates also, for example, to the use of bank lines of credit behind commercial paper issuance.[22]

Another example of central bank concern with incomplete financial contracts and potential liquidity — immediacy crises is the case of the Spanish commercial paper market. In response to the rapid growth in bank credit during 1990 the Spanish central bank placed restrictions on bank lending. Unexpectedly, the private commercial paper market rapidly replaced bank credit, leading to an even faster pace of private credit growth. The Bank of Spain expressed concern not only over the growth of private credit but the fact that investors in their opinion were unaware of the credit risk attached to the commercial paper, some of which did not appear to be bearing interest rates (risk premiums) consistent with the underlying risks involved.[23] This can be read (my reading) as a central bank concern with the incompleteness of the financial contracts represented by the commercial paper and the reluctance of the central bank to provide the role of market-maker in the event of a liquidity (immediacy) crisis in the commercial paper market. In contrast to the Spanish central bank's attention to the private holdings of commercial paper ('private holdings increased by a startling 1,778 billion pesetas'), their concern with commercial paper holdings by UCITS (undertakings for collective investment in transferable securities) was much less, 'largely as a result of the need for a (bank) liquidity guarantee certificate (which ensures marketability in the secondary market) to hold this type of financial instrument'.[24]

The ability of the central bank to ensure payment through its willingness to act as the market-maker of last resort, that is, its potential to absorb credit risk during periods of incomplete contract market failure, brings with it a moral hazard risk. This risk may be greater when the financial system is more intermediated (i.e. banking dominance) than when there are good

---

[22] This point is argued in Peter Garber and Steven Weisbrod, 'Banks in the Market for liquidity', NBER Working Paper No. 3381, June 1990.

[23] See Banco de España, 1990 Annual Report, pp. 86-89 and 'Paper Mountain Thwarts Madrid', *Financial Times*, 31st May 1990.

[24] Ibid, Banco de España, p. 87.

alternatives to bank credit, private market-makers in immediacy. The rise of securities markets, together with derivative markets, should, other things being equal, reduce the moral hazard problem of the central bank. Nonetheless, as the October 1987 equity market crash revealed, the central bank does not escape its role of ultimate provider of liquidity (market-making) even in a highly securitised financial system. Supposedly negotiable contracts can lose liquidity and immediacy in circumstances of great uncertainty. Regardless of the structure of the financial system the central bank cannot avoid the important role of periodic market-maker in major financial assets when private market-makers withdraw. We have seen this in the case of the Japanese equity market during the mid-1960s, the USA commercial paper market during the Penn Central crisis and most recently during the 1987 international equity market collapse.

4.4 FINANCIAL ORGANISATION: STRUCTURAL vs. PRUDENTIAL REGULATION

This section looks briefly at the structure of financial systems, in particular the 'integration' of various financial services under the same corporate umbrella, as an attempt to deal with incomplete contracts. Structural regulation in banking concerns issues of banking organisation, the provision of financial services and the pricing of these services. Traditionally banking has been an activity where integration has been frequently restricted in order to limit the rights of control or influence of particular parties in order to ensure its stability. Commercial banking, investment banking and insurance activities are common separations. One of the strongest separations is that between commerce and banking.

Industrial organisation theorists have emphasised that vertical integration may be viewed as an organisational means of minimising transactions costs when complete contracts between separate legal entities are difficult to write or enforce. Vertical integration can also be used to eliminate bilateral moral hazard problems. Moreover, even if the transaction cost of writing contracts does not warrant organisational integration, integration may thought to be desirable if it more efficiently distributes the residual rights of control over assets which could not be included in a contractual relation.[25] In addition, opportunistic behaviour on the part of parties to a contract may be reduced and mutually advantageous information exchange increased where organisational integration is possible. (No doubt there also exists the risk with some organisational integrations of conflicts of interest, as in the combination of

[25] See Sanford J Grossman and Oliver D Hart, 'The Costs and Benefits of Ownership: A Theory of Vertical and Lateral Integration', *Journal of Political Economy*, 1986; Paul L Joskow, 'Asset Specificity and the Structure of Vertical Relationships: Empirical Evidence', *Journal of Law, Economics and Organization*, Spring 1988; and Paul L Joskow, 'Contract Duration and Relationship-specific Investments: Empirical Evidence from Coal Mines', *American Economic Review*, March 1987.

commercial and investment banking.) These are presumably some of the advantages of universal banking and Japanese-style keiretsu corporate groupings centred on a main bank. Economies of organisation revolve around efficiencies in the use of information and distribution of control rights between different financial institutions and between financial institutions and their non-financial customers. In contrast, the most common reason given for limiting integration in the banking industry is to prevent the use of government insured liabilities in support of non-banking activities. Thus we observe in some countries the requirement that certain financial activities be conducted in separately capitalised subsidiaries of a bank holding company. How close then or distant ought to be organisational ties between banking and non-banking financial enterprises, assuming the distinction can be well defined, and between banking and industry/commerce?

Restrictions on organisational structure in banking and the provision of related financial services across countries reflect differences in philosophies of financial structure, specifically, philosophies regarding business information flows and the control of financial and non-financial enterprises. Differences in financial structures between countries can be said to depend on a 'philosophy of finance', which includes: (i) the content and perceived merits of public disclosure of information on performance, ownership, financial structure and control of enterprises; (ii) the strength of belief in the allocative efficiency of financial markets versus conglomerate (horizontally and vertically integrated) financial institutions; (iii) the desired structure of and market for the ownership and control of companies, both non-financial and financial; (iv) perceptions of the existence and ability of public policy to exploit any trade-off between financial stability and efficiency and between efficiency and 'fairness' in the allocation of capital;[26] (v) the culturally related structure of contract law and the required use of the courts to settle business contract disputes; and (vi) the desired role of the government in the ownership and control of financial enterprises. All of these factors influence the organisational structure and regulation of banking. A basic argument regarding the origin of financial intermediaries and the need for their regulation rests on problems of incomplete information in credit contracts. Differences in philosophies of financial structure rest heavily on differences in information disclosure (e.g. bank secrecy laws, business public disclosure requirements, external audit rules, rights to information privacy and

---

[26] On the issue of 'fairness' in the provision of financial services, see Michael Mussa, 'Competition, efficiency and fairness in the financial services industry', in George G Kaufman and Roger C Kormendi (eds), *Deregulating Financial Services*, Ballinger Publishing Company, 1986; and Hersh Shefin and Meir Statmen, 'Fairness, Efficiency and the Regulation of Financial Markets', manuscript, Department of Finance, Santa Clara University, 1991. The latter argue that regulations are partly motivated by the demand for fairness, defined as equality of opportunity, i.e. 'all parties in a fair market are entitled to equal access to information relevant for asset evaluation'. The access to business information is an important factor which distinguishes financial systems.

consumer protection laws) and the permissible control of firms exercisable
by financial intermediaries.

Arguably the clearest example of banking structure organised in order to
minimise the problems of incomplete financial contracts is the universal
bank. The term universal describes its ability to engage in traditional short-
term deposit-taking, lending, portfolio management and trust business
together with the underwriting and distribution of corporate securities. The
definition of bank universality along these lines may, however, be too
narrow: the above definition hinges on the nature of the dual and possibly
conflicting responsibility of the bank to depositors and to fiduciary-related
(portfolio management) customers and as an agent in the underwriting and
sale of marketable financial assets. (Non-universal banks are defined by the
restrictions on their permissible product range which reduce the moral
hazard problem for bank customers.) An alternative characterisation of this
type of banking organisation would appear to derive from its information
and control relationship with its loan customers. The 'long-term'
relationship that is said to characterise, for example, German banks with
their customers is a sign that the relationship is in part structured to
compensate for the incompleteness of the standard loan contract — the
anability to prespecify provisions for all future contingencies. By this
definition Japanese banks would be more universal than generally argued
and German banks possibly less, given the modest use of equity and bonds
by German enterprises.

Implicit in the relational loan contract is the exercisable residual right of
control by the lender over the assets and activities of the borrower.[27] (A
residual right of control goes to the lender on default of the borrower. The
relational contract may extend some form of residual control for the lender
during the contract period.) Relational contracting is also dependent on the
size of the loan, since the size of the loan will influence the strategic power of
both parties. That is, for large loans the threat of debt repudiation passes to
the borrower some residual control over the lender. The size and uniqueness
of the loan (asset specificity) create the possibility that the loan is implicitly a
strategic bargaining contract.[28] Recognising the implicit residual rights of
control each party to a loan contract has over the other party may then induce
risk-sharing behaviour, such as a mutual exchange of shares or explicit
subsidies from one party dependent on the performance of the other. The
ability in some universal banking systems for the bank to take an equity stake
in the borrower firm and to act in a managerial capacity under certain
conditions (either on the board of directors, as an executive of the firm in
case of serious difficulty which prevents satisfaction of the loan contract, or

---

[27] This issue and related issues regarding the relationship between financial systems and firm behaviour are discussed in Colin Mayer, 'The Assessment: Financial Systems and Corporate Investment',
Oxford Review of Economic Policy, Winter 1987.

[28] The strategic nature of loan contracts is analysed in Douglas Gale and Martin Hellwig, 'Repudiation
and Renegotiation: The Case of Sovereign Debt', *International Economic Review*, February 1989.

through an informal corporate group information relationship) also can be viewed as an attempt to efficiently handle the fact that the original contract was incomplete. Bank ownership of shares may facilitate the bargaining implicit in large loan agreements, where the probability of loan contract renegotiation is high. Alternative forms of relationship between the borrower and lender are, in a sense, forms of organisational integration which seek to distribute efficiently the residual rights of control should some conditions to the original loan contract prove unable to be satisfied.[29]

The long-term bank/firm relationship also permits the establishment of insurance-like risk-sharing relationships, which allow the firm to avoid open market financing or having to switch banks when there is the risk that potentially uninformed creditors may misinterpret the true potential and performance of the firm. This may be particularly true for young firms which have not established a market reputation and can easily be crowded out of financial markets when credit conditions tighten and a sharp tiering of credits arises.[30] (The payment of fees to banks for the availability of credit lines for issuers of commercial paper can be regarded as a sort of credit availability insurance contract.)

From this vantage point we can characterise two financial (banking) systems of regulation/integration. The first is one in which banking regulation is primarily structural and there is a strict ownership/control separation between banks and non-bank enterprises. The separation is often demanded to promote fairness in the provision of financial services (i.e. to limit informational conflicts of interest). There are restrictions on financial vertical integration (strict separation of banking and non-banking activities and firms) which restrict the ability to deal with incomplete contracts through integration: that is, through risk and information-sharing. Complete contracts, or at least the ability to approach them, are left to markets. Futures, swaps and options markets are thus found first in the less integrated (less universal) financial markets, such as in the USA and the UK. The emphasis in this system is on strong public disclosure requirements and Glass Steagall (USA), Article 65 (Japan) type legal separations between commercial and investment banking. (It is sometimes argued that market contracting, since it requires greater public disclosure than internal (relational) contracting, minimises the potential for conflicts of interest. However, public disclosure may be less efficient than internal disclosure brought about by vertical integration if the information can be more effectively used by internal specialists.) Consistent with this financial structure are restrictions on the

[29] The exercise of residual rights of control by banks, for example, by direct representation on corporate boards, is a contentious issue, particularly when it is clearly greater than the role of minority shareholders. A recent illustration is that of the financial difficulty of Nobel Industries AB in Sweden and the residual right of control exercised by Swedish banks. See 'Nobel's move raises issue of banks' role', *The Wall Street Journal*, 8th October 1991.

[30] Akiyoshi Horinchi emphasises the role of risk-sharing in the Japanese main bank system. See 'Information Properties of the Japanese Financial System', *Japan and the World Economy*, 1989.

investment and corporate control activities of institutional investors.[31] This financial structure would view as desirable an open market in corporate control. Financial intermediaries are not viewed as instrumental in carrying out corporate governance. This is a role left to individual shareholders. An important element influencing this financial structure is the role played by fiduciary law, as opposed to contract law, which may influence disclosure requirements and limit the ability of major creditors to exercise residual rights of control over firms. The legal elements influencing the structure and power of financial intermediaries thus depend on the country's tradition of common law.[32]

A second financial system might be characterised as one in which structural regulations are absent or modest and prudential regulations (balance-sheet requirements such as capital and liquidity ratios) dominate. In this stylised model some integration between banks and firms is permitted, such as bank holding of shares in industrial/commercial enterprises with banks taking either formal or informal managerial roles in firms. Capital markets in this structure are implicitly incorporated within banks, which are permitted to provide most financial services. Little effort is made to secure 'corporate separateness' between different functional activities of the bank. This second model emphasises long-term relational contracting between banks and firms and does not stress the allocative efficiency of market contracting. (Indeed, there may be a strong suspicion that market contacting is less efficient.) Information in the system is more internal than external, with little emphasis on public disclosure requirements or major concern with fairness (e.g. equal access to information). (The fact that insider trading is not a criminal offence in some continental European countries partly reflects the predominance of internalised contracting, seen in the heavily interme-diated financial system.) Financial intermediaries are viewed as central ele-ments in corporate governance. Open markets in corporate control are discouraged; cross shareholding by firms is viewed as desirable to protect the stability of domestic industry/commerce and finance. We can appreciate some of these biases by simply comparing typical US and continental Euro-pean business contracts. US contracts usually are more explicit and detailed, with provisions made for possible future contingencies, i.e. more complete contracts. Many continental European business contracts are much more open-ended and less explicit, with clear understanding that unanticipated disruptions to the agreement will be resolved by horse-trading, i.e., the typical contract is more relational.

These two stylised financial systems can be viewed from an industrial organisational vantage point: what are the advantages and costs of

---

[31] See, for example, Mark J Roe, op. cit.

[32] The subject requires a lawyer with knowledge of both economic and legal agency theory. See Robert C Clark, 'Agency costs versus fiduciary duties', in John W Pratt and Richard J Zeckhauser (eds), *Principles and Agents: The Structure of Business*, Harvard Business School Press, 1985.

integration in terms of information and enterprise control? In the second structure, the enterprise control aspect works in two directions: the bank may be able to influence the behaviour of the borrower in a strategic manner during the contract period and the borrower may seek help from the bank during difficult periods or in order to ward off takeover attempts. Cross-shareholding between banks and commercial/industrial firms, as with both German Haus banks and Japanese keiretsus, are both means of mutual protection and ways to minimise transactions costs where incomplete loan contracts need to be periodically renegotiated.[33] The equity investment by the bank may credibly commit the bank to the long-run financing of the firm, particularly in difficult periods. The close association between bank and non-bank enterprises, reinforced by bank equity holdings, reflects the symbiosis between the two groups. The integration of the bank and the enter-prise serves both as a protective device and as a means of internalising the problems of revolving contract dispute — the resolution of problems raised with incomplete contracts. Organisational theorists in recent years have emphasised the reduction in transactions costs created by vertical inte-gration, particularly when it is difficult to write long-term contracts.[34] This difficulty is greater when (Arrow-Debreu contingent claims) complex contracts, contingent on uncertain future events, are costly to negotiate and costly to legally settle when disputed. The integration of financial and non-financial activities in the second banking system helps to fill the gap presented by the absence of such contracts. The transactions costs involved here are not simply the costs associated with the writing and execution of contracts, but also the costs associated with hold-ups, the ability of a supplier (or a purchaser) to extract a quasi-rent from an investment by the firm by threatening to delay or suspend delivery (purchase) of a good. The cost is greater the larger and more specific the firm's investment (for which the product may be an input in production). Vertical integration and long-term contracts thus can be viewed in certain cases as substitutes.

With banking vertical integration is often not an option. Firms cannot own banks and bank ownership of non-financial enterprises is often restricted. Yet banks can hold up firms by refusing to continue the financing of a project. (From the point of view of the firm, bank ownership of its shares may reduce financing hold-up threats.) Changes in the state of nature often will require some recontracting, which may be difficult when the bank cannot efficiently monitor or observe the debtor. An uncertain state of nature (a recession) may cause the bank to pull in its loans and suspend lending. Thus there exists a bilateral moral hazard problem between the bank and the firm. Some sort of integration may be sought to reduce this problem, by forcing

---

[33] An analysis of the strong banking/industry ties in Germany is reviewed in Claude Dupuy and Fran-çois Morini, 'Le Coeur Financier Allemand', *Revue d'Economie Financière*, Summer 1991.

[34] See Benjamin Klein, 'Vertical Integration as Organisational Ownership: The Fisher Body-General Motors Relationship Revisited', *Journal of Law, Economics and Organization*, Spring 1988.

the other party to reveal more information. It is not surprising to find public disclosure by firms and legal public disclosure requirements more prevalent in less bank-intermediated financial systems.

Because of the legal inability of non-financial firms to sufficiently vertically integrate banking and commerce in some countries and the difficulty (or cost) of precommitting the bank to a long-term lending contract, some firms have attempted to build a quasi in-house bank. An example is IBM Credit Corporation, which offers the IBM Money Market Account. This account permits cheque writing facilities and mutual fund investment services. According to recent testimony by the President of the American Bankers Association, the IBM Money Market Account receipts are placed entirely in IBM Credit Corporation Paper.[35] IBM is hence funding itself with a money market fund. General Motors is said to have a similar funding scheme. Hence an alternative for the firm to the establishment of a long-term relationship with a bank, supported by bank ownership of enterprise shares, is the creation of an internal bank, a money market fund with deposit and short-term investment characteristics backed by the firm's own short-term debt. (For example, at the close of 1990 the IBM Money Market Account held about $600 million of IBM Credit's floating rate notes, equivalent to 14% of the firm's total short-term indebtedness.) Other examples of the vertical integration of financial services into the non-financial firm are readily available (e.g. Sears, General Electric Financial Services). While these examples may not match identically all the services offered by commercial banks, their ability to engage in commercial lending and to offer short-term money market investment facilities has undercut the strength of traditional commercial banking in the USA. Hence a third financial system structure is one in which some financial intermediation functions are developed by a non-financial firm without the integration of an external bank. While the subsidiary may be called a finance company, it performs many of the services of commercial banks and without many of the structural or prudential regulations applied to banks.

This section has emphasised that differences in financial structures between countries can be characterised by certain attributes, which comprise what we call the 'philosophy of finance'. These attributes deal in various ways with the difficulty of writing and enforcing long-term (incomplete) loan contracts and with handling the implicit residual rights of control in loan agreements. We suggest that a useful way to contrast financial systems, aside from the usual distinction between intermediated and non-intermediated systems, is from the vantage point of vertical integration (or internal organisation). Vertical integration, in general, is thought to result when transactions costs are high and there is a great deal of specificity of investments. Similarly, the argument can be applied to banking and the competing

---

[35] Statement of Richard A Kirk on behalf of the American Bankers Association to the Senate Banking, Housing and Urban Affairs Committee, US Senate, 9th May 1991.

services provided by securities markets. (Low transactions and a lack of investment specificity would favour the growth of capital markets over banks.) Internal organisation in finance (Haus banks) may reduce the problems of incomplete contracts, the need for costly ex post contract bargaining and opportunistic behaviour (hold-up behaviour), where long-term loan contracts are difficult to negotiate. This may be especially true for the financing of investment with a high degree of specificity, or what some call irreversibility (e.g. long-term investment). However, public policy concerns with the power of banks, fairness, informational conflicts of interest and legal distinctions between debt and equity contracts (debt viewed as a complete contingent contract and equity as a fiduciary contract) have in many cases prevented close relationships between banks and firms, without necessarily increasing the stability of banks. Add to this that as a result of structural deregulation in finance, the availability of financial instruments which more greatly span the 'contract space' and the decline in financial transactions costs, banks in some countries are losing their predominant role as deposit-takers and lenders to enterprises.

The strongest regulatory reaction to the diminished role of banks, and in recognition of the capital weakness in banking partly induced by restrictions on vertical integration, has been the recent US Treasury's proposal to permit banks to form affiliations with a wide range of financial firms under the umbrella of financial service holding companies. In stark contrast to the history of US financial legislation, under the Treasury's proposal these financial holding companies could be owned by commercial enterprises.[36] While not wishing to debate the merits of the US Treasury proposal, it appears to face squarely the need to increase efficiency in the financial system by permitting a closer (vertical) integration and governance structure between users and suppliers of financial services. The proposal carries with it, however, the major risk of expanding the government's safety net.[37]

Consider now the general issue of banking regulation. The purpose of financial regulation is often placed in such a broad framework that it is difficult to consider it analytically (e.g. 'The working of the (financial) system depends so completely on public confidence in the ability and willingness of institutions to carry out the contracts which they have entered that the authorities must always seek to prevent failures and to contain the effects of those failures that are inevitable. The supreme purpose (of regulation) is the safety of the financial system'[38]). To make the issue somewhat tractable, we start

---

[36] See 'Modernising the Financial System: Recommendation for the Safer, More Competitive Banks', The Department of the Treasury, Washington, February 1991, pp. 54-61.

[37] A strong argument against commercial ownership of banks is E Gerald Corrigan, 'Balancing Progressive Change and Caution in Reforming the Financial System', Federal Reserve Bank of New York, *Quarterly Review*, Summer 1991.

[38] Jack R S Revell, 'The Complementary Nature of Competition and Regulation in the Financial Sector', in Albert Verheirstaeten (editor), *Competition and Regulation in Financial Markets*, Macmillan, 1981, p.27.

with the Coase theorem, which states that resources can always be optimally allocated through the market mechanism, irrespective of the assignment of legal liability, when information is perfect and in the absence of transactions costs.[39] The applicability of the Coase theorem to banking is limited to some degree by the inability to write complete contracts: because of the need for repeated bargaining when both parties to a contract have limited information on the actions of the other party, and because of transactions costs and externalities.[40] Hence government intervention, such as public disclosure requirements, restrictions on the risk-taking by banks and requirements for self-insurance against risk taking (capital requirements), is justified if those dealing with banks cannot jointly limit the risk-taking of a bank which could expose them to some damage (negative externality) for which they were unable to extract compensation.[41]

This general argument for government intervention is not specific enough to apply uniquely to banking, where we define banks to be short-term deposit-taking institutions. The lack of depositor information on the activities of bank management is unlikely to be greater than someone with an investment placed with an insurance company. The example of the troubles of Swedish finance companies' investments in real estate illustrates the problem of asymmetric information. Commercial paper holders had no less of a problem in evaluating the risk of these finance companies than did depositors in Swedish banks. Hidden information and actions of financial institutions, particularly when they are numerous and engage in a wide variety of activities, geographically and functionally, makes prudential self regulation difficult. What makes banks require special regulations?

Historically, one of the central reasons for bank regulation has been the entrustment of the payment system with banks, in which all transactions are finally settled with bank liabilities, coupled with the liquidity difficulties of the institution — banks typically borrow short and lend long. The justification for bank regulation and supervision based on its payments system function remains. However, regulation justified by the illiquidity of bank balance-sheets and the strategic role of banks in the intermediation process seems more difficult to argue today. Banks increasingly are able to raise funds with marketable instruments and are capable of converting individual non-marketable loans into bundles of readily tradable instruments. No doubt securitisation has its limits. But the traditional argument for regulation/ supervision based on illiquidity has weakened. As we have seen recently in the USA, there can even occur runs on insurance companies.

[39] R H Coase, 'The Problem of Social Cost', 1960, reprinted in *The Firm, the Market and the Law*, The University of Chicago Press, 1988.

[40] A discussion of the failure of the Coase theorem in certain cases is contained in Jean Tirole, *Theory of Industrial Organisation*, MIT Press, 1989.

[41] See Jeffrey C Marquardt, 'Financial Market Supervision: Some Conceptual Issues', BIS Economic Paper, No. 19, Bank for International Settlements, May 1987.

The move to the greater marketability of bank assets and liabilities raises the question not only of the forms of future regulation and supervision but also of its limits. While bank regulation may be justified by the need to protect the payments system and to restrict undesirable access and abuse of the safety net, it appears clear that greater attention should be paid to the basic Coase proposition, suggesting greater regulation of banks by market participants, fostered by greater public information disclosure.

More complete loan contracts are now capable of being written and transactions costs in financial contracting have declined. This serves both to change the nature of bank services and to weaken their traditional position as financial intermediaries. For example, the creation in the USA of loan-backed securities with a bank guarantee attached (securitisation with recourse) changes the risk exposure of large uninsured depositors and their residual rights of control by giving the previously unsecured depositor a senior claim on bank assets.[42] At the same time it alters the risk to which the US bank deposit insurer is exposed, by leaving on the balance sheet of banks less desirable assets. Regulations designed to increase protection of the payments mechanism by strengthening bank capital may be insufficient to alter risk-taking when banks are capable of writing contracts which provide greater security for purchasers of non-insured bank liabilities and expose the deposit insurer to a weaker bank balance sheet. Put simply, the fundamental nature of banking in many countries has changed. Only by understanding the 'nature of the bank' can one suggest what regulations might be desirable.

4.5 'THE NATURE OF THE BANK':
FINANCIAL DEREGULATION AND THE
RESTRUCTURING OF CORPORATE CAPITAL

In 1937 R.H. Coase addressed the question of the definition of the 'firm' by contrasting the direction of production via the price system in the market with a private organisation in which transactions took place without an explicit market price mechanism. The basic question raised by Coase can be raised with respect to the definition and scope of activities of a 'bank'.

Outside the firm, price movements direct production, which is co-ordinated through a series of exchange transactions on the market. Within a firm these market transactions are eliminated, and in place of the complicated market structure with exchange transactions is substituted the entrepreneur — co-ordinator, who directs production. It is clear that there are alternative methods of co-ordinating production. Yet, having regard to the fact that, if production is regulated by price movements, production could be carried on without any organisation at all, well might we ask, why is there any organisation? . . . The main reason why it is profitable to establish a firm would seem to be that

---

[42] On this issue see Lawrence M Benveniste and Allen N Berger, 'Securitisation with Recourse', *Journal of Banking and Finance*, 1987.

there is a cost of using the price mechanism. The most obvious cost of 'organising' production through the price mechanism is that of discovering what the relevant prices are. This cost may be reduced but it will not be eliminated by the emergence of specialists who will sell this information. The costs of negotiating and concluding a separate contract for each exchange transaction which takes place on a market must also be taken into account. . . . It is true that contracts are not eliminated when there is a firm, but they are greatly reduced.[43]

Coase points us in the direction of considering the costs and availability of contracting and information in order to understand the nature of the firm. The same can be said of the nature of the bank, with one additional element. The products provided by the bank, credit and deposit services, are not simply separate inputs into the production process. With the supply of credit comes an important residual right of control over the assets and activity of the firm. The hold-up costs imposed on the borrower firm can result in illiquidity and, potentially, failure. Hence, in addition to financial transactions costs, the nature of the bank is *jointly determined* with the structure of corporate capital and the governance relationship the managers of the firm desire or are legally required to have with their sources of financing.

The most recent notable upheaval in banking and corporate financial structure has occurred in the USA. The interdependent restructuring of banking and corporate finance has included the increased indebtedness of US corporations, particularly with commercial paper, medium-term notes and low quality bonds, the large retirement of equity, the substantially reduced role of US banks in directly financing US corporations and the increased concentration of non-financial corporate equity ownership with institutional investors.[44] In addition to the tax advantages of debt finance and the reduced creditworthiness of certain US banks, some of these changes have occurred because of the rise of non-bank money market mutual funds, the desire for changes in corporate governance and the decline in financial transactions costs. Corporate capital restructuring may also have been the result of the managerial inefficiencies related to a weak corporate governance structure, which, some argue, increased debt burdens may help to correct. It is also important to note that the reduced corporate financing role of US banks has been just as much a result of the private placement market as the use of public capital markets. In both 1988 and 1989 privately placed issues were greater than the volume of bonds publicly offered.[45] Hence commercial banks have lost ground to non-deposit financial intermediaries as well as to the capital markets. Firms have substituted one form of incomplete relational contract, bank loans, for credit contracts with non-deposit intermediaries.

---

[43] R H Coase, 'The Nature of the Firm', *Economica*, November 1937, reprinted in R H Coase, *The Firm, the Market and the Law*, The University of Chicago Press, 1988.

[44] See L E Crabbe, M H Pickering and S D Prowse, 'Recent Developments in Corporate Finance', *Federal Reserve Bulletin*, August 1990, and Joseph Bisignano, 'Structures of Financial Intermediation, Corporate Finance and Central Banking', manuscript, Bank for International Settlements, December 1990.

[45] Crabbe, Pickering and Prowse, op. cit., p.603.

At the same time that US banks have lost loan business to capital markets and the private placement market, they have increasingly offered insurance-like contingent claims contracts and fee-generating off-balance-sheet services (interest rate and foreign exchange swaps, futures and options). Offsetting the reduced lending to firms, US commercial banks have become heavily involved in lending related to corporate mergers and acquisitions and commercial real estate, the latter the source of many of their present difficulties. In the last few years the outstanding volume of commercial banks' real estate loans has exceeded their commercial and industrial loan portfolio.[46] US commercial banks have increasingly engaged in activities which are, on the one hand, more like brokerage and insurance activities, and, on the other, more asset-specific and relational (corporate merger and acquisition and real estate lending), but in which their residual rights of control may be subject to legal limits.

The fundamental change in the risk characteristics of US bank assets and the greater use of brokered deposits have led some to suggest that the nature of the bank which is protected by the safety net should be redefined; specifically, the high risk activities of deposit-taking institutions should not be underwritten by the government. Quite in contrast to the US Treasury's 1991 proposal to allow well-capitalised banks to have a wide variety of financial affiliates, others are suggesting that the scope of activities of an insured bank be radically reduced. Proposals have recently been made to establish core banks with insured deposits which carry out transactions deposit business, saving and money market account activities and limited risk lending.[47] The core bank concept, the antithesis of the so-called universal bank, appears to be a response to the growth of securitised finance, the growth of non-bank intermediaries and the new capital structure — corporate governance of American firms, coupled with the desire to limit the central bank's exposure to payments and securities settlement risk.[48] Yet it is questionable whether these risks really can be avoided, given the central bank's fundamental role of liquidity guarantor in times of crisis. It is also doubtful whether the core bank proposal really alters the central bank's fundamental requirement to provide security in payments settlement. What has changed is the locus of the liquidity market, from predominantly the banking system narrowly defined to a myriad of securities and derivative markets in which banks are active, together with banks' traditional role as providers of payments services.[49]

---

[46] See J V Duca and M M McLaughlin, 'Developments Affecting the Profitability of Commercial Banks', *Federal Reserve Bulletin*, July 1990.

[47] The 'core bank' proposal is described in Lowell L Bryan, *Bankrupt: Restoring the Health and Profitability of our Banking System*, Harper Business, 1991.

[48] The concern with the stability of the payments and security settlements system in a securitised world is the focus of the paper by David Folkers-Landau and Peter M Garber, 'The ECB: A Bank or a Monetary Policy Rule', presented at the CEPR/Paolo Baffi Centre for Monetary and Financial Economics, 'Monetary Policy in Stage Two of EMU', Bocconi University, Milan, 27th-28th September 1991.

[49] Regarding the potential problems posed by banks' increased activities in securities and derivatives, see 'Thoroughly Modern Safety Net', *Economist*, 26th October 1991.

Alternative proposals call for the corporate separation of banks from other affiliates of financial holding companies and the regulation and safety net protection of only banks.[50] Such proposals see banks as essentially protected mutual funds with insured deposits, where investments only in marketable securities or low-risk non-marketable loans are permitted. Note that such proposals would, in effect, attempt to detach almost completely the payment system from the financial services institution, insuring stability by establishing minimum capital ratios and greatly limiting bank investment opportunities. The end product of the above proposals would be the creation of a government-protected (insured) transaction payments services company with limited liability creation and risk investment activities. The government would not attempt to achieve the stability of the financial intermediation process by regulation and insurance but only provide the payments system. The 'bank' would have a limited ability to create incomplete relational contracts and severely circumscribed ability to exercise any residual rights of control over non-financial enterprise activities. 'Banking', now very narrowly defined under the Bryan-Pierce proposals for US financial reform, would result in a radical reduction in the risk diversification, monitoring and control ('agency cost reduction') functions of regulated and insured deposit-taking intermediaries. These proposals imply that the moral hazard costs of internalising relational financial contracts within banks seem to be too high, given the inability of the banks and their umbrella agency, the central bank, to exercise sufficient control over the risk-taking activities of their clients.

The joint determination of banking structure with corporate capital and governance structures is also seen in Japan. With the opening of opportunities for Japanese firms to finance themselves in foreign capital markets, given the administrative and transactions costs in the domestic capital market, and the ability to convert freely foreign exchange into yen (yen swap limits) the Coase question regarding financial organisational form takes on particular relevance: what to do with large financial institutions some of whose primary functions have been largely taken over by market-traded financial contracts.

Although Japanese firms' dependence on commercial banks continues, deregulation has placed in question the role of Japan's long-term credit banks. These institutions were charged with making long-term (industrial development) loans to industry and, given their ability to issue debentures, acted as Japan's capital market before deregulation, similar in some ways to the internalisation of the long-term credit market within Germany's universal banks. With the ability to tap international capital markets after

---

[50] On the subject of corporate separateness, see James L Pierce, *The Future of Banking*, Yale University Press, 1991 and Sam Chase; 'Comment on bank regulation and monetary policy', *Journal of Money, Credit and Banking*, 1985.

deregulation, some argued that the long-term credit banks have become functionally superfluous.[51] The decline in the need for long-term bank loans has pushed long-term credit banks into the securities area, primarily as underwriters of Euro-bond issues. It may also be a factor in their financing of speculative real estate and equity investment activities. Japan too needs to confront the issue of the nature of the bank.

Japan's long-term credit banks raise three practical problems in a deregulated environment. Firstly and fundamentally, should long-term credit banks really be considered and regulated as banks, since they are not primarily depository institutions subject to the usual concerns with liquidity and the risk of bank runs? (The same question applies to Italy's specialised long-term lending intermediaries.) At present commercial banks cannot issue time deposits with maturities greater than three years and long-term credit banks are not able to issue debentures with less than a five year maturity. The question is whether a bank should be defined by the maturity of its liabilities. Secondly, seeing that recent proposals for financial reform in Japan recommend giving long-term credit banks the same ability to establish securities subsidiaries as city and regional banks, as well as the ability to establish trust and ordinary banking facilities, should Japan follow the earlier example of France and eliminate the definitional segmentation of the banking industry?[52] Aside from issues of how to define a bank and what might be its activities lies a third question: what should be the relationships between non-bank financial intermediaries and banks and how ought they to be regulated? In Japan and in several other countries it has been non-bank banks which have been a major source of weakness in the financial system.

Much of the speculative activities in real estate and equity markets in Japan are related to non-bank banks, primarily credit and finance companies. Many of these institutions have been largely financed by banks and have been only modestly regulated and supervised. In May 1991 the Diet gave to the Ministry of Finance the power to regulate these vaguely defined non-bank financial institutions. While not issuers of deposits these institutions have been important in providing loans to small and medium-sized enterprises. The recent legislation will require the largest 300 non-bank banks to itemise their loan portfolios, presumably to give regulators the ability to discourage certain types of lending.[53] The issue of the supervision and regulation of non-bank banks is a politically sensitive one because of the division of financial intermediary supervisory and regulatory responsibility in Japan.

Note that the new legislation regarding Japanese non-bank banks does not give them the ability to issue commercial paper. Hence commercial banks retain an important avenue for their lending, and possibly the ability to

[51] Aron Viner, *Inside Japan's Financial Markets*, The Economist Publications Ltd., 1987, p.170.
[52] See 'Bank Reform to Fall Short of Full Liberalisation', *The Nikkei Weekly*, 19th October 1991.
[53] See 'Diet Bill Gives MOF Power Over Non-banks', *The Japan Economic Journal*, 18th May 1991.

indirectly circumvent restrictions on certain activities by use of their non-bank intermediaries. In this case we see banks attempting politically to block the use of capital markets by their customers. It is obvious that by continuing to restrict the use of the commercial paper market by non-bank banks and giving the Ministry of Finance only limited, even if expanded, power to regulate these intermediaries, Japanese banks are in effect being protected by regulation from competing directly with non-bank intermediaries.

Given the major dependence of non-bank intermediaries on banks for financing, one can reasonably ask whether the theoretical definition of a Japanese bank ought to be expanded to include their non-bank financial activities, since, in an industrial organisation context, some banks appear to exercise considerable residual rights of control over their non-bank financial affiliates. As argued above, ownership is not necessary to exercise economic control. The ability of the bank to hold up financing of the dependent non-bank intermediary and its ability to extract quasi-rents from the non-bank's investments in real property may imply that the bank owns the intermediary in an economic sense, i.e., it can explicitly influence the non-bank's investment activities.[54] This argument would imply that the economic definition of a bank ought to be broadened because of the close interdependent relationship between the bank and the non-bank intermediary and because of the former's significant residual rights of control over the latter. That is, the true bank is more universal in nature than the legal definition of the institution.

The issue of the nature of the bank and its close relationship with less regulated or supervised non-bank intermediaries is important in understanding the instability recently displayed in several Nordic countries. While the details of the instability in the financial systems of Sweden, Finland and Norway are different, there are several common threads related to regulatory structure, non-bank intermediaries and the residual rights of control exercised by banks.

One thread common to the cloth forming Nordic banking systems was the government policy of limiting competition in banking. In Sweden, for example, no charter was granted for the creation of a new private bank between 1945 and 1983. Banking policy also was characterised as having 'a type of over-regulation motivated by the desire to avoid bank collapse'.[55] Over-regulation in turn gave rise to a non-regulated financial sector: finance houses, both partly financed and in some cases owned by banks, were legally permitted to engage in greater risk-taking than banks. Between 1980 and 1987 the number of finance companies more than doubled and their share of

[54] The relationship between the residual rights of control and ownership is examined in Hart (1988) and Grossman and Hart (1986), op. cit.

[55] Lars Joung, 'Financial Deregulation in Sweden', *Skandinaviska Enskilda Banken Quarterly Review*, No.4, 1986, p 17.

total market advances increased from 6 to 11%.[56] The rapid growth and later weakness of the less regulated finance institutions in Sweden has close parallels with the finance/credit intermediaries in Japan. Both appear to have been heavily financed by banks and to have engaged in activities possibly designed in part to circumvent restrictions on bank lending. The rapid growth of finance companies was further aided by the removal of regulations on household borrowing, which was encouraged by high marginal tax rates and the tax deductibility of interest payments. The Swedish banks were earlier encumbered further by high 'liquidity ratios', requiring them to maintain sizable portfolios of public sector bonds, which helped to crowd out their lending to private enterprises.[57] The much less regulated and very competitive finance companies, on the other hand, engaged in substantial lending collateralised with mortgaged property. Compounding these difficulties was a government policy designed to hold down long-term interest rates. The risky lending by finance companies eventually led to a crisis in the finance industry with some rather severe consequences for banks. Between 1988 and October 1990 the number of finance companies declined by almost 50%.

Similar to earlier behaviour in the UK, banking deregulation in Sweden restulted in excess credit demand: bank balance sheets doubled between 1986 and 1990. Increasingly banks grew dependent on interbank funds and short-term market borrowing, both more expensive than non-bank deposits.[58] The increased competition induced by deregulation cut sharply into the rate of return on bank equity. Between 1989 and 1990 the return fell from 18.8% to 12.6%. And the collapse in property prices resulted in the largest loss ever by a Swedish commercial bank: the second largest bank, 71% state owned. The new coalition government proposed the sale of the government's large stake in the bank. The interrelated dependencies between Swedish banks and finance companies suggests that the nature of the bank was probably better defined by the nature of the residual rights of control of the two institutions than by the ability to accept deposit liabilities.

The story in Norway has certain parallels with the problems in Sweden and even with the turmoil in the Australian financial industry. The removal in 1984 of direct bank lending regulations occurred during a period of high marginal tax rates, when interest payments were deductible from gross income for tax purposes and the economy was growing strongly. At the same time banks were unfamiliar with the environment of aggressive competition and are said to have had inadequate credit review procedures. Moreover, as in Sweden and Australia, while deregulation was at one point welcomed, politicians were reluctant to accept or failed to recognise the need for an

[56] Marianne Bilyer, 'Finance companies — structural changes', *Quarterly Review*, Sveriges Riksbank, Stockholm, No.3, 1991.

[57] Peter Englund, 'Financial Deregulation in Sweden', *European Economic Review*, 1990.

[58] See Bo Dahlheim, Peter Lageslöf and Per Anneström, 'Profits in Commercial Banking', *Quarterly Review*, Sveriges Riksbank, Stockholm, No.2, 1991.

increase in interest rates once non-price credit rationing had been reduced. The result was an explosion in domestic credit, much of it real estate and equity market related. All of Norway's three major banks met with difficulties. The significant weakness in some Nordic commercial and savings banks has required substantial government financial support. In some cases the end product of banking deregulation has been *de facto* nationalisation.[59]

From Norway to Australia and from Japan to the USA problems of adjustment to financial deregulation are widespread and for some common reasons. Countries have sought to move from structural to prudential banking regulation with the expectation that efficiency would be improved while remaining regulation would lead to competitive neutrality. What was not expected was the degree of difficulty institutions would have in a competitive environment and the costs of adjustment to financial deregulation, big bang has led at times to 'big bust'.

Countries have not been neutral in their restructuring of liquidity and safety net support systems in the face of financial deregulation. It is often argued that it is the banks which are most in need of liquidity back-up support and the payments system which most needs to be protected.[60] Yet the increased use of marketable securities and the related shrinkage in the lending role of some banking systems necessarily expands the role of the central bank in its liquidity support function outside of the traditional banking system. That is, the increased volume of financial contract (securities) trading that takes place in markets and not within bank intermediaries shifts the arena in which the authorities need to prevent liquidity insolvency, not least because banks are now heavily involved in securities and derivative markets.

The Coase question regarding the nature of the firm is central to the definition of the role of the central bank in ensuring the liquidity of certain incomplete contract markets. Coase's characterisation of the 'price mechanism as a co-ordinating mechanism' competing with the 'co-ordinating function of the 'entrepreneur'', is closely related to the characterisation of intermediated versus non-intermediated finance, i.e., the role of the (capital) markets in allocating credit as opposed to allocation by financial institutions, some of which accept deposit liabilities. In the desire to promote efficiency, or in recognition of their inability to prevent it from occurring endogenously, regulators have removed many of the restrictions on the prices, quantities

[59] See Karen Fossli and John Burton, 'Banking Crisis Echoes in the North', *Financial Times*, 15th October 1991; and Karen Fossli and Robert Peston, 'The troubles of Norway's bankers', *Financial Times*, 25th October 1991.

[60] This view is forcefully expressed in E Gerald Corrigan, 'Financial market structure: a longer view', *Federal Reserve Bank of New York Annual Report*, February 1987. Regarding the increased use of security markets and the trade-off between capital market efficiency and the monitoring role of 'traditional intermediation', Corrigan argues, 'Thus, as events seem to work in the direction of unbundling the credit process there is at least a question as to whether that unbundling yields results which will preserve the integrity of the decision-making process *as a whole,* while still providing an institutional mechanism that can solve problems and provide liquidity in a manner consistent with the dictates of profitability and stability' (p. 20).

and variety of services of competing intermediaries. The disturbances we are observing in financial institutions worldwide are a result both of the removal of these restrictions and of the continued attempts by some intermediaries to get around those that remain. As we have argued, this restructuring of financial institutions has gone hand-in-glove with the restructuring of non-financial corporate balance sheets and the expansion in household leverage potential. The question these adjustments give rise to is whether governments can actually afford the financial systems they view as most efficient. This question is being addressed in some Nordic countries where we observe the government in one case attempting to sell off its holdings in one of the country's largest banks and in other cases governments forced to invest large amounts in institutions to save them from insolvency. As in the USA, the adjustments to a more deregulated financial structure are causing some countries to call for a shrinking of the government's safety net, while requiring the same countries to invest enormous sums to save parts of the system from collapse.

4.6 'REPUTATIONAL CAPITAL', REAL CAPITAL AND THE SHRINKING OF THE SAFETY NET

If we look at a financial intermediary as the locus of financial information and indirect (i.e. residual rights of) control of the productive capital of firms and individuals on which they hold claims (loans, bonds, shares), we are forced to examine the nature of these claims (contracts) and the claims on the intermediary in determining its stability. It appears clear that some continental European and Japanese financial systems have historically preferred to permit considerable contracting within institutions, broadly defined, so that the information advantages of intermediaries improved control, monitoring and contract enforcement compared with open market contracting. As financial institutions themselves hold only modest real assets as a percentage of their total assets, since the bulk of their assets are claims on others, the reputational capital of the intermediary derives from the stability of the contract relationship it has with its debtors and creditors.

Internalised contracting in some countries is thought to reduce transaction costs and minimise opportunistic behaviour of parties by implicitly integrating financial and non-financial activities through organisational structures, thereby strengthening contract relations. The internal contracting is a source of stability for some intermediaries, even though potential informational conflicts of interest may exist. A large German or Japanese bank, for example, may be identified with its ownership and control of specific firms or industries. (Hence public concern is sometimes expressed regarding the power of banks.)[61] The philosophy of financial development in these countries thus has been one of ensuring the enforcement of certain financial claims through the internal organisation of control, information and risk-sharing.

Where close informational and control relationships between intermediaries and non-financial firms are discouraged, both by legislation and by the courts, the reputational capital of the financial institution is likely to depend in greater part on the intermediary's own capital and on the explicit support provided by government agencies which stand behind them. (In universal banking systems some governments actually discourage the advertising of deposit insurance so as to reduce the problems of moral hazard.) Although the contract enforcement mechanism leans more on market forces and the courts, rather than on relationship contracting, the government often plays the role of bank liability guarantor in cases of market failure. The stability of an intermediary will then depend on the credibility of an explicit government guarantee, such as deposit insurance or lender of last resort, rather than the institution's claims on the real capital of enterprises.

Where the liabilities of bank intermediaries are short-term, because of the difficulty of outsiders to identify real bank capital or to value the quality of bank assets, the reputational capital of all of them may be questioned when any one bank has difficulty establishing its credibility (e.g. contagious bank runs). Well-developed financial markets thus present a direct challenge to bank intermediaries, the threat of disintermediation. This threat increases the lower securities transactions costs, since if primary securities are perfectly divisible the intermediary's risk-pooling ability may be mimicked by an individual investor.[62] The need to build up reputational capital by banks is one reason why governments have in some cases restricted competition in banking and even retarded the growth of securities markets. [For example, in some countries small denomination private financial assets or government securities are unavailable to investors. In Germany money market mutual funds are still unavailable.] The need to guarantee stability of deposit flows has caused some countries to discourage the creation of direct competitors with bank deposits.[63]

One factor differentiating financial systems and financial regulatory structures among countries is the manner in which business information and corporate control is organised. The reputational capital of intermediaries,

---

[61] For example, see 'Zur Diskussion um die Macht der Banken', *Bundesverband Deutscher Banken*, September 1989.

[62] See Michael A Klein, 'The Economics of Security Divisibility and Financial Intermediation', *Journal of Finance*, September 1973. Note, for example, that securities transactions costs were only recently removed in Germany and are still in force in Switzerland, both predominantly bank-intermediated systems.

[63] Preventing the creation of direct competitors for bank deposits can be argued for both monetary control and prudential regulation reasons. See Virginie Coudert, 'Monnaie et Finance en Allemange Fédérale', *Revue d'Economie Financière*, No.3, 1991.

especially banks, depends on this business information/control structure. Banks will lose reputational capital if open financial markets can utilise information on enterprises and create and enforce credit contracts more efficiently. It is not surprising then to find public disclosure of business information generally modest in systems which are heavily bank-intermediated. Banks may further lose ground to financial markets where low transactions costs permit the enforceability of credit contracts to be enhanced by the collateralisation of specific assets of the firm, such as asset-backed commercial paper.

The result of financial deregulation and the technically induced decline in transactions costs has been to reduce the supposed advantages banks had over securities markets in the establishment, monitoring and enforcement of credit contracts and in resolving so-called problems of information asymmetry. The absence of the assumed superior loan contract monitoring and enforcement abilities of banks in some countries has been exposed by their widespread difficulties in operating in a less protected and regulated environment. This has been most apparent in the excessive lending to real property investors and placements in over-valued equity markets. It has become clearer that the problem of asymmetric information which deposit-taking intermediaries were assumed to resolve exists for them as well. Banks with modest capital bases and difficult to value assets in some cases have had greater information asymmetry problems with their creditors that the firms to whom they lend. The consequence has been the realisation that the reputational capital of some large financial institutions may derive less from their superior monitoring and informational advantages over capital markets than from the implicit capital support lent to them by government guarantees. In the opinion of some, banks in certain cases have undesirably leveraged the implicit safety net provided by governments. With the decline in the franchise value of banks, the banking systems in some countries are shrinking and with them a desire to reduce the government's explicit safety net of support.

Financial regulators, supervisors and central banks have responded to the implicit leveraging of the safety net by calling attention to the decline in bank capital and to the moral hazards associated with the safety net. Federal Reserve Chairman Alan Greenspan recently stated,

> ... the safety net has been constructed by government because private market decisions cannot adequately incorporate the perceived costs to the economy of systemic risk. ... The safety net lowers the risk premium on bank liabilities, permitting banks to operate with lower capital or with higher risk asset portfolios. ... By giving governmental assurances to bank depositors of the availability of their funds, the safety net enables banks to have larger, riskier asset portfolios than would be possible in a market-driven inter-mediation process.[64]

---

[64] Alan Greenspan, Chairman, Board of Governors of the Federal Reserve System before the Annual Conference on Bank Structure and Competition, Federal Reserve Bank of Chicago, 10th May 1990.

While a redefinition of the appropriate and affordable banking safety net is desirable, it is less apparent that a shrinking of the safety net and demands for greater bank capital will by themselves be sufficient to restore the reputational capital some banking systems once possessed. Even if more than a decade old, financial deregulation and enterprise financial restructuring have only begun and in the process of transformation we are likely to see further costly periods of adjustment. We still observe in many countries considerable segmentation in financial institutional structure and associated inefficiencies. At the same time we are witnessing programmes aimed at increasing competition in many areas of financial services. Without serious analysis and carefully designed financial structural reforms, governments' problems of moral hazard in banking may not decline, nor may the safety net be allowed by events to shrink. The occurrence in recent years of serious weaknesses in some banking systems appears, if anything, to be widening the safety net. The rhetoric of the long-run merits of financial deregulation has had to yield to the short-run fact of financial instability and in some cases failure. It is little wonder that bank supervisors have responded with demands for greater bank capital.

Discussion

CHARLES A. E. GOODHART

Let me begin with some comments on Sydney Key's joint paper with Hal Scott on 'International Trade in Banking Services'. I regularly tell graduate students preparing to write a dissertation that a great deal of time needs to be spent on working out the *structure of the paper*. If the structure is good, the paper will then largely write itself. Here the structure of the paper is excellent; it has been built around the banking matrix, a simple, visual framework that nevertheless allows a number of complex issues to be presented in a beautifully lucid and succinct fashion. Because the structure has been so well established, the paper does flow clearly, simply and persuasively.

I am not here primarily to compliment the author, though that is a pleasurable exercise, but also to pick holes and to raise doubts. Let me start with the choice of rows in the matrix (Chapter 3 Fig. 1), the policy objectives. Here I have two queries. First, where is the externality or market imperfection that requires the authorities to have concern with the safety or soundness of individual banks *unless* it may lead onto a systemic threat. Could not these two rows have been telescoped together? Second, is there not a more general obligation, policy objective, of regulators to prevent illegal behaviour by banks, e.g. fraud, money laundering, tax evasion, etc?

Let me now turn to the columns. Here the authors have achieved simplicity, in itself a highly desirable outcome, by assuming that banking services, however defined, are only produced by banks, however defined. Key and Scott note from time to time the problems arising from the difference in the range of permissible banking activities available to banks in Europe as compared to those in the USA and Japan, but what about competition from non-banks, foreign or domestic, in the provision of banking services? I shall revert to that issue when I turn to Joseph Bisignano's paper.

Having cast a critical eye on the make-up of the rows and columns, let me come to the elements of the matrix itself. The elements in column 1 are clear enough. The regulation of cross-border services has to be by the home country, except where advertisement and disclosure in the host country is concerned.

Again, there would seem to be a clear and simple *principle* for the elements of columns 4 and 5 relating to subsidiaries. Since subsidiaries are separately incorporated under the laws of host countries, it might seem that they could, and should, be dealt with purely under host country regulations.

There is, however, more of a problem than this simple principle allows. The health and functioning of subsidiaries can be, and perhaps generally is, so intertwined with that of its parent bank that concerns over systemic risk, and the access of its domestic creditors, and insured depositors to funds in the case of bankruptcy, cannot be sensibly addressed without confidence in the state of the parent bank. Remember BCCI. Key and Scott recognise this problem by reference to the application of a source-of-strength doctrine. Now my concern with that is that one can apply an objective test whether a home country has adopted the appropriate international regulations *formally*, but how can one objectively test whether the regulators, and/or the accountants and auditors, in another country are applying and enforcing such rules adequately and effectively. One incentive for them to do so would be to make deposit insurance home based for subsidiaries abroad as well as for branches. That would put the onus for deciding on the adequacy of supervision abroad on the home, rather than the host, regulator. Would that be desirable?

Finally we come to the even more difficult area of the regulation of foreign branches. Here the authors noted a problem, before it was translated into the headlines, that there are no generally accepted rules in the case of international bankruptcies — a fertile and prosperous hunting ground for lawyers. Their preferred solution would have been harmonised home country deposit insurance, but in the absence of such harmonisation, they settle for host country rules with additional requirements. But, so long as disclosure is mandatory, does it matter if deposit insurance schemes do differ from bank to bank?

The authors have clearly identified some pressing problems, but when they turn to procedural methods for addressing these difficulties, they find it difficult to make much progress. In particular, I do not share their apparent preference for the OECD, a somewhat toothless body, as the appropriate forum, over the BIS, where the absence of government officials may perhaps be regarded as a plus rather than a minus.

Not only have Key and Scott identified some key problems that need urgently to be addressed, not least in the light of recent events, but they have greatly clarified our thinking. My main criticism is that their matrix implicitly assumes away some difficulties by treating both banking services and banks as being reasonably easily separately identified. In practice deregulation and competition are progressively blurring the dividing lines, which brings me neatly onto Bisignano's paper. This paper is filled with excellent ideas, a wide range of practical examples, flashes of insight and recurrent themes.

His first theme concerns the well-known, indeed in my view even exaggerated, dichotomy between the relational banking system in Germany and Japan, with most corporate finance being intermediated and corporate governance being largely in the hands of the banks, and the more market-orientated systems in Anglo-Saxon countries, with corporate governance subject to a wrestling match between the current managers and potential market raiders. Bisignano shares the common enthusiasm for the improvement in information flows, efficiency and long-term commitments of relational banking, but, in addition to the privileged access to insider information that this gives the financial intermediaries involved, where the resulting ethos may have played some role in recent events in Japan, he also suggests that the maintenance of a successful bank-intermediated relational system may require either the conscious suppression of competing financial markets and/or at least a willingness to accept an existing oligopolistic system in which competition in financial markets is severely limited. If that is so, which will succeed, the more efficient system, or the more competitive fair and transparent system?

What is less clear is exactly how this then relates to the current topic, the need, nature and form of regulation. The link is suggested in section three where he states that the connecting thread is 'the role of the central bank in indirectly providing liquidity to the market for certain financial assets with incomplete contracts, e.g. bank loans'. But there is a problem here. On the face of it the intermediated relational banking systems would seem to involve much more in the way of illiquid assets than the more market oriented Anglo-Saxon systems. So one might, therefore, expect the German/Japanese model Central Banks to be much more concerned with systemic risks, Lender of Last Resort activities, bail-outs, etc., than the Central Banks, say, in the USA or UK. Yet the reverse is true.

The solution to this puzzle is, I think, that the relational banking systems require, and have largely obtained, structural regulation which maintains the key banks in an exceptionally powerful oligopolistic position, with secure regular profits and no serious internal competition. Hence, they do not need much or any additional Central Bank support.

Indeed, the next theme is that the banks in the Anglo-Saxon countries have been increasingly exposed, in part by the process of structural deregulation, to competition from other sources, both from other markets and from non-bank competitors, and hence have lost market share, profitability and stability. Their position has thus become much more fragile, a fragility enhanced on occasions by regulatory errors, such as 100% deposit insurance and limitations on functions. Such weakness in the banking industry, involving a consequential decline in bank credit ratings, and some remaining comparative competitive disadvantages, e.g. in the shape of reserve and capital adequacy requirements, then leads to typical areas which had been previously bank financed either moving to competitors, e.g. the large in-house financial intermediaries of large corporations, Scandinavian finance houses etc., and/or off-balance sheet, i.e. in the shape of securitised asset markets.

The current fragile state of Anglo-Saxon type banking, and the shift of what was previously banking business elsewhere, has then led to two diametrically different proposals. The first is the narrow, or core, bank proposal, for which Robert Litan is perhaps the best known proponent, which is to force banks effectively to abandon making traditional bank loans altogether, and hold only 'safe' assets. The argument then is that the Central Bank need only protect these narrow banks, leaving the provision of all previously bank-type assets to the free and unfettered play of the market.

Bisignano rejects that option, as he must, if he adheres, in my view correctly, to the view that the Central Bank's role is to provide liquidity to the markets for incomplete financial assets. Consequently, he is driven to the opposite conclusion that the shift of banking business to non-bank competitors and to other markets, such as the commercial paper market, requires the Central Bank to assume a wider range of responsibilities than heretofore. This widening of their responsibilities, beyond the ring-fence of authorised banks is resisted by Central Banks which worry, inter alia, that there is then no clear limit to what they may be held responsible for, the width of their safety net.

Here I accept both Bisignano analysis and I appreciate Central Banks' reluctance to assume wider responsibility, at any rate formally. This then remains a problem, and hence a good point to conclude.

Part III

Regulating Financial Institutions in a Global Context

Chapter Five

Regulating Banks' Securities Activities: A Global Assessment

RICHARD DALE

5.1 INTRODUCTION

There is widespread agreement among policy-makers, regulators, academics and members of the financial community that banks should be free to engage in securities activities. Indeed, the EEC has adopted the universal banking model in its second Banking Co-ordination Directive, the UK and Canada have recently removed barriers between the banking and securities industries, and the USA and Japan are considering proposals for ending the statutory separation of commercial and investment banking.

However, there is no international consensus on the new regulatory framework that should govern combined banking/securities businesses. National authorities have adopted divergent approaches which reflect fundamental differences of view as to how financial markets behave, how different institutional structures respond to financial shocks and what kinds of regulatory safeguards best serve the twin objectives of stability and efficiency. The result is that banks will soon be conducting their international securities business on the basis of incompatible national regulatory arrangements, implying significant competitive distortions as well as uneven lender of last resort coverage for financial institutions operating in different jurisdictions.

The purpose of the present paper is to identify the key differences in national regulatory policies with respect to combined banking/securities businesses and to assess potential dangers and competitive disparities associated with regulatory diversity in this area. The first section examines the policy alternatives, the second section focuses on the divergent

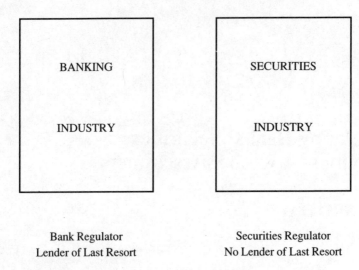

Bank Regulator   Securities Regulator
Lender of Last Resort   No Lender of Last Resort

Fig. 1. Formal separation — Financial stability but economies of scope foregone.

regulatory approaches adopted in Europe, North America and Japan and the final section assesses the broader policy implications.

5.2 POLICY CHOICES

Essentially, there are three alternative regulatory regimes for banking and securities businesses. The first, very simply, is to prohibit the combination of these two businesses within a single organisation. At the opposite extreme regulatory authorities may allow banking and securities business to be freely intermingled, as in the case of universal banks. Finally, by way of compromise, an attempt may be made to construct a financial market regime in which banks undertake securities business on terms which segregate the risks incurred by the bank and its related securities entity.

Statutory Separation

Separation of the banking and securities industries through the imposition of statutory barriers involves heavy but unquantifiable costs in the form of economies of scope foregone and the apparatus of enforcement. Among other disadvantages of this approach is the difficulty of defining banks' permissible activities in a situation where the distinction between traditional bank lending and securities operations is becoming increasingly blurred. Furthermore, even statutory barriers cannot prevent banks being exposed to securities markets through, for instance, lending to securities firms. Indeed,

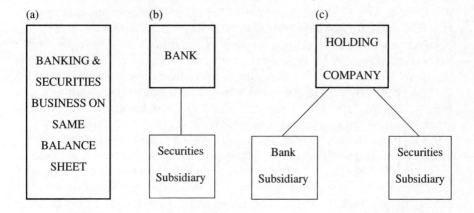

Institutional Regulation — No Firewalls — Lender of Last Resort Extended to
Securities Markets

Fig. 2. Universal Banking — Economies of scope but banks at risk.

such exposure was a major concern during the stock market crash of 1987.[1]
Nevertheless, a complete prohibition on the riskier types of securities activities, including dealing in and underwriting equities, does limit the scope for
risk-taking by banks while confining the lender of last resort function to deposit-taking institutions undertaking conventional banking business. Under
this regime regulation is strictly functional, with bank and securities market
regulators having separate, non-overlapping responsibilities (see Figure 1).

Universal Banking

The universal banking model lies at the opposite end of the spectrum[2]. Here
economies of scope can be maximised and it is left to the bank to decide
whether it can conduct its securities business more efficiently through separately capitalised subsidiaries, through a holding company structure or
through the bank entity itself (see Figure 2). Whatever the corporate structure there are no regulatory constraints on intra-group financial transactions
(though 'Chinese Walls' may inhibit transfers of information) and risks are

---

[1] An SEC report noted that some broker-dealers experienced problems obtaining credit during the
week of 19th October 1987 — to the point where the Federal Reserve Bank of New York felt obliged to
encourage certain City banks to support the securities industry. See the October 1987 Market Break, US
Securities and Exchange Commission, February 1988, pp.5-24 to 5-30.

[2] For recent discussions of universal banking see, George Benston, *The Separation of Commercial and
Investment Banking*, op. cit. pp.179-214; Richard Herring and Anthony Santomero, The Corporate Structure of Financial Conglomerates, *Journal of Financial Services Research*, Vol.4, No. 4, Dec. 1990,
pp.471-497; and Alfred Steinherr and Christian Huveneers, *Universal Banks: the Prototype of Successful
Banks in the Integrated European Market*, Centre for European Policy Studies, 1989.

permitted to flow freely from one part of the conglomerate to any other part. In other words, the bank is exposed to all risks incurred within the group.

Under a universal banking regime it is important that the regulatory/ supervisory function be organised along institutional lines. Since major problems arising in a bank's securities arm would expose the bank itself to the risk of insolvency, it makes no sense from a prudential standpoint to regulate the two functions separately. Therefore, a single agency should be given regulatory responsibility for the activities of the whole group.

An argument could be made for requiring such mixed banking-securities businesses to adhere to more stringent capital adequacy standards than specialist stand-alone banks and securities firms. The capital 'penalty' would reflect the additional social costs associated with the higher risk of bank failure and the fact that, in the case of banking conglomerates, the lender of last resort function would have to be extended to securities activities since these would be inseparable from the banking function. Indeed, the strongest argument against universal banking, to be set against its undoubted merits in terms of operational efficiency, is that it widens the official safety net to non-bank activities.

Risk Segregation through Firewalls

Policy makers are therefore faced with a dilemma. On the one hand formal separation of banking and securities business may involve costly inefficiencies; on the other hand, a permissive regime in which the two businesses can be freely mixed creates risks for the financial system, for the deposit insurance fund and for the lender of last resort. And because neither approach meets the twin policy objectives of efficiency and safety, much attention has been given to devising a third option which might enable banking groups to diversify into securities business while containing securities market risks within the bank's securities unit. Any such scheme which claims to resolve the apparent conflict between efficiency and safety deserves particulary careful consideration.

The first step in seeking to insulate a bank from the risks incurred by its securities operations is to separately incorporate those operations. Whether this should be done through a holding company structure, in which the bank and the securities firm become subsidiaries of the holding company and affiliates of each other, or whether the securities firm should be a subsidiary of the bank, is a matter for debate.[3] The preferred view appears to be that there is less risk of legal separation being overturned by the courts and the bank found liable for the obligations of its related securities firm, if a holding

---

[3] See, for instance, 'Bank Powers: Insulating Banks from the Potential Risks of Expanded Activities', US General Accounting Office, April 1987, pp.26-41; and 'Mandate for Change: Restructuring the Banking Industry', Federal Deposit Insurance Corporation, August 1987, pp.105-125.

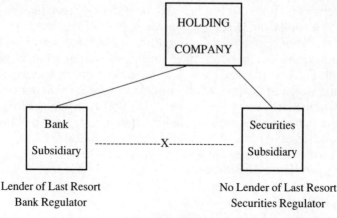

FIREWALLS:
a) legal – separate incorporation
b) commercial – funding restrictions
c) market perception – no joint marketing

Fig. 3. Risk segregation with firewalls. — Bank insulated from risk [?] but limits on economies of scope.

company structure is used (see Figure 3). In other words such a structure makes it less likely that the courts will 'pierce the corporate veil'. As one US commentator has put it:

> ... piercing cross-wide [through the holding company] would be less likely than piercing upward [through the bank]. That is, if a non-bank subsidiary failed, the likelihood that a banking subsidiary would be held liable for its debts is considerably smaller than the (already small) likelihood that the parent holding company would be held liable.[4]

Whatever form of corporate structure is chosen, the next step is to construct firewalls between the bank and its related securities firm to ensure, so far as possible, full legal, economic and market separation. Broadly, these firewalls are of three kinds: they may place restrictions on intra-group financial transactions, they may seek to separate the identity of the bank and securities firm, and they may require separate management.[5] In addition, Chinese Walls may be introduced which aim to prevent conflict of interest abuses by restricting information flows within the group.

[4] Samuel Chase, 'The Bank Holding Company — A Superior Device for Expanding Activities?', in *Policies for a More Competitive Financial System*, Federal Reserve Bank of Boston, June 1972, p.82.

[5] For an assessment of firewalls see 'Using 'Firewalls' in a post-Glass-Steagall Banking Environment', Statement of Richard Fogel, Assistant Comptroller General, before the subcommittee on Telecommunications and Finance, Committee on Energy and Commerce, US House of Representatives, April 13, 1988.

Restrictions on financial transactions, or 'funding firewalls' are intended to prevent a bank from becoming directly exposed to its securities affiliate/subsidiary through extensions of credit or the acquisition of bad assets.[6] Funding firewalls do, however, have several shortcomings as an insulating device. In the first place a bank, under the pressure of events, may well breach the walls, in contravention of the law. Second, situations may arise where a securities firm may need the support of its banking affiliate/parent and where denial of that support could trigger a collapse. The President of the Federal Reserve Bank of New York, Mr Gerald Corrigan, has suggested that in such circumstances funding firewalls could become 'walls of fire'.[7]

Thirdly, while funding firewalls seek to prevent contagion through the assets side of a bank's balance sheet, the more serious problems are likely to arise on the liabilities side — that is through confidence-induced deposit withdrawals. Even if effective asset insulation were achieved this would not ensure protection on the liabilities side. Finally, funding firewalls involve important costs. They are difficult to enforce and they deny to diversified financial groups the benefits of a group funding role for the in-house bank.

Firewalls may also be used to separate in the public mind the identity of a bank and its related securities firm. Such separation is intended to prevent contagion via confidence effects in the event that the securities firm should experience publicised financial difficulties. Restrictions under this heading may include (in the extreme) prohibition on joint marketing of bank and securities firm products, separate premises for the two businesses and a ban on the use of similar names. Where joint marketing is permitted, a minimum safeguard would be contractual documentation making it clear that the bank is not liable for the obligations of securities firm products. The major disadvantage of this class of restriction is that it limits economies of scope on the marketing side and, in the case of a separate premises requirement, adds very significantly to operating costs.

Finally, firewalls may require separate management of a bank and its related securities firm, by prohibiting common directors, officers or employees and mandating separate accounts and record-keeping. Such restrictions are aimed primarily at reinforcing legal separation of the two businesses. However, once again the costs may be heavy, since a fragmented management structure is hardly conducive to successful exploitation of economies of scope. Furthermore, in times of crisis — the very contingency

---

[6] In addition, funding firewalls may be advocated as a means of preventing banks using cheap insured deposits to fund their securities affiliates, thereby allegedly conferring a competitive advantage on bank-related securities firms. However, to the extent that independent securities firms also have access to bank finance this arguments for firewalls is unpersuasive.

[7] Statement before the Senate Committee on Banking, Housing and Urban Affairs, May 3 1990, p.38.

for which firewalls are built — it may be too much to expect that management will remain separate.[8]

In addition to these prudential safeguards, it is likely that regulators of
banking conglomerates will wish to establish Chinese Walls designed to prevent conflict of interest abuses and unfair competition. In particular, a bank
may be prevented from disclosing to its related securities firm any non-
public customer information relating to the creditworthiness of an issuer or
other customer of the securities firm. From the point of view of securing
competitive equality such a restriction may be desirable, but it also erodes
the potential benefits to be derived from financial diversification.[9]

In summary, the separate incorporation of securities activities, buttressed
by firewalls that seek to insulate the related bank legally and managerially as
well as in terms of corporate identity, may go some way towards protecting
the bank from non-bank risks. In such a regime the hope would be that the
lender of last resort function could be confined to the bank. And to the extent
that risks were segregated in this way regulation could be organised along
functional lines — although any doubts about the effectiveness of the insulating mechanism would call for some form of institutional supervision.

Other Forms of Risk Segregation

From this brief review it is obvious that the effectiveness of firewalls in insulating a bank from the risks incurred by a related securities firm will depend
on the height of the walls and the rigour with which they are enforced. At the
extreme, firewalls may impose such severe constraints on intra-group financial, marketing and managerial relationships as to negate the benefits of
diversification — in effect internalising Glass-Steagall-type barriers within
the diversified group and thereby eliminating all economies of scope. Even
so, there can be no assurance that a bank will not be adversely affected by
any problems experienced within its securities subsidiary/affiliate. Indeed,
recent episodes involving, inter alia, Drexel Burnham Lambert (see below)
and British and Commonwealth Merchant Bank, not to mention numerous
earlier US cases, suggest that cross-infection on the liabilities side may
defeat all efforts to insulate the banking entity. Certainly, this is the view of
several leading regulators, as typified by the following comments of Mr
Gerald Corrigan, President of the Federal Reserve Bank of New York:

> ... what the marketplace tells us with almost unfailing regularity is that in times of
> stress, some parts of a financial entity cannot safely be insulated from the problems of
> affiliated entities. Investors, creditors and even managers and directors simply do not

[8] See the example of the Amoco Cadiz cited by the Chairman of the Federal Reserve Board, Mr Paul
Volcker, in evidence to the Subcommittee on Commerce Consumer and Monetary Affairs of the Committee on Government Operations, US House of Representatives, 11th June 1986.
[9] An assessment of the information advantages enjoyed by universal banks is provided by Alfred Steinherr and Christian Huveneers, op. cit. pp.6-7.

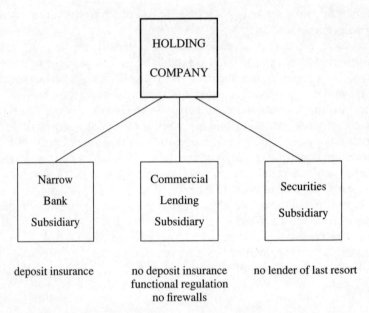

deposit insurance   no deposit insurance   no lender of last resort
                         functional regulation
                         no firewalls

Fig. 4. Risk segregation through 'narrow banks'. — Financial stability [?] plus economies of scope

generally behave in that fashion and the larger the problem the less likely they are to do so. Because this pattern of behaviour seems so dominant and because the authorities throughout the world generally frame their policies with this in mind, there seems to me little doubt that taken to an extreme, absolute firewalls can aggravate problems and instabilities rather than contain or limit them.[10]

It would seem, then, that attempts to reconcile the conflicting objectives of efficiency and safety through the use of firewalls are unlikely to succeed — and may even be counter-productive. In recognition of this fact, a number of ingenious proposals have been put forward in an attempt to square the circle.

One such proposal is based on the idea of the 'narrow bank'.[11] Under this scheme financial holding companies (FHCs) would be free to engage, through separate subsidiaries, in any business activity (including non-financial activities). However, a bank entity within the FHC structure would be required to operate as an *insured* money market mutual fund, accepting insured deposits and investing in highly liquid, safe securities in the form of government obligations. In effect the deposit-taking function would be separated from the lending function, the latter being conducted by separately incorporated FHC lending subsidiaries wholly funded by uninsured liabilities such as commercial paper (see Figure 4). The bank could not, legally, bail out a non-bank affiliate (since its assets would have to consist

[10] Statement before the Senate Committee on Banking, Housing and Urban Affairs, May 3 1990, op. cit. p.39.
[11] See Robert Litan, '*What Should Banks Do?*', Brookings Institution, 1987, pp. 144-189.

entirely of government securities), the possibility of contagion would be minimised if not altogether eliminated and deposit insurance, although retained for confidence reasons, would not be strictly necessary.

A variant of the narrow bank proposal is the idea of a 'secure depository'.[12] Here banks would be able to hold only high-quality marketable assets traded on well-organised exchanges. Regulatory capital would be calculated daily and subject to immediate corrective action in the event of any shortfall — an approach similar to that currently adopted by securities market regulators. All liabilities of the bank would be insured although, as with the narrow bank, prompt corrective action would make deposit insurance very much a second line of defence. The secure depository could be part of a financial conglomerate whose non-bank activities would not need to be circumscribed in any way. The commercial lending function would have to be undertaken by a separate non-bank affiliate whose obligations would be uninsured. Transactions between a secure depository and an affiliate could not threaten the solvency of the depository since the latter's assets would be marked to market daily. Therefore there would be no need for firewalls.

The authors of the secure depository proposal have also suggested as an alternative the 'secured deposit' approach.[13] Under this scheme banks would be able to conduct any activity they wished but their deposit liabilities would have to be collateralised with marketable assets which would be placed in the legal custody of a third party. Loans that could not be securitised would be funded by uninsured liabilities. Rather than ensuring the safety of the corporate entity that accepts deposits, the purpose here would be to ensure the safety of deposits within a larger corporate entity. The secured deposit scheme would therefore do away with the need for separate incorporation of risky activities and allow financial institutions to function as German-style universal banks, with no activity constraints or firewalls.

The great difficulty with each of these proposals, apart from the fact that they involve a major restructuring of banking as we know it, is their failure to ensure broad-based financial stability.[14] A newly defined core banking system, embracing high-quality marketable assets funded by insured

---

[12] See George Benston, Dan Brambaugh, Jack Guttentag, Richard Herring, George Kaufman, Robert Litan and Kenneth Scott, *Blueprint for Restructuring America's Depository Insitutions*, The Brookings Institution, Washington D.C., 1989, pp.19-23.

[13] Ibid. pp.23-25.

[14] A proposal advanced by Gerald Corrigan is vulnerable to the same criticism. He would distinguish between banks authorised to accept insured transaction deposits and financial holding companies authorised to offer uninsured transaction accounts. Under the proposal commercial activities could be combined with non-bank financial activities and non-bank financial activities could be combined with banking, but commercial activities could not be combined with banking. Commercial-financial conglomerates would not have access to the lender of last resort but since the financial activities of these groups would be integrated with the non-commercial financial-banking sector, there would be every possibility of cross-infection spreading within the financial system whenever the financial unit of a commercial concern failed. See Gerald Corrigan, 'Financial Market Structure: A Longer View', *Federal Reserve Bank of New York Annual Report 1986*, pp.3-54.

deposits, would be protected. But the key problem for bank regulators has always been the funding of non-marketable commercial loans. Under each of these schemes commercial lending would be conducted outside the core banking system but would presumably be funded, as at present, by short-term liabilities. These would be uninsured deposits in all but name. The familiar problems of deposit runs, forced asset disposals and contagious crises of confidence would therefore be merely shifted to other areas of the financial marketplace.

For instance, under the secure depository proposal commercial lending could be undertaken by a finance affiliate whose obligations would not be insured. Such finance companies would be far more vulnerable to funding crises than are present day banks enjoying the protection of deposit insurance. Furthermore, it is far from clear that a multiple collapse of finance companies would be any less devastating for the financial system and the economy as a whole than would be the multiple failure of conventional banks. Finally, in times of stress it is reasonable to expect that there would be a massive transfer of funds from the uninsured to the insured financial sectors, as lenders sought to safeguard their assets. The potential for such large-scale destabilising movements of funds would, arguably, increase the fragility of the financial system and defeat the whole purpose of the proposed reforms.

It is difficult to avoid the conclusion that there is a problem here without a solution. Policy-makers may give precedence to the safety and soundness of the financial system by separating the banking industry from securities markets — with whatever loss of efficiency and competitiveness that such a division may entail. Alternatively, they can give priority to efficiency and the exploitation of economies of scope by allowing banks to engage freely in securities activities — while accepting a much greater potential for contagious financial disorders and a correspondingly larger role for the lender of last resort. However, attempts to achieve both safety and efficiency by using the apparatus of firewalls, separate legal entities and other risk insulation techniques promise neither safety nor efficiency — and quite possibly achieve the worst of all worlds by combining costly restrictions with hard-to-detect risk 'seepage'.

5.3 NATIONAL PRACTICE

Having analysed the various policy alternatives for regulating banks' securities activities it is necessary to review national practice in this area. One clear trend to emerge from the discussion that follows is the increasing determination of national authorities to permit banks to participate in securities markets. However, there is no common approach to managing the risks associated with financial diversification, within individual countries policy

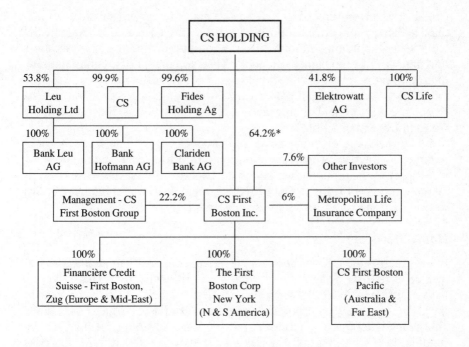

Fig. 5. Credit Suisse Holding Company structure (end 1990). — * CS Holding owns 73.5% of the voting rights. N.B. Percentages shown are capital stakes not voting rights.

has tended to shift erratically and the latest moves towards liberalisation generally lack a firm analytical base.

Germany and Switzerland

Germany and Switzerland are traditional universal banking countries where securities business is typically, but not always, conducted off the banks' own balance sheet. Regulation is institutional rather than functional with the Federal Banking Supervisory Office, in the case of Germany, and the Federal Banking Commission, in the case of Switzerland, responsible for supervising a bank's securities as well as its banking business.

Swiss and German banks have been forced to separately incorporate their US securities activities in order to conform to the Glass-Steagall Act but even here risks are free to flow between the securities entity and its related bank. This key point was underlined recently when Credit Suisse sought to reduce its regulatory capital requirements by creating a holding company structure (see Figure 5) in which Credit Suisse and its US investment banking arm, Credit Suisse First Boston (CFSB), became affiliate companies owned by CS Holding (CSH) (previously CFSB had been an indirectly held subsidiary of Credit Suisse). However, in October 1989 the Federal Banking Commission ruled that the new holding company structure did not exempt

Credit Suisse from providing full capital cover for group subsidiaries and that the bank would have to consolidate itself with CSH as if it and not CSH were the group holding company. The reasoning behind the Commission's decision was that the bank would be obliged as a matter of commercial self-interest to support CSFB if the latter should get into difficulties, even though there was no legal obligation to do so. The Commission's decision, and its reasoning, were upheld on appeal by a ruling of the Swiss Federal Supreme Court in December 1990.[15]

It is clear, therefore, that universal banks cannot escape from the risks incurred by their securities operations, and it follows that capital adequacy rules apply to the group rather than to the bank. A further, though less explicit, consequence of this denial of risk segregation is that the lender of last resort function extends to banks' securities activities.

United Kingdom

In broad terms the UK has adopted the universal banking model as a consequence of the Big Bang restructuring of securities markets. That is to say, banks are free to undertake securities business off their own balance sheet or through a separately incorporated securities subsidiary. Furthermore, if they choose the latter there are no formal restrictions preventing UK banks from funding their securities subsidiaries — i.e. there are no firewalls and risks may flow through from the securities subsidiary to the bank.[16]

However, the universality principle is subject in the UK to two major qualifications. In the first place, gilt-edged market makers are 'ring-fenced' within the banking groups to which they belong. Such market-makers must be separately capitalised, they can generally have no subsidiaries operating in financial markets (downstream protection) and they are supported by comfort letters from their major shareholders (upstream protection). These mechanisms of risk insulation are justified, inter alia, on the grounds that gilt-edge market-makers have direct access to the Bank of England as lender of last resort, although it seems somewhat incongruous that firms operating in the gilt-edged market are protected in a way that the banks which own them are not.

A second important qualification arises from the statutory distribution of regulatory responsibilities in the UK. Parliament chose to divide responsibility for regulating combined banking/securities businesses between the Securities and Investment Board (SIB) and the Bank of England: the SIB

[15] For a summary of the Court's decision see 'Credit Suisse loses its Supreme Court appeal', IBCA, London, January 1991. It should be noted that because Swiss law gives the Banking Commission regulatory authority only over banks, and not over their holding companies, the Commission had to deal with CSH at one remove via Credit Suisse. Hence the requirement that Credit Suisse consolidate itself with CSH for regulatory purposes.

[16] For a detailed description of the UK's financial regulatory structure see Richard Dale, 'UK Regulation of Financial Conglomerates After Big Bang', Discussion Paper No.91-11, Department of Accounting and Management Science, University of Southampton, May 1991.

being responsible for regulating businesses authorised to conduct securities/ investment activities under Section 25 of the Financial Services Act of 1986, while the Bank is responsible for supervising the banking activities of those firms authorised to undertake such business under the Banking Act of 1987. In other words combined banking/securities businesses are subject to functional rather than institutional regulation, with different parts of the same financial group being treated separately for regulatory purposes.

This division of regulatory responsibilities presents serious difficulties given the integrated nature of risks incurred within combined securities/ banking businesses and the consequent need for an overall assessment of such businesses' financial condition. In other words, functional regulation cuts right across the universal banking model. In order to alleviate this difficulty the Bank of England and the SIB have between them developed the concept of 'lead regulator' whereby each UK supervisor retains statutory responsibility for the institution it authorises, while the lead regulator for the group promotes exchanges of information between supervisor and co-ordinates any necessary remedial action. While the lead regulator innovation does introduce an institutional element into the functional statutory framework, it cannot hope to deliver the same quality of prudential supervision as would a regime in which all parts of a financial group are subject to consolidated supervision by one overall group supervisor (assuming, of course, that the group supervisor commands the necessary expertise).

Europe

In launching its single European market programme the European Commission at the outset adopted a financial regime based on the Swiss/German universal banking model. That is to say, banking is defined broadly to include securities business, questions of corporate financial structure are left to individual banking organizations to decide as a purely commercial matter, and no attempt is made to segregate banking from non-banking risks within financial conglomerates.

Having prescribed a universal banking regime the European Commission ran into difficulties when it sought to formulate a capital adequacy directive for mixed securities/banking businesses.[17] On the one hand it was recognised that banks, unlike securities firms, are vulnerable to contagious funding crises and should therefore be subject to a stricter definition of regulatory capital than that applied to securities houses. On the other hand, in the interests of competitive equality, the Commission proposed that supervisors should be able to apply a more permissive definition of regulatory capital to a bank's own securities trading book. The effect of this hybrid capital adequacy test, which allows more liberal use of subordinated debt as capital backing for securities activities, is that the burden of absorbing losses on a

---

[17] See Richard Dale, 'The EEC's approach to capital adequacy for investment firms', *Journal of International Securities Markets*, Vol. 4, September 1990, pp.1-9.

bank's trading book may have to be borne by the equity capital that supports the rest of the bank's business. Therefore under the EC regime banks that engage in securities business may carry a higher risk of insolvency than specialist banks.

To put it another way, under the proposed EC scheme, banks and their securities activities are fully integrated from the point of view of risk exposure but treated separately for the purposes of capital adequacy assessment. An important — and incongruous — element of functional regulation is thereby introduced into a pooled risk regime that surely calls for an institutional approach to prudential regulation.

A further difficulty arises from the multifarious arrangements within the EC for regulating banks' securities business. In general, securities activities carried out by banks on their own balance sheets are regulated by the banking supervisor but this is not necessarily so — for instance UK banking and securities supervisors have overlapping responsibilities in such cases. Furthermore, where banks' securities business is conducted through separately incorporated subsidiaries, the securities subsidiary may be the primary responsibility of the securities supervisor (as in the UK and Spain).[18]

USA

The Glass-Steagall Act represented an unequivocal decision by the US Congress to separate the risks associated with commercial and investment banking. However, the statute left an important loophole in overseas markets which US regulatory authorities were happy to tolerate in order to strengthen US banks' competitive position abroad. Furthermore, the strict segregation of domestic banking and securities business was relaxed during the 1980s as a result of a number of decisions by the Federal Reserve Board, exercising its discretionary authority under the Bank Holding Company Act.[19]

These moves culminated in the decision of September 1990 to allow a bank holding company's 'Section 20 subsidiary'[20] to underwrite corporate debt and equity securities on a limited scale and subject to detailed firewall requirements. On the face of it the Federal Reserve Board appeared to be giving its support to a new regulatory regime, in which risk segregation techniques such as separate incorporation and extensive firewalls were to be used as a means of allowing banks expanded securities powers without widening the official safety net.

[18] See *Systemic Risks in Securities Markets*, OECD, 1991, pp.37-38.
[19] See Richard Dale, 'US Banking Reforms: Repealing Glass-Steagall', *Journal of International Securities Markets* Vol. 5, Summer 1991, pp.105-111.
[20] Under Section 20 of the Glass-Steagall Act, a bank may not be affiliated with any company 'principally engaged' in securities business. However, bank holding companies may establish 'Section 20 Subsidiaries' which undertake securities underwriting and distribution on a limited scale that does not amount to being principally engaged in securities business.

However, the reality was somewhat different. The quantitative limits imposed on securities business undertaken by Section 20 subsidiaries are designed both to meet the statutory wording of the Glass-Steagall Act and to minimise the overall risks incurred by the securities subsidiary. In other words, bank holding companies are being allowed to engage in potentially risky securities activities but on a scale that would be highly unlikely to jeopardize the solvency of the securities subsidiary, still less the bank. In this situation firewalls are being employed only as a back-stop, rather than as a central mechanism for segregating risks. The Section 20 subsidiaries there-fore represent a hybrid solution to regulating banks' securities activities — involving both costly firewalls and a severe limitation on the extent of banks' participation in securities markets.

The Bush Administration's proposals for repealing Glass-Steagall, intro-duced in February 1991, rely much more heavily on risk segregation.[21] This is to be achieved through a financial services holding company (FSHC) structure in which the bank and its securities affiliate would be separated by firewalls and the official safety net would be explicitly confined to the bank. In the Treasury's words, 'creditors of the FSHC or [non-bank] financial affiliates should receive no federal protection in the event of FSHC insolvency'.[22] In contrast to the limits currently placed on bank holding companies' Section 20 subsidiaries, a bank's securities affiliate could, under the Administration's scheme, undertake securities business on whatever scale it chose — subject, of course, to the SEC's regulatory capital require-ments for securities firms. Consistent with this risk segregation regime, regulatory responsibilities would be allocated on a functional basis (Figure 6).

The authors of the Administration's proposal evidently harbour some doubts about the effectiveness of their attempts to segregate risks. Thus, in order to allow for the possibility of cross-infection, banks which choose to have securities affiliates will have to maintain especially high capital ratios.[23] Furthermore, the bank regulator is to be given 'umbrella oversight' of the holding company, thereby providing an element of institutional regu-lation designed to detect and correct problems within non-bank affiliates that could pose a threat to the bank. In short, the apparatus of risk segregation is in this case being combined with other safeguards more properly associated with the universal banking model — with adverse competitive implications for US banks (below).

However, the main criticism of the Administration's proposal is that the holding company structure and firewalls which lie at the heart of the scheme

---

[21] See 'Modernising the Financial Services System: Recommendations for Safer, More Competitive Banks', USA Treasury Department, February 1991.

[22] Ibid. p.58.

[23] The statutory basis for this premium capital requirement is set out in draft legislation ('The Financial Institutions Safety and Consumer Choice Act of 1991') placed before Congress by the USA Administration.

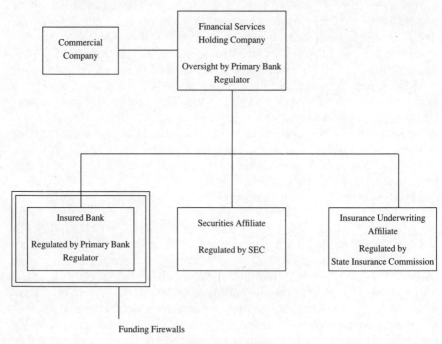

Fig. 6. Proposed financial structure.

are likely to prove redundant. There is already ample evidence to suggest that a bank will be quickly infected by a non-bank affiliate's problems, fire-walls or no firewalls, the most recent and spectacular example being pro-vided by the collapse of Drexel Burnham Lambert.

On 13 February 1990 Drexel Burnham Lambert Group, Inc. ('Drexel'), the holding company parent of Drexel Burnham Lambert Inc., a major securities firm, and Drexel Burnham Lambert Government Securities Inc., a registered government securities dealer, filed for Chapter 11 bankruptcy.[24] Drexel had become increasingly dependent on short-term credit markets, borrowing as much as $1 billion on an unsecured basis, largely through the issuance of commercial paper. In December 1989 Standard and Poor's had reduced its rating on Drexel's commercial paper, with the result that Drex-el's borrowing from this source dried up. But because a large proportion of Drexel's assets were not readily marketable (in particular it had a large port-folio of 'junk' bonds) its balance sheet could not be contracted in line with its reduced funding capacity. The result was an acute liquidity crisis, described by the Chairman of the Federal Reserve Board, Mr Alan Greenspan, in the following terms:

[24] For a full account of Drexel's collapse see Statement of Richard Breeden, Chairman US Securities and Exchange Commission, before the Committee on Banking, Housing and Urban Affairs, US Senate, concerning the Bankruptcy of Drexel Burnham Lambert Group Inc., 1 March 1990.

As doubts emerged about the ability of Drexel to meet its obligations in a timely and predictable way, it suffered what in banking terms would be called a 'run'. The run extended across the various units that make up Drexel — including both regulated and unregulated affiliates, and including affiliates that seemed to be solvent, as well as those whose status was in doubt.[25]

Of particular significance was the fact that Drexel's government securities subsidiary, which was adequately capitalised, stringently regulated and apparently soundly run, found its access to funds cut off when questions were raised about the health of the parent company. The unmistakable implication is that all parts of a financial conglomerate that rely on short-term borrowing become vulnerable when confidence in *any* part of the organisation is shaken.

This unwelcome message from the markets appears to have had a major impact on the thinking of at least some regulators. In July 1990 Mr Greenspan delivered the following congressional testimony, revealing his own deep misgivings on the whole risk segregation issue:

The Board has for some time held the view that strong insulating firewalls would both protect banks (and taxpayers) from the risk of new activities and limit the extension of the safety net subsidy that would place independent competitors at a disadvantage. However, recent events, including the rapid spread of market pressures to separately regulated and well-capitalised units of Drexel when their holding company was unable to meet its maturing commercial paper obligations, have raised serious questions about the ability of firewalls to insulate the unit of a holding company from funding problems of another. Partially as a result, the Board is in the process of re-evaluating both the efficacy and desirability of substantial firewalls between a bank and some of its affiliates. It is clear that high and thick firewalls reduce synergies and raise costs for financial institutions, a significant problem in increasingly competitive financial markets. If they raise costs and may not be effective, we must question why we are imposing these kinds of firewalls at all.[26]

Despite the lessons of the Drexel affair and growing official scepticism about the effectiveness of firewalls, the US Administration has proposed a new financial structure in which the stability of the US banking system may depend on the ability of firewalls to insulate banks from securities market risks. At the same time the requirement that banks with securities affiliates must have additional capital will undermine US banks' competitiveness vis-à-vis their European counterparts without doing anything to neutralise the most potent source of cross-infection — namely, confidence-induced withdrawals of funding.

[25] See Testimony before the Subcommittee on Economic and Commercial Law, Committee on the Judiciary, US House of Representatives, 1 March 1990, p.14.

[26] See Testimony before the Committee on Banking, Housing and Urban Affairs, US Senate, 12 July 1990, p.14.

Canada

Historically, Canada's banking and securities industries were separated under the 'four pillars' policy which established formal legal barriers between banking, insurance, securities and trust business.[27] These domestic restrictions did not, however, prevent Canadian banks, like their US counterparts, from conducting investment banking operations through their subsidiaries in London and elsewhere. Banks have been permitted to acquire domestic securities subsidiaries since 1987 but regulatory policy governing the relationship between a bank and its related securities entity has undergone important changes during the course of this liberalisation process.

The Government's 1985 Green Paper setting out its proposals for financial reform followed a risk segregation approach, utilising a holding company structure and strict firewalls between a bank and its non-bank affiliates. This was similar to the scheme now adopted by the US Administration. However, in a major policy switch the Government, in its subsequent 1986 Blue Paper, abandoned the risk segregation model in favour of a more permissive regime in which banks would be able to diversify through securities subsidiaries with relatively few restrictions on intra-group financial transactions (in effect low firewalls). The legislation submitted to Parliament in 1990, by lifting these residual restrictions, marked a further shift towards the universal banking model — although the outer shell of risk segregation was retained in the form of a separate incorporation requirement for banks' securities (and other non-bank) business.

Consistent with this approach, the Government has attempted to introduce an institutional element into its supervisory arrangements, in particular by reaching accords with the various provincial authorities that regulate banks' securities subsidiaries. In effect these agreements give the federal bank regulator the right to be consulted on regulatory matters affecting the solvency of a securities subsidiary. Nevertheless, the federal/provincial division of regulatory responsibilities for banks and securities firms makes it very difficult to achieve a satisfactory institutional oversight of banks' securities activities.

Japan

After the Second World War the USA, as occupying power, imported the main restrictions of the Glass-Steagall Act into Japan. Nevertheless, the separation of banking and securities business has been less complete in Japan, where banks, unlike their US counterparts, are empowered to invest in equity securities and Japanese banking groups have been able to acquire

---

[27] For a review of Canada's changing regulatory structure see Richard Dale, 'The New Financial Regulatory Framework in Canada', *Journal of International Banking Law*, Vol. 3, Issue 3, 1988, pp.117-126.

major interests in securities firms through a complex web of cross-shareholdings.[28] These differences apart, the Japanese authorities have in effect extended the official safety net to major securities houses which typically have direct access to the Bank of Japan's discount window. Paradoxically, therefore, statutory risk segregation has failed to confine the lender of last resort function to the banking sector.

Since the mid-1980s the Japanese authorities have been considering proposals for dismantling the present constraints on banks' securities activities. In June 1991 the Ministry of Finance appeared to be favouring a proposal under which banks would be able to establish separate securities subsidiaries but the question of what, if any, firewalls might be required remained undecided — as did the more fundamental issue of whether the new structure should continue to segregate bank from non-bank risks. Indeed, in the Japanese context the whole debate about banks' securities powers is linked to concepts of fairness rather than to the more familiar Western policy goals of safety and soundness and efficiency. Thus the Ministry of Finance is evidently inclined to limit the pace at which City banks can expand their securities activities because of the marketing advantages they enjoy in the form of extensive branch networks — an approach that turns on its head the traditional case for expanded securities powers based on economies of scope. More paradoxically, the Ministry has proposed that banks' securities subsidiaries should be allowed to engage in underwriting (a high-risk activity) but excluded from brokerage business (a lower risk activity).[29]

5.4 CONCLUSION

From the above survey it should be apparent that in addressing the issue of financial diversification national policy makers and regulators have only one thing in common — a desire to extend the boundaries of banks' permissible securities activities. How this should be done, whether risks should be segregated and what the role of the lender of last resort should be — all these matters are the subject of divergent and often confusing national initiatives.

The policy disarray surrounding the key issue of financial market structure has disturbing implications for the stability of the international banking system. In particular, it is clearly unsatisfactory that the EC and the USA should be moving in opposite directions on the question of risk segregation. Within Europe it must be assumed — as the Swiss court did in the Credit Suisse case — that a bank will always stand behind a related securities firm.

[28] See, generally, Richard Dale, 'Japan's "Glass-Steagall" Act', *Journal of International Banking Law*, Vol. 3, 1987, pp.138-146.
[29] See Naoyuki Isono, 'Recommendations Point to Liberalising Financial System', *Japan Economic Journal*, June 15 1991, p.1.

In the USA, the Administration's proposed holding company and firewall structure is explicitly designed to ensure that a troubled securities firm is *not* supported by its bank affiliate. There is a further implication that within Europe the lender of last resort function may have to be extended (directly or indirectly) to bank-related securities firms. In contrast, the US Administration's scheme is intended to confine the official safety net strictly to the banking sector.

The coexistence of these diametrically opposed regulatory structures is fraught with difficulties. In times of global financial stress there may be a temptation, within Europe, for lenders to shift their exposure from stand-alone to bank-related securities firms, on the grounds that the latter are more likely to receive official support. More importantly, in such circumstances there will be a strong inducement for lenders to withdraw funding from US securities firms (whether or not bank-related) in favour of securities firms affiliated to European banks. In the meantime US banks which are part of diversified financial groups will face a competitive disadvantage *vis-à-vis* their European counterparts because of their mandatory holding company structure, higher capital requirements and restrictive firewalls.

Chapter Six

International Corporate Finance and the Challenge of Creative Compliance*

DOREEN McBARNET
CHRISTOPHER WHELAN

6.1 REGULATION AND THE INTERNATIONALISATION OF CAPITAL MARKETS

Internationalisation of capital markets has underlined two key inter-related issues in the regulation of corporate finance. First, demands for access to reliable financial information have escalated as international financial risks have grown. The sums involved in corporate deals grew exponentially in the 1980s. The leveraged buyout of RJR Nabisco in 1988 cost $25.08 billion, resulting in borrowings for the new RJR of $22.08 billion, more than the combined national debts of Bolivia, Uruguay, Costa Rica, Honduras and Jamaica.[1] The need for transparency in financial reporting has been further highlighted by recent major corporate and banking crashes, such as the Bank of Credit and Commerce International, British and Commonwealth, Rush and Tompkins, Polly Peck, Bond Corporation and Maxwell Communications Corporation.

Subsequent analysis of some of these has revealed that the reliability of

---

* This chapter is based on research in the UK, France, Germany and Brussels. We are grateful for the funding contributions of the European Commission, French Commissariat du Plan, and Jacob Burns Socio-legal Fund.
[1] *Sunday Times*, 4 September 1988.

the financial information disclosed prior to collapse was suspect while the transparency of corporate financial activity was undermined by the use of 'havens' throughout the world where secrecy rather than disclosure is the norm. The suddenness, at least as far as the public was concerned, of many of these crashes, as well as the 'mega' sums involved, both testify to the fact that, in practice, investors are not always properly informed of the real financial risk to which they are exposed.

Secondly, calls for international harmonisation of the rules governing disclosure have increased as markets have opened up to international capital. The demand is for harmonisation which allows the players in capital markets to genuinely compare the financial results disclosed by different companies in different countries, and creates a 'level playing field', in which all the players are subject to the same rules. In an international capital market, the argument runs, there are dangers in differences in national rules, dangers, for example of creating what has been called a 'Delaware effect'. In the USA, the advantageous rules of the state of Delaware attract corporate registration of companies which actually operate elsewhere — at the time of our research only one major US corporation operated out of Delaware but 56% of the top 500 US corporations, and 45% of all companies whose shares were listed on the New York Stock Exchange, were registered there.[2]

Concern has been expressed that in an international market, different national rules can likewise create competitive advantage. Companies in one country might attract investment on the basis of high profitability or net value which is a product of advantageous rules on financial reporting and disclosure rather than genuine superiority of performance. The Securities and Exchange Commission recently announced a review of US accounting standards to determine whether they were 'adversely affecting the ability of US companies to compete internationally with foreign companies whose home country's accounting rules may be less stringent than US standards'.[3]

Different rules in different regimes may well distort the level playing field as when UK accounting rules have given UK companies an edge in takeovers, allowing them to offer higher bids for acquisitions than otherwise equally placed competitors. So, for example the spate of takeovers in the 1980s of US corporations by UK companies, often large US companies by smaller UK companies, has been put down in part to the comparative advantage given to UK companies by rules on accounting for goodwill. When Blue Arrow acquired the US corporation, Manpower, it could, under UK accounting rules, project annual profits of $30.1 million. A US bidder operating under US rules would have had to deduct at least $30 million each year from profits to write off goodwill, allowing a projected profit of only

---

[2] W Landau (1989), 'The Federal and State Roles in Regulating US Business Corporations', in B Wachter et al., *Harmonisation of Company and Securities Law*, Tilburg University Press.

[3] 22 Sec Reg and Law Rep (BNA) 1111, July 27, 1990.

$1.1 million. This could make it harder to sell the bid to shareholders and to raise finance.

How advantageous this competitive advantage was, might with hindsight be questioned, where overbidding and major financial difficulties have resulted.[4] However differences in rules have provided fuel for complaints and for the rhetoric of the need for harmonised rules and a level playing field in international capital markets. Can harmonisation and comparability, and the perhaps more fundamental goals of transparency and reliability, be achieved? This chapter addresses the issue by drawing on our research on law and accounting in the Single European Market.[5]

The creation of the Single European Market (SEM) provides us with a case study in regulation aimed at harmonisation. Fundamental to its idea of a free competitive market is the removal of those rule-based competitive advantages which act as prohibited trade barriers and their replacement with single community rules. The harmonisation programme of the SEM is a regulatory response to the problem of divergent rules within an international market. The tool being used in this strategy is European Community law. The SEM is thus a prime example of an attempt at using law to achieve international integration into a single market based on a level playing field. How successful has it been? How successful can it be?

In practice there have been major problems in the EC's programme of integration and regulation. Some are familiar problems with any regulation, although they are exacerbated by the international context. We will explore these in the specific context of the regulation of the financial reporting, briefly reviewing the familiar problems of legislation and enforcement, then focusing on the particular challenge we identify as 'creative compliance'.

6.2 CONTROLLING COMPETITIVE ADVANTAGE: THE CASE OF THE SINGLE EUROPEAN MARKET

Harmonisation of disclosure of financial information in the SEM has been tackled via the company law directives, particularly the fourth directive on company accounts and the seventh directive on group accounts. It has been no easy task.

The process of political compromise which has marked EC legislation generally has led to problems. There is the problem of settling for the lowest common denominator in standardisation. While the playing field may then be level, the EC rules are too weak. Worse, they may have been substituted for strong national regulations. Thus, fears have frequently been expressed that high standards of protection — for investors, employees, consumers,

---

[4] *Sunday Times*, 7 October 1990.

[5] Based on analysis of law and financial techniques and interviews with leading practitioners and regulators in the UK, France, Germany and Brussels.

etc. — in particular member states will be 'jeopardised in pursuit of economic integration.'[6] Then there is the tolerance of options within apparently harmonised rules. This can take the form of permission for member states to derogate from or to choose whether to implement certain terms of the measure. It seems, for example, that only the UK has implemented the option in the Seventh Directive which declares a parent-subsidiary relationship to exist where there is a participating interest and the actual exercise of dominant influence (discussed further below).

Compromise can also lead to gaps. It has been argued that a mergers regulation has been possible only on the basis that it concentrates on the competition aspects and ignores the social effects of mergers.[7] There is also the problem of delay with the result that by the time old problems are sorted out new ones have appeared. In an accounting context, the new practice of transferring goodwill to intangibles such as brands is possible 'as a result of the absence of any requirement to the contrary within EC directives'.[8] Such problems of the political and legislative process have undermined the quality of the rules themselves and their value as an instrument of genuine harmonisation. In short, while EC Directives are binding on all member states as to the end to be achieved and uniform standards may be mandated, significant deviations in the actual rules of member states remain in practice.

In the particular context of the disclosure of financial information, the European Community was confronted with marked differences in the basic purposes and philosophies of accounting in different countries. Indeed, even after the implementation of the fourth directive there remain considerable variations between member states, as Touche Ross's recent study[9] indicates.

This study demonstrated how a hypothetical company's performance could be reported in line with the national rules of different European Community countries. The reported profits for the same company undertaking the same transactions in the course of a year could vary from a lowest achievable ECU 27 million under German rules to a highest achievable ECU 194 million under UK rules. The most likely German result was only two thirds of the UK's (ECU 133 million in Germany, compared with ECU 192 million in the UK). Yet this was the same company reporting exactly the same business. This is a striking example of the difficulties involved in making international comparisons of company performance on the basis of disclosed financial information when the rules governing that disclosure are so diverse.

The Touche Ross study attributed a key role in this to the different orientations of member states to accounting for the capital market or accounting for tax. Where UK and Netherlands accounting separates tax and market

[6] See, e.g., A. McGee and S. Weatherill (1990), 'The Evolution of the Single Market — Harmonisation or Liberalisation', 53, *Modern Law Review*, p.578, p.585.

[7] Ibid. p. 591, n.90.

[8] Touche Ross (1989) *Accounting for Europe*, Touche Ross, p. 18.

[9] Ibid.

accounts, in other countries, such as Germany, ta ، and market accounts are the same so that companies wishing to claim tax allowances must present the market with accounts with the appropriate claims deducted from profits. This leads to an inbuilt conservatism in German accounts which distorts comparability.

One can see just how difficult comparison can be by considering the accounts of German motor manufacturer BMW at the time of our research of Germany. BMW was taking full advantage of tax benefits such as the 100% first year allowances for investments in West Berlin, involving accelerated depreciation, which appeared as such on the accounts. The result is that one could not even sensibly compare a Berlin company's financial accounts with those of a Hamburg company. Yet even for the international market, BMW did not (and was not required to) disclose the effect this had on profits, noting merely that 'full advantage is taken of tax concessions regarding depreciation charges'[10]. As one (then) Big 8 accountant observed: 'this tells you they are extremely prudent but does not tell you much else'. How then are investors to compare BMW's performance with that of companies based elsewhere in Europe, or for that matter in the world? Continued variation in rules, and in accounting purposes and philosophy, undermines comparability.

This situation has been compounded by problems of enforcement and non-compliance even with compromised rules. Enforcement of law is a perennial problem even within the nation state. Effective enforcement is constrained by organisational problems, by lack of resources, by problems in detecting violation or non-compliance. Enforcing *international* regulation is more complex still.

In the European Community there are policing problems at two levels. First there is the problem of ensuring member states who have agreed to the substance of specific directives in fact implement them. European Community law comes in different forms. While 'regulations' are directly applicable in member states, the more frequently used 'directives', have, for the most part, to be implemented into their own domestic law by member states before they take effect. The organisation of the European Commission has been focused more on making than on enforcing legislation.

Then there is the problem of how closely member states themselves police compliance among companies falling under new regulations. Politics can play a part here too. Implementing law, but failing to enforce it, can result in the 'law in the books' bearing no relation to actual practice, and reduce the appearance of regulation and harmonisation to the merely symbolic.

In Germany, for example, the fourth directive was extremely unpopular. Many small and medium sized companies had not hitherto been required to produce public accounts. The implementation of the fourth directive meant

---

[10] BMW annual report to December 1987.

340,000 companies would now have to do so for the first time, this in a country where in 1985 there were only about 6,000 and in 1990 only 12,000 qualified auditors (Wirtschaftsprufer and Vereidigte Buchprufer).[11] Germany was five years late in implementing the directive and has throughout lobbied (successfully)[12] for a change in the directive to exempt many of these companies. In the meantime enforcement appears to have been somewhat ineffective. Less than 10% of German companies complied with the requirement to register company accounts in the prescribed time.[13] Harmonisation of member state legislation did not necessarily mean harmonisation — or transparency — in practice.

What are the solutions to such problems? The routine reaction is to demand a regulatory response, calling for better rules, better enforcement to achieve more effective rules and real compliance. Yet even if they could be achieved, better rules, better enforcement may not produce transparency or comparability. A great deal of effort — in policy- making, enforcement and research — is expended routinely on the objective of securing compliance. But even achieving this objective may not solve the problem. Securing compliance may not be enough.[14]

Formal compliance by those subject to regulation with even tough rules, cannot necessarily be equated with effective achievement of declared regulatory goals. Compliance far from being a solution to a regulatory problem may itself pose a regulatory problem. This is what we see as the paradox of compliance. Regulatory problems have been defined for too long as problems of non-compliance. The problem we focus on is the problem of compliance, and particularly the problem of 'creative compliance'.

Focusing on compliance as a problem involves a switch of perspective, from the regulatory response, to the response of the regulated. After all, those on the receiving end of rules do not simply receive them passively; they react and respond. They can respond by lobbying for change or by non-compliance, taking the risk of sanctions if law is enforced.

But the regulated can also respond in another way, setting lawyers and other advisers to work to develop responses to regulation, which do not simply accept the impact of the rules but which circumvent them. This involves using the rules themselves in innovative ways to avoid and manage regulation. This is why we have to switch perspective in another way too, from issues of politics and enforcement, to closer scrutiny of the nature and role of law and regulation. Law and regulatory rules are amenable to use not only as instruments for implementing regulation but as instruments for

---

[11] *The Wirtschaftspruferkammer* (1991), Wirtschaftspruferkammer, Dusseldorf.

[12] 90/604/EEC.

[13] Senior official, German Ministry of Justice.

[14] D. McBarnet (1992), 'The Construction of Compliance and the Challenge for Control: The Limits of Non-compliance Research,' in J Slemrod (ed.), *Who Pay their Taxes and Why?*, Michigan University Press.

resisting it. Such resistance to law through law is epitomised in the strategy of 'creative compliance'.

6.3 CREATIVE COMPLIANCE

Creative compliance means complying with rules in form without complying in substance, meeting the letter but not the spirit of the law. This is not an enforcement problem. On the contrary enforcement is pre-empted because control is avoided without breaking the rules. Creative compliance means operating within loopholes in the law, beyond the reach of the law, or using the fabric of the law itself to create loopholes or innovative techniques which comply totally with the requirements of the rules but nonetheless completely undermine the policy behind it.

So for example when Germany implemented the fourth directive requiring disclosure of financial information for many companies for the first time, one response for the companies concerned was to lobby for change; another was simply not to comply. These strategies posed practical enforcement problems and political problems for regulators. There was, however, another response possible, and it posed a more fundamentally legal problem. That was to change the legal structure of the business to remain outside the ambit of the law, and so avoid disclosure by creative use of law.

In Germany there are a number of different legal forms available for the conduct of business. Those affected by the 1987 implementation of the fourth directive were mainly GmbHs. However, those who wished to escape the requirement of the directive to disclose financial information could reorganise into a different legal form, into a GmbH & Co or a GmbH & Co. KG, often via highly complex legal routes.[15] The advantage lay in the fact that the GmbH & Co and GmbH & Co.KG were commercial partnerships which were not required to disclose financial information like other German corporate structures (Aktiengesellschaft, Kommanditgesellschaft auf Aktien, and GmbH). Disclosure could thus be escaped without non-compliance, via legal lateral thinking, via creative compliance.

This particular loophole has been closed by new rules[16], not least because of EC fears that what was defined at the time as a local German problem might be used more widely, fear, indeed of a Delaware effect, despite apparent legislative harmonisation by regulators. As a senior European Commission official put it: 'It would be iniquitous and contrary to the spirit and aims of the Fourth and Seventh Directive to allow those particular kinds of partnerships and unlimited companies to evade the accounting requirements

[15] Strobl, Killius and Vorbrugg (1988), *Business Law Guide to Germany*, 2nd ed., CCH Editions Ltd, Bicester.

[16] Directive extending the scope of the Fourth Directive on annual accounts and the Seventh Directive on companies, adopted Nov 1990. Implementation date is 1 January 1993, but it need not apply until 1995: 90/605/EEC.

applicable to other undertakings having limited liability.'[17] The regulatory response was not enough; the regulated could respond in turn to find new sources of rule-based competitive advantage, requiring further regulatory response in a cat and mouse game which is repeated in tax avoidance, the regulation of financial institutions and elsewhere.[18] And the game is not yet over. European Community law has itself provided other business structures which, we would suggest, might in turn be used to avoid disclosure. Certainly, even where such structures are set up for other reasons, non-disclosure of financial information is one consequence.

So, when Airbus criticises British Airways (BA) for being anti-European by buying its engines from America and even hints that 'sweeteners' may have underpinned its decision-making,[19] BA cannot easily retaliate. Airbus is a French Groupe d'Intêrets Economique (GIE). As such it does not have to publish accounts. Its liabilities, its sweeteners, government subsidies or whatever are hidden, legally, from view.

The GIE is only available in France. But it was the model for the new business structure available since July 1989, throughout the EC known as the European Economic Interest Grouping (EEIG).[20] The EC Regulation on EEIGs was designed to facilitate cross-border business cooperation within the Community by removing the need to operate in an unfamiliar system of law. But the EEIG is not only freed from legal obstacles, it is also freed from the obligation to disclose financial information. An EEIG has the advantage of flexible forms of funding. There is no capital requirement and liabilities can be hidden. The EEIG may thus offer route to escape from harmonised disclosure rules.

It is paradox enough that the 'strongest' form of EC law, a Regulation[21], can be used as a means of escaping from EC Directives, but there is more. While the Regulation provides for a uniform framework throughout the EC, it leaves to national law a number of matters it could not cover without seeking to impose a uniform system of private law. EEIG members are free to register it in any member state where it has a business presence or where it has its central administration. It will then be subject to the law of that state. The perceived and actual differences in national law, such as tax provisions, and in national legal systems — common law/adversarial versus civil/inquisitorial — re-emerge then as factors in determining where to register the EEIG. The effect of the Regulation may thus be that the choice of location will be distorted, 'Delaware' fashion, to the most favourable state.

---

[17] K Van Hulle, (1987), *Developments in Financial Accounting and Reporting of the European Community*, p.14, (KPMG, Amsterdam).

[18] D. McBarnet, (1988), 'Law, Policy and Legal Avoidance', *Journal of Law and Society*, Spring; and see E. Kane on the 'regulatory dialectic' e.g. in 'Impact of Regulation on Economic Behaviour', *Journal of Finance*, Vol.xxxvi no.2, May 1981.

[19] *The Times*, 27 November 1991.

[20] Regulation 2137/85.

[21] That is, it is directly applicable in member states.

This may be the least regulated. Whether this will pose a significant problem remains to be seen.

Escaping disclosure requirements altogether is one way to throw transparency and comparability, but of course if a company wants to enter the market it may have to disclose information. Indeed, in practice there may be more harmonisation than the formal rules would imply. French companies often voluntarily produce accounts following US GAAP (Generally Accepted Accounting Principles) for the simple reason that they want to enter the US market. Companies may produce multiple accounts for different markets or show how accounts prepared under one set of rules would have to be adjusted in another context.

But that is where we come to the underlying issue of the reliability of the information that is being disclosed. Creative compliance affects the reliability of financial information and, in doing so, it also affects its comparability. One area of creative compliance currently attracting regulatory attention is that of off-balance sheet financing (OBSF). This refers to the raising of finance in ways which do not appear in the accounts at all or do appear in the accounts but fail to make clear the real exposure involved.

OBSF can take many forms. It can involve the creation and use of complex and innovative financial instruments, which have posed a challenge for accounting rules worldwide. It is often unclear just how they should be accounted, measured or categorised, and this provides an opportunity for creative accounting. But OBSF can also involve the use of legal structures which avoid disclosure of awkward information. One UK example which has stimulated extensive regulatory response is the 'quasi-subsidiary'.

In the UK, and with the implementation of the seventh directive throughout the European Community, groups of companies are required to produce consolidated accounts showing the assets and liabilities of the group as a whole. However the techniques known as the non-subsidiary subsidiary, quasi-subsidiary or orphan subsidiary, have been used to avoid the requirement to consolidate financial information, thus hiding liabilities, manipulating performance indicators such as earnings per share, and, according to the reported figures, making the company stronger on the market, more creditworthy to lenders, and more powerful in the takeover market, in short, creating a potential competitive advantage based on manipulation of rules rather than performance or value.

The form used depends on the rules in play. In the UK under the rules of company law prior to the 1989 Companies Act, a subsidiary's accounts had to be included in the group's accounts (subject to some exceptions) if the parent company owned more than 50% of the shares and controlled more than half of the board of directors. A number of legal structures were created with varying degrees of complexity to retain control of a company while avoiding meeting those two requirements and so avoiding the need to include the quasi-subsidiary in the group's accounts. With the quasi-subsidiary safely off the balance sheet it could be used to carry debts or other awkward financial information in *its* accounts without affecting the balance sheet or earnings per share ratios of the group.

Such vehicles were used for many purposes by many household name companies including Cadbury Schweppes, Dixons, Burton, Storehouse, Habitat, S & W Berisford and Beazer.[22] Maxwell Corporation's acquisition of Macmillan and the Official Airlines Guide (OAG) for $2.6 billion and $750 million respectively, in 1988, used off-balance sheet structures. Macmillan was bought through shell company Mills Acquisition. OAG was bought by Pergamon, which as a private company, was not included in Maxwell Corporation's balance sheet. If the companies had been bought directly by MCC and included in the group's balance sheet there would have been seriously adverse effects on the earnings per share ratios of the group with possible knock on effects on share prices. The interest costs involved in servicing the enormous debt incurred would also have affected MCC's pre-tax profits.

Purchasing through an off-balance sheet structure provided a window in which to try to sell off assets to reduce the enormous burden of debt before bringing the acquisitions onto MCC's accounts. MCC's broker was reported in the press offering reassurance that the timing of the transfer of ownership of MacMillan would ensure there was no dilution of group earnings per share.[23] In reality, neither the debt nor the interest costs went away. But they were kept off MCC's reported assets and profits, even though MCC remained ultimately exposed to the financial risks involved.

The quasi-subsidiary in the particular forms constructed in the 1980s is no longer possible. These have been caught by new rules in the Companies Act 1989. However, the form employed is dictated by the rules in play at any given time. New rules can simply mean adaptation and new techniques. Even before the 1989 Act was on the statute book, the practitioners we were interviewing claimed to be constructing new techniques with the express purpose of meeting the requirements of the new rules yet still avoiding consolidation of riskier ventures in group accounts.

The deadlocked joint venture is one of several current techniques, carefully designed in a bid to escape the new law. The criteria for consolidation of a company's results in the larger group's accounts moved in the 1989 Act towards broader criteria, aimed more at capturing the economic substance of corporate relationships and not just their formal legal structures.[24] The new criteria were, first, participating interest (which was broadly but clearly defined) and second, control defined more vaguely in terms of 'actual dominant influence'.

The deadlocked joint venture is geared to avoiding this criterion of

---

[22] For a detailed analysis of Bearer's use of a quasi-subsidiary for the acquisition of Koppers, see McBarnet and Whelan (1992). Law Management and Corporate Governance, in J. McCahery, S. Picciolo and S. Scott (eds), *Corporate Control and Corporate Accountability*, forthcoming.

[23] *Financial Times*, 5 November 1988.

[24] See McBarnet and Whelan (1991), 'The Elusive Spirit of the Law', *Modern Law Review*, November.

control, being based on a 50-50 partnership with neither partner controlling. Deadlocked joint venture companies have been used as vehicles for property development, and the discovery, after its sudden collapse, of a claimed £700 million of debt in joint ventures involving construction/property development group Rush and Tompkins clearly reveals how the joint venture can work to hide liabilities. The receivers at Rush and Tompkins have suggested many of its 50 joint ventures were joint in name alone with Rush and Tompkins carrying most of the risk.[25]

The regulatory response continues with the accounting profession's efforts to produce a new accounting standard to ensure the reality of risks and rewards is disclosed. But the approach is controversial. The standard has been in process since 1987 and is still at draft stage, in Exposure Draft 49 (ED49).[26] There must also be doubts as to the feasibility of effectively and sustainedly enforcing the 'spirit of the law' rather than ensuring merely formal or creative compliance.[27] Off balance sheet financing is not a UK phenomenon nor even just a European phenomenon, but a regulatory headache in the corporate sector and in banking internationally.[28]

Such creative compliance has relevance for both transparency and comparability in financial reporting. A company which can raise finance in ways which protect its balance sheet and earnings per share ratios may not only distort its own financial image but may create for itself a competitive advantage over those who offer fuller disclosure of debt and risk.

6.4 THE CHALLENGE OF CREATIVE COMPLIANCE IN A COMPETITIVE MARKET

When issues arise perceived as requiring a regulatory response, then, however powerful that regulatory response may be, it may still be rendered ineffective by the response of the regulated. Even if we could achieve harmonised rules and formidable enforcement it would not be the end of the regulatory story but the beginning of the next chapter, the regulated's response. In the context of international capital markets, variation in the stringency of different nation's laws and regulations has been pointed to as a source of competitive advantage. Indeed there are often powerful economic incentives for governments to promote a 'Delaware effect' so long as they are benefiting. But law can provide a means of competitive advantage in another way, less dependent on governments or regulators. Law must be

---

[25] Christopher Morris of Touche Ross, *The Times*, 30 April 1990.

[26] Accounting Standards Committee (1990), ED49: Reflecting the Substance of Transactions in Assets and Liabilities, Accounting Standards Committee.

[27] See McBarnet and Whelan (1991) op cit., note 24.

[28] For example, Bank of International Settlements (1986), *Recent Innovations in International Banking*, BIS.

recognised not just as a means of regulatory control but as a raw material[29] with which the competitors themselves can create rule-based advantage.

Indeed there is a paradox in using law or other forms of regulation to remove rule-based competitive advantage and create a level playing field for fair competition. The situation needs to be viewed from the perspective of the players in the competition. From this perspective the level playing field may well be something seen as an unqualified good — *for one's competitors*. For oneself, there may be other ambitions, such as the vantage point of a little molehill of competitive advantage in the middle of that level playing field. In the competitive environment which is the goal of the SEM, there may be every incentive to use creative compliance to stay one step above levelling law.

Paradoxically, regulation, intended to remove artificial competitive advantage can also create opportunities to gain competitive advantage. A legally based level playing field opens up new sources of competitive advantage, with some more able than others to creatively escape even harmonised regulatory restrictions. The rules of the level playing field themselves become obstacles to some but not all. Regulation in effect becomes a further stimulus for innovative use of law both to defeat unwelcome regulation and to secure advantage over competitors.

This produces a dilemma for regulatory authorities, bent on a policy of free competition. How are they to encourage companies to take advantage of a competitive environment while at the same time discouraging them from gaining a competitive edge by getting round the restrictions of the rules themselves? One irony of the Single European Market is that the European Commission uses law to establish a level playing field for competitive market activity, producing, indeed, 'an immense corpus of law'.[30] But in a competitive market law may become just one more market obstacle to be overcome by the legal creativity of the regulated. The same paradox is likely to be repeated in regulation of international capital markets more generally. As one of the then Big 8 accountants we interviewed put it: 'What we are seeing is competition based on comparative creativity rather than on financial strength or traditional business links.'[31]

The significance for the international capital market is not, however, just a matter of a level playing field, perhaps always something of a holy grail. It is also a matter of risk. Global markets imply bigger deals, more volatility and more risk. The reality of the risk that was there in the creativity of the 1980s is under the spotlight in the recession of the 1990s. Creative compliance poses a challenge not just for a competitive market but for the exposure to, and indeed creation of, risk in that competitive market. It also poses a major

[29] McBarnet (1984), 'Law and Capital: Legal Form and Legal Actors', *International Journal of the Sociology of Law*, August.

[30] P. Sutherland, 'Address by Mr Peter D. Sutherland', in Irish Centre for European Law (ed.), *The Legal Implications of 1992* (1990), p.4.

[31] Head of Treasury Practice Group, International Accounting firm, London.

challenge for regulation, with no easy solution in sight. Yet unless the challenge of creative compliance can be effectively met, there can be little realistic prospect of achieving comparability in the market or of ensuring adequate disclosure of financial risk.

Discussion

ANTHONY G. HOPWOOD

We are increasingly conscious of the difficulties facing regulatory endeavours. Trying to influence the behaviour of interested, opportunistic and thoughtful individuals is never an easy task. Almost invariably the regulated attempt to outwit the regulators, and often succeed in doing so. The institutional structures of the modern world are also extremely complex, usually presenting enormous challenges to regulatory efforts to engage with them. Frequently the aims and understandings of regulation are expressed in terms that are relatively simple compared with the diversity of the institutional and administrative contexts they are trying to address. Regulatory intentions thereby do not map unproblematically on to the organisational terrain of the regulated. Options, uncertainties and gaps in understanding inevitably exist, creating very real constraints on the effectiveness of almost any regulatory endeavour.

Such difficulties are well illustrated by the papers of Dale, and McBarnet and Whelan. Analysing in detail the regulation of the risks stemming from the extension of banking activities into the securities area, Dale sets out both the range of regulatory strategies and the diverse institutional structures through which these are implemented in different countries. When seen in such comparative terms, even so focused a regulatory aim can result in wide range of institutional arrangements, with as yet only modest insights into their relative effectiveness. Dale also notes the potential interaction of different regulatory efforts and the ways in which the consequences of different strategies are dependent upon how they interact with the wider institutional context in which they are embedded.

Looking at a wider range of regulatory activities in the capital market area, McBarnet and Whelan also point to the difficulties facing the regulator. Although noting the active politics which determine the shape of the regulatory regime, they place most emphasis on the ways in which the regulated creatively respond to the initiatives of the regulators. An active market in creative compliance emerges in which concerns with satisfying the form of regulations and rules takes precedence over complying with the substantive nature of their intent. However well intentioned regulators might be, McBarnet and Whelan nevertheless leave us with a rather pessimistic view of the possibilities of them effectively engaging with the complex and proactive domains which they seek to influence.

In their different ways both papers emphasise a number of important themes. First, of course, they illustrate in rich detail the very real difficulties facing regulators. Both McBarnet and Whelan, and Dale discuss how some of the difficulties emerge because of the sheer complexity of the institutional procedures and processes with which regulation must engage. Doing what you want to do is rarely easy. Second, both papers discuss the diversity of national institutional and thereby regulatory forms. In so doing, they both point to the inadequacy of our present understandings of both the potentially different rationales built into different regulatory structures and their relative effectiveness. Finally, both Dale, and McBarnet and Whelan also emphasise the importance of understanding the close interdependency between bureaucratic regulatory mechanisms and market responses. Regulations disturb and disrupt market processes but they rarely constrain them. Rather market forces actively respond to the regulatory efforts, creating an often complex pattern of second order adjustments which only rarely enter into regulatory rationales and debates about the effectiveness of different regimes of control.

If nothing else, the analyses offered by both the papers point to the specificity of particular regulatory problems and solutions. If there is to be any real engagement with the complexity of institutional and market life, abstract conceptual notions of regulatory aims and practices will continue to have a distant relationship to how effective regulation is actually done. As Dale illustrates so well, to have any chance of being effective regulation must engage with detailed administrative and organisational arrangements. It needs to build on understandings of how organisations actually function rather than how they should or even might function.

Faced with such clear evidence of the difficulties which regulators must confront, it is useful to note some of the reasons why effective regulation is so elusive. The main one, of course, is that responses to regulation are invariably interested and opportunistic ones. Indeed they are likely to become more so as the expansion of market processes undermines many of the previous organisational and social constraints on industrial behaviour. What was once tempered by the dictates of the community, the club or the guild, can now be more fully a reflection of individual interest.

However, such opportunistic behaviour is only one of the reasons why we still have only a limited understanding of the actual range of consequences that can result from regulatory initiatives. A great deal of regulation is still an experiment with the unknown. Cause and effect relationships in many areas of regulation are poorly understood. The complexities of tracking regulatory initiatives through the administrative processes of large and multifaceted organisations are very real ones. One particular problem relates to the pervasiveness of unanticipated consequences. Regulatory interventions in any complex institutional system invariably will have a range of ramifications that never entered into their original justification. I sense, however, that if regulators were a little more sensitive to the operation of real-life organisations, the range of the unanticipated might be reduced a little.

When trying to understand the effectiveness of regulation, we also need to be conscious of the political processes which we give to particular regulatory regimes and institutions. McBarnet and Whelan make this quite explicit. Often real effectiveness may not be one of the primary goals of a regulatory authority. Regulatory institutions, themselves reflecting the outcomes of compromises between the interested parties can sometimes be established in ways which constrain their ability to act in an effective manner and often are subject to regulatory capture.

Institutions for the regulation of corporate disclosures and accounting standardisation are often illustrative of such tendencies. In the United Kingdom, for instance, the Accounting Standards Committee was established by the audit industry to prevent more rigorous modes of State intervention in the accounting field. Once in existence, it tended to respond to crises which had the potential to destabilise the form of professional rather than State control over accounting that it represented. Rather than seriously trying to lay down a programme for the more effective regulation of corporate accounting, the Accounting Standards Committee had a history that was more oriented to the preservation of the status quo and the legitimation of the profession's modes of self regulation.

Some of the more internationally oriented accounting regulatory bodies have similar origins and also operate in ways that do not always place a priority on the effective execution of their stated rationales. The International Accounting Standards Committee (IASC), for instance, was established by the agencies of the international audit industry to counter pressures for a more legalistic regulation of accounting and corporate reporting that might have resulted from the United Kingdom's membership of the European Community. Once this perceived danger passed, the IASC tended to focus more on the articulation of modest statements of accounting expectations that might be suitable for newly developing countries. The situation only changed when the International Organisation of Securities Commissions exerted pressure on the IASC. Again fearing a loss of control over accounting standards, the international audit industry entered a renewed period of activity — a period in which it is still engaged.

Not all regulatory bodies are subject to the same dangers as those involved with the standardisation of accounting disclosures, not least because not all regulatory authorities have been so subject to the influence of those whose behaviours should be regulated by them — in this case, the auditors. But even so, such examples reinforce those provided by Dale, and McBarnet and Whelan in pointing to the very real difficulties involved in regulating market activities.

Perhaps, not surprisingly, McBarnet and Whelan concluded on a rather pessimistic note, not being sure whether the challenge of creative compliance can adequately be met. I have many sympathies with their concerns. Certainly the effectiveness of grandiose and highly generalised regulatory attempts is almost bound to be limited. If any form of regulation is to have any chance of success, the implications of the careful and thoughtful analyses offered by both papers is that regulation should seek to be highly specific, most likely modest in intent and based on a detailed knowledge and understanding of the institutional and administrative practices with which it seeks to engage.

I am tempted to suggest two further attributes of effective regulation. The first is that regulation should strive to focus on the actual activities and processes that it seeks to influence. This may seem like a very obvious suggestion. But so frequently it is set aside. Consider the case of the regulation of corporate disclosures. This is an area where a great deal of emphasis is placed on accounting disclosures and within accounting, on forms of standardised practice. However both of these concerns are derivative ones, the latter from the concern with accounting and that concern, in turn, from the wider concern with disclosure. I would be tempted to argue that we should try to worry less about accounting and more about the multifaceted ways in which firms disclose to active markets in corporate information. And that leads me to my second attribute of more effective regulation, namely that regulatory strategies should, whenever possible, seek to build on the advantages of markets rather than trying to supersede or displace them. Again appealing to the area of corporate disclosure, I would be tempted to argue that far too much emphasis has been put on the bureaucracy of accounting and on accounting itself rather than the wider concepts of information, disclosure and corporate transparency.

We already know that capital markets can actively use and compare a wide range of information sources. Such abilities should be built on rather than displaced by a range of more bureaucratic accounting concerns. We should seek to stimulate a wider range of corporate information flows and even competition between them. In other words, let accountants not only believe in markets but live in them!

That very thought perhaps illustrates how some regulatory questions have been subjected to the interested attentions of too narrow a range of professional concerns. It is refreshing to have the complex institutional issues at stake in regulation subjected to the attention of at least different and possibly more perceptive minds. The observations of Dale, and McBarnet and Whelan are therefore very welcome ones.

Part IV

The Effects Of Regulation

Chapter Seven

Financial Regulation: The Contribution of the Theory of Finance*

STEPHEN M SCHAEFER

7.1 INTRODUCTION

A combination of high levels of price volatility, technological change and the move towards a single market in financial services in the EC ('1992') has meant that the recent history of the financial services industry has been a turbulent one. Against this background, financial regulation has been changing too, particularly in the context of 1992. Faced with the pressure to react rapidly to changing circumstances, it is not surprising that regulators have not found much opportunity to reflect on the principles and objectives which underlie the rules. This paper attempts to provide some of the perspective which such reflection might bring. It analyzes the motivation for and the design of financial regulation, particularly in the context of the rules governing the financial resources which financial firms have to maintain.

The paper also attempts to say something about the 'contribution of the theory of finance', a somewhat ambiguous phrase which covers both those

* In preparing this paper I have benefitted greatly from my experience as an independent board member of the Securities and Futures Authority (SFA) and, before that, of the Securities Association (TSA). Advice and help from the staff of SFA/TSA is gratefully acknowledged. The views expressed are, however, purely personal. The paper was substantially revised during the period I spent at the Dipartimento di Scienze Economiche of the Università degli Studi di Venezia as the Cassa di Risparmio di Venezia Visiting Fellow. I thank my colleagues in the department for their warm hospitality and the bank for their generosity in funding the Fellowship.

areas where finance has arguably already made a contribution (a rather small set) and also those areas where it could have a contribution (a rather larger set). The areas of potential relevance run the whole gamut from broad questions about the objectives of regulation to rather technical issues to do with the assessment of risk; and from issues to do with regulatory competition and the market for regulators to the effect of capital adequacy requirements on resource allocation. To date the most obvious contributions have been of a somewhat technical nature in the areas of risk assessment but, if finance, or simply economics, has a distinct contribution it is, I think, in providing a framework for analyzing some of the most basic questions about the objectives of regulation and the extent to which a particular regulatory design is likely to meet its objectives.

While my main theme is the regulation of capital I shall argue that the design of capital requirements has implications for other regulatory issues and, in particular, for the question of functional versus institutional regulation and for the so-called 'level playing field' doctrine. The idea of the 'level playing field' is that the capital requirements, and indeed other regulatory requirements, should be equalised across different *types* of financial institutions providing the same services. Thus, if both a bank and a securities firm offer equity trading services, the 'level playing field' doctrine would calculate required capital for this activity on the same basis for both types of institution.

The justification which is claimed for the 'level playing field' approach is fair competition. For example, in a recent speech to securities regulators Sir Leon Brittan said:

> With regard to strengthening the stability of the natural markets, my second priority for the 1990s is to ensure that security traders have sufficient capital to provide a buffer against the price and foreign currency risks they take on their books in volatile global markets.

> Within the Community , we are making good progress in the negotiations on the capital adequacy directive, not least in overcoming the difficult problem of providing a broadly *level playing field* for bank and non-bank players in the market.

And, in the same speech, he said:

> At the same time, due to the narrowing profit margins, the market players also want to be sure that they are competing on level terms with their competitors in global markets' (italics added)[1]

In the same spirit the Chairman of the SIB, Sir David Walker, referring to the work of IOSCO (the International Organization of Securities Commissions), said:

---

[1] Address by Sir Leon Brittan, Vice President Commission of the European Communities to the International Organization of Securities Commissions Annual Conference Constitution Hall, Washington, DC. Reported by Federal Information Systems Corporation; Federal News Service, September 24, 1991.

The second strand is the *level playing field* strand. Assuming the securities supervisors are agreed amongst themselves, how we can have a level playing field between the banks' and securities firms' haircuts in respect of both debt and equity instruments? (italics added)[2]

Determining regulatory requirements on the basis of the nature of the product rather than on the type of institution implies an approach to regulation which is 'functional' rather than 'institutional'. At first sight the approach appears sound. To be against the 'level-playing field' would be seem to oppose fair competition. To support an institutional approach to regulation raises at least two problems. First, if regulatory requirements for the same activity differ across institutions, it gives rise to a form of 'regulatory arbitrage' where the regulatory burden can be changed merely by changing institutional form. Moreover, should regulators be in the business of encouraging or discouraging particular institutional forms? Is that not a job better left to the market? Second, in a world where technology and financial products change rapidly, the regulator will find it difficult to decide on the proper allocation of institutions to categories.

However, as I shall attempt to show, these arguments do not bear close examination; the 'level playing field' approach is flawed and, despite the difficulties, the institutional approach is fundamentally consistent with the aims of capital regulation while the functional approach is not.

7.2 THE 'WHY' OF CAPITAL REGULATION

It is common ground, at least among economists, that the principal reason for regulation in any market is to alleviate market failure. In the case of capital regulation the market failure relates to externalities, 'systemic costs', which arise in the event of financial distress. The standard example given here is the case of bank failure and the risks which this carries of bank runs and consequent disruption of the payments mechanism. In the USA the 1930s showed that disruption of the payments mechanism is much more than an academic possibility and the structure of current US bank regulation owes much to events of this period (although it now seems that much of this structure may be changed by the US Congress over the next few years). Left to themselves, it is argued, banks would gear up to the point where the marginal benefit of further gearing was equal to the *private* costs associated with failure (the costs of 'financial distress' in the jargon of corporate finance). In order to achieve the correct social tradeoff, which takes account of the *public* (systemic) costs, it is necessary to induce to force banks to hold higher capital.

---

[2] Sir David Walker, 'The FRR Interview,' *Financial Regulation Report*, The Financial Times Limited, April 1991.

This description of the process begs the question of the benefits which banks obtain from higher gearing. There are a number of possibilities. First, banks may regard non-deposit forms of funding as more expensive than deposits. We discuss this view, which clearly implies a particular theory of the relevance of capital structure, in more detail below. A second possibility is connected with the presence of implicit guarantees against failure (e.g. from a central bank) or explicit, but underpriced, deposit insurance.[3] I return to this point later but, for the time being, we focus on the issue of 'systemic' risk.

Let us assume that there are indeed significant social costs associated with bank failure (though some would wish to debate even that point). The next question is: does increasing the quantity of capital which, for these purposes I shall define to include all non-deposit sources of funding, by itself reduce the expected social costs of failure? The answer, quite clearly and as the regulators have recognised for some time, is that it does not. In order to say something about the probability of failure of an institution we have to consider not only its capital structure (and, in particular, its gearing ratio) but also the risk of its assets. For example, if a bank has only one percent of capital but has assets which consist entirely of Treasury bills, its risk of failure would be essentially zero. If the same bank had ninety percent of its assets in unsecured loans to real estate developers (to take a contemporary example) its risk of failure would be substantial. In other words we need to assess the adequacy of capital in the context of a 'risk-adjusted' measure of the assets. This much is common ground although, as I discuss later, the manner in which the risk assessment should be performed is not.

Accepting the idea that the capital ratios need to be measured in a way that adjusts for the riskiness of assets, it is also generally agreed that changing capital requirements will change the probability of failure and, as a consequence, the expected social costs of failure. This is illustrated in Figure 1 which shows the expected systemic cost as a declining function of the capital ratio. These costs depend on both chance of failure and also on the particular consequences of failure for a particular institution or category of institution. It may not be simple, or even possible, to assess accurately what these costs might be but there is, equally, no reason at all to suppose that they are constant across all types and sizes of institution, even among those where there is some overlap between the types of businesses being carried on. As I have already mentioned, it is traditional to cite the threat to the payments mechanism as a reason to regulate capital in the banking industry. But the character and magnitude of the systemic risks depend on the nature of the firm and its role in the payments mechanism and, more broadly, in the economy, rather than on the presence of certain activities in its portfolio. The nature of these costs must surely depend on features such as firm size as well

---

[3] See, for example, R C Merton (1977), 'An Analytic Derivation of the Cost of Deposit Insurance and Loan Guarantees: An Application of Modern Option Pricing Theory,' *Journal of Banking and Finance*, June, pp. 3-11.

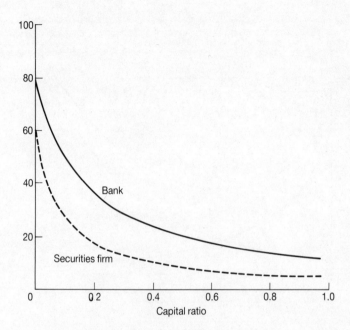

Fig. 1. Expected systemic costs for 'bank' and 'securities firm'.

as firm type and, in particular, the costs associated with a securities firm are not necessarily the same as those for a bank (though it is a moot point as to which would give rise to higher costs). For the present discussion it does not matter which are the higher, it is sufficient to agree that the costs are not necessarily the same across institutional types.

In Figure 1 I have sketched the expected systemic costs for two types of institution, which I have labelled 'bank' and 'securities firm'. As it is drawn, the systemic costs for the bank are higher than those for the securities firm but the argument does not depend on the ranking. At this point we may usefully ask an apparently naive question which Figure 1 suggests: 'If the expected social costs fall with the capital ratio, why not set the required capital ratios at sufficiently high levels, if necessary 100%, effectively to eliminate the chance of failure?' The answer to this question has to do with the supposed private benefits of gearing and, without it, the design of actual capital adequacy rules cannot be understood.

The Benefits of Gearing

There is much casual evidence that practical bankers, and indeed regulators, believe that, even on a risk adjusted basis, capital is a more expensive form of funding than non-capital sources (e.g. deposits). If we maintain this view it

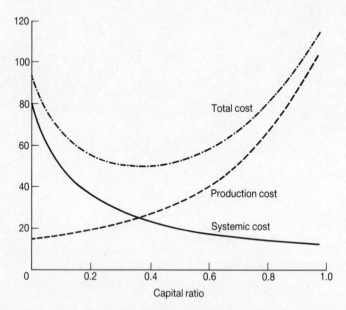

Fig. 2. Expected systemic cost, production cost and total cost.

follows that: (a) the weighted average cost of capital increases with the fraction of capital or non-deposit liabilities (the 'capital ratio'), and (b) in order to minimise the average cost of funding, banks will increase gearing to the point that the marginal disbenefit of further gearing, e.g., limitations in access to credit, just offset the marginal benefit of a lower funding cost.

Debate between bankers and economists is often difficult on this point: most bankers consider it self evident that non-deposit liabilities are more costly while most financial economists would view such a claim with scepticism. I do not intend to become involved in that debate here beyond noting that standard corporate finance theory in the shape of the Modigliani and Miller ('MM') proposition, would predict that the weighted average cost of capital is *independent* of the capital ratio.

For the present, however, I assume that practical men are right and that capital is costly in the sense the weighted average cost of funding increases with the capital ratio. The attitude that the regulator should take to these costs depends on who pays them and, on the reasonable assumption that the industry is competitive, the customer will pay. If the required return on capital liabilities is higher than on deposits, an increase in capital requirements will increase the 'production cost' of financial services and, depending on demand elasticities, reduce the size of the industry to some extent. Thus the capital ratio is also a determinant of the price of financial services. The social benefits of higher capital requirements take the form of reduced expected

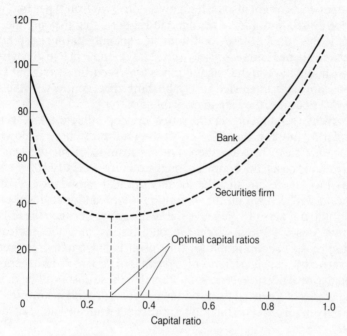

Fig. 3. Expected systemic costs for 'bank' and 'securities firm'.

systemic costs offset by the social disbenefits of higher 'production costs' (i.e., prices) for financial services. The regulator's task is to take both into account and achieve the best tradeoff.

The regulator's problem is illustrated in Figure 2 which shows the systemic and 'production' costs separately and also aggregated. The socially 'optimal' capital ratio, and the one which the regulator should choose, is the one which minimises total costs. This is the point at which the marginal benefit of reducing systemic costs and the marginal disbenefit of increasing production costs are equal. While the analysis is entirely standard, the motivation for the existence of capital regulation and what it is designed to achieve is perhaps less often made explicit.

This simple account of the motivation for capital regulation depends on two main assumptions: (i) that failure imposes social costs which are institutionally dependent and (ii) that the risk adjusted required return on capital funds is higher than on deposits. The assumptions are, of course, open to question and below I discuss the implications of relaxing each assumption in turn. For now we take the assumptions as given and analyze capital requirements for different types of firm to show that optimal capital ratios, if not firm specific, are specific to a firm type. For example, the case illustrated in Figure 1 assumes that the expected systemic costs for banks are higher than those for securities firms. To derive the 'optimal' capital ratio for the two firm types we must add the output cost to the expected systemic costs. Of course output costs might also differ between the two firm types but, for the purposes of illustration, I have assumed in Figure 3 that they are the same. The result is that, under these conditions, the socially optimal capital ratio differs between banks and securities firms. The example I have given implies that banks should have higher capital ratios than securities firms but I stress again that I am only interested in establishing that, contrary to the 'level playing field' doctrine, they are in principle different.

In the event that higher capital ratios do not influence the weighted average cost of funding (the MM case) the total cost curve is downward sloping. In this case, because there are no costs to offset the benefit of reduced systemic costs, the optimal capital structure is clearly 100% capital.

We conclude, therefore, that the socially optimal capital requirement for an institution will depend on the institution's type and that 'level playing field' rules will not generally achieve the best balance between the reduction of systemic costs through higher capital ratios and the increase of 'production' costs. The intuition for this result is that capital requirements are motivated by considerations of systemic risk which are themselves institutionally dependent. It seems unlikely that these costs will be the same for all categories of financial firms or that the costs depend in any direct way on the activity involved (the 'function') as distinct from the nature of the firm as a whole.

As described above, the analysis rests on two main assumptions: first that the motivation for capital regulation is the mitigation of institutionally specific systemic costs associated with financial distress and, second, that the reason that capital requirements are not set at levels which reduce the probability of failure to arbitrarily small levels is because higher capital levels impose a cost on financial institutions and ultimately on consumers. Below I consider the implications of relaxing these assumptions.

If, however, both assumptions are correct then, for the reasons I have already given, there is a *prima facie* case for capital regulation to be institutionally rather than functionally based, in other words to abandon the level playing field approach. One implication of this result is that the output cost may vary by institutional type and that lower capital requirements may give certain categories of firm a cost advantage. This, in turn, may result in that category of firm capturing most or all of the market. This is the situation illustrated in Figure 4 which shows the output cost implications of the optimal capital ratios derived in Figure 3. For example, giving a lower capital requirement for equity trading activities to securities firms rather than banks may result in all equity trading being carried out by securities firms. This may appear to be distortionary in just the way that the 'level playing field' is supposed to avoid but of course it is not. Imagine two chemical plants manufacturing the same product, one of which (A) produces no pollution while the other (B) has a 'smoking factory chimney'. If we agree that it is appropriate to tax the polluter, does it make sense, as the level playing field approach would imply, to tax plant A, which produces no pollution, to 'avoid unfair

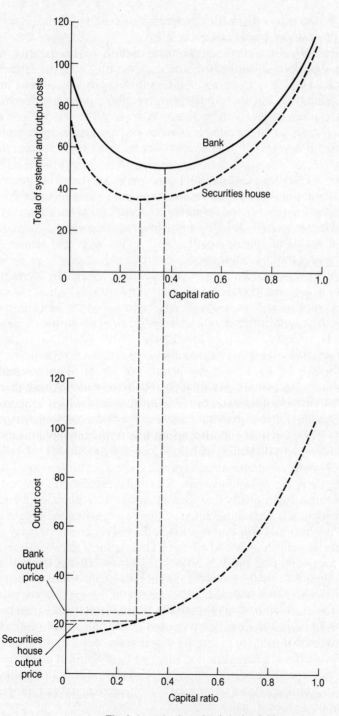

Fig. 4. An optimal non-level playing field.

competition'? Institutions for which systemic costs are lower are 'low cost producers' from the perspective of social costs.

Suppose, however, that one of the two main assumptions is incorrect and, in particular, that there are no social costs[4] associated with the failure of financial institutions[5]. In this case it is difficult to justify any regulation of capital at all. There are, of course, other possible motivations, e.g., the existence of information asymmetries between buyers and sellers of financial services which give rise to the need for consumer protection. However, it is difficult to see the 'level playing field' approach as an appropriate solution to this problem.

Next, suppose that the second assumption is wrong and there are in fact no additional costs imposed by higher capital requirements. In this case Modigliani and Miller are right and the solution is simple: capital requirements for banks should be set at 25% or 50% or whatever is necessary to reduce the chance of failure to arbitrarily small levels. (This will also require the regulator to control the risk of assets.)

In summary, we conclude that there are three internally consistent positions which may be adopted regarding the regulation of capital[6], none of which corresponds to the 'level playing field' approach. First, if the purpose of regulating the capital of financial intermediaries is about balancing the benefit of reduced systemic costs against the disbenefit of an increased funding cost, then capital requirements should generally vary with institutional type. Second, if increasing the quantity of capital does not reduce systemic costs, or if systemic costs are zero, then why regulate capital at all? In this case capital decisions should be left to the market. Third, if MM holds, then increasing capital requirements imposes no extra costs on financial intermediaries and the socially optimal solution is to set capital requirements at levels which are sufficiently high to make the possibility of failure essentially zero.

7.3 THE 'HOW' OF CAPITAL REGULATION

If the 'why' of capital regulation is a rather vague and intangible business dealing with quantities such as systemic costs and marginal costs of capital which are difficult to measure, the 'how' is a much more concrete affair where the problems relate directly to well developed theory and to extensive empirical research. If the 'why' leaves much for judgement, and even

---

[4] I disregard the straw man possibility that costs of failure are entirely independent of institutional type.

[5] Exploitation of deposit guarantees should be included as a social cost to the extent that the costs are borne by the public.

[6] We ignore for the time being the information asymmetry motivation for capital regulation.

politics, the 'how' leaves less room: here the financial economists are on their home ground and, potentially, have a great deal to offer. However, progress so far has been modest and in some important areas of EC legislation we seem to be in the process of going backwards. In this section I shall briefly review the basic ideas involved and then compare some actual and proposed capital adequacy schemes with the approach which a financial economist might take.

To assess the probability of insolvency for an institution, it is necessary to be able to describe the probability distribution of its capital or net worth, C. For an institution with assets of value A and non-capital liabilities of value L, the rate of return on capital is given by:

$$\tilde{r}_C = \tilde{r}_A(G + 1) - \tilde{r}_L G \tag{1}$$

where r_A, r_L and r_C denote the rates of return on assets, non-capital liabilities and capital, respectively; a tilde denotes a random variable, and $G = L/C$ represents the gearing ratio. If we regard the value of the non-capital liabilities as fixed then the volatility of the return on capital is given by:

$$\sigma_C = (G + 1)\,\sigma_A \tag{2}$$

where σ_C and σ_A are the volatilities of the rates of return on capital and assets respectively. Thus, to calculate the risk of insolvency, we must estimate the variability of the assets as well as the gearing ratio. These two parameters are indeed the ones with which regulators seem concerned[7] though, in assessing the practical usefulness of this simple analysis, three points should be considered.

First, uncertainty in net worth may stem not only from asset risk but also from uncertainty in the value of liabilities. For example, in the case of a bank, the liabilities may consist at least partly of certificates of deposit and other fixed rate instruments whose value is influenced by interest rate changes. In a securities company some of the liabilities may be options which the firm has written. In either case, the risk which attaches to capital will be influenced by the risk characteristics of the non-capital liabilities. Of course, if the non-capital liabilities are positively correlated with the assets (i.e., if the liabilities act as a hedge for the assets) then the risk which attaches to capital may be lower than in the case where the liabilities have no risk.

Second, it is clear that the formula given above (2) for the risk of the capital is based on the market values of assets and liabilities. Estimates based on balance sheet values, which do not attempt to reflect market conditions, are inappropriate and may be misleading. Third, for a given asset risk and gearing ratio, the probability of failure is a function of the time period over

---

[7] See, for example, the Bank of England's gearing and risk asset ratio tests. Bank of England, (1980), 'The Measurement of Capital', *Bank of England Quarterly Bulletin*, September, pp. 324-30, and Bank of England, (1985), 'The Future Structure of the Gilt Edge Market', *Bank of England Quarterly Bulletin*, April, pp. 250-82.

which the value is measured. Thus, in choosing a probability of failure, the regulator also chooses the frequency of monitoring. This should depend on both the liquidity of the assets and the costs and difficulty of assessing asset and liability values. These two characteristics will often be related. Assets for which there is a ready secondary market will generally possess higher liquidity and, because the market revalues such assets frequently, it is also easier to assess their market value. Broadly, the assets of securities firms will tend to fall into this category while many bank assets will not.

Although some of the inputs may be difficult to estimate, assessing the risk of a portfolio of assets is, in principle, a straightforward application of portfolio theory. The character of the problem depends on the composition of the assets. If the assets have significant idiosyncratic risk (e.g., equities or corporate loans which are prone to default) then the most important parameters are the covariances between asset values and, in well diversified portfolios, the covariances will dominate the own variances. If most of the risk is systematic then covariation is less important and, in the particular case where the main source of risk is interest rate movements, a duration approach will provide a good first approximation. Both types of risk assessment have been extensively researched by both academics and practitioners over the past 40 years.

With one notable exception, the approach taken by regulators to the assessment of asset risk is not based on portfolio theory. The exception is the treatment of equity position risk by the SFA (and formerly by its predecessor the TSA) and by the SIB in the UK whose rules are based on a simplified version of Markowitz' portfolio theory[8]. The objectives of the SFA/SIB method are clear: it is supposed to measure the volatility of the portfolio rate of return and the evidence is that it has done a good job, even through the crash of October 1987[9].

In contrast, the methods used by bank regulators to measure the risk of bank asset portfolios have little to do with a modern understanding of portfolio risk. Their approach divides assets into classes (claims on central government, claims on banks, mortgages, claims on the private sector etc.) and assigns to each category, k, a 'risk weight', α_k. The 'risk adjusted' total of assets, V_T, is then the sum of the balance sheet values, V_k, weighted by the risk weights:

$$V_T = \sum_k \alpha_k V_k \qquad (3)$$

[8] The 'SFA', the Securities and Futures Authority, is one of four self regulatory bodies in the UK and has responsibility for regulating dealing in securities, derivatives and commodities. It was formed in 1991 as a result of a merger between The Securities Association (TSA) and the Association of Futures Brokers and Dealers (AFBD). The SFA derives its authority from the Securities and Investments Board (SIB) which is a statutory body.

[9] See E. Dimson and P. Marsh (1992), 'The Risks of UK Equity Market Makers' Books', Working Paper, London Business School.

Required capital is then a fraction of the total of risk assets, V_T , and in order for this quantity to produce a given probability of insolvency, V_T must proxy for the volatility (e.g., the standard deviation) of the asset value. The connection between this and a modern portfolio theory approach is, at best, tenuous since it is well known that risk does not aggregate in the linear manner implied by the formula. I am not aware of any formal empirical evidence on the performance of this scheme as a proxy for the risk of bank portfolios[10], but it is difficult to understand what is gained by ignoring a commonsense theory, namely portfolio theory, that has been shown to work well in a variety of contexts.

Why has portfolio theory been largely ignored by regulators? Let me suggest two reasons. First, there is a perception that portfolio theory is 'complicated' and, while it is true that some years ago portfolio theory was relatively unfamiliar to practitioners, this is much less true today. More importantly, complication should be judged in terms of functionality. Portfolio theory provides a powerful method for solving a certain class of problem and this justifies the 'complication'. In the same way, and even though it is mathematically much more complicated than portfolio theory, option pricing theory is widely used in the financial services industry precisely because it has proved itself useful. Second, it appears that there is a certain amount of misunderstanding on the part of some regulators about the extent to which portfolio theory based estimates of risk may be approximated by simple functions such as the risk adjusted total of assets used by bank regulators. In general these linear risk measures will behave in an entirely different way from the portfolio theory formula. I provide some evidence on this point below.

Before I leave this topic, it is a disturbing feature of the present situation that, after much protracted negotiation, the linear 'risk weight' approach has been readopted by the G10 countries as the basis on which international convergence of bank capital adequacy standards is to proceed[11]. This approach is essentially the same as that introduced by the Federal Reserve Board in 1956 and known as the 'ABC' (Analysis of Bank Capital) approach. However, 1956 was only four years after Harry Markowitz had published his path-breaking article on portfolio theory which, at that time, was essentially unknown in the financial services industry. In 1956, then, a risk-weight approach to risk assessment was, from a practical point of view, 'state of the art'.

The same cannot be said of that approach today. In 1991 portfolio theory is not only widely known but widely used, if not in the banking industry then certainly in the securities industry. Moreover, the substantial reduction in

---

[10] In part this is surely due to the difficulty in obtaining reliable measures of the value of bank assets.

[11] See, e.g., Bank of England (1985), 'The Future Structure of the Gilt Edged Market', *Bank of England Quarterly Bulletin*, April, pp. 250-82.

computing costs over this period has made the application of portfolio theory much less costly.[12]

Just how important are the details of portfolio theory? To put this in perspective Figure 5 compares the capital requirements for a sample of UK equity market makers' books under two position risk requirement ('PRR') regimes: the current SFA/SIB portfolio theory[13] method and an approach which has been proposed in the context of the forthcoming Capital Adequacy Directive and which would implicitly estimate the risk of a portfolio as a weighted sum of the gross and net portfolio values (the '$x + y$' rule). The SFA/SIB rules use a simplified version of the Sharpe diagonal model to compute portfolio variance. Thus if the fraction of the portfolio devoted to asset k is w_k, $k=1,2, ..., K$, the portfolio standard deviation σ_p is calculated as:

$$\sigma_P = \sqrt{A + B \sum_{i=1}^{K} \sum_{j=1}^{K} w_i w_j} \tag{4}$$

where A is an estimate of the variance of the market portfolio and B is an estimate of residual risk[14]. The capital requirement is then set as a fraction of the estimated standard deviation of the portfolio return multiplied by the net value of the portfolio, V_T. In the '$x + y$' approach the required capital is set equal to:

$$V_T \left(x + y \sum_{i=1}^{K} |w_i| \right) \tag{5}$$

The adequacy of the 'simple' expression (5) depends on whether it gives a good or a poor approximation to the portfolio theoretic formula in (4). Some evidence on this question, for a sample of actual portfolios, is given in Figure 5. Here, for the '$x + y$' calculations, the weights are 2% on the gross amount for more liquid equities, 4% on the gross amount for less liquid equities and 8% on the net amount. The relation between this quantity and the portfolio based measure is very poor: the correlation coefficient between the two is only 0.39. It is also quite wrong to regard one measure as intrinsically more 'conservative' than the other: the level of the capital requirements is determined by the choice of the parameters: x and y in one case and A and B in the other. With the parameters used in Figure 5 there are actually four portfolios

---

[12] Perhaps an even more telling sign of the extent to which 'complicated' portfolio theory is no longer the preserve of ivory tower economists came in the Economist magazine which published a lucid and accurate account of portfolio theory in its section addressed to *schoolchildren*. 'Risk and Return', (1991), *The Economist*, 2 February, pp. 86-87.

[13] For details of the SFA/SIB method see, e.g., SFA Rules, Chapter 3 'Financial Rules'. See also S.M Schaefer (1990), 'The Regulation of Banks and Securities Firms', *European Economic Review*, 34, pp. 587-97.

[14] Effectively, the model assumes that all 'betas' are unity and all residual risks are the same.

with capital requirements under the SFA/SIB rules, sometimes claimed to be intrinsically 'lax', which are over 15% of net worth higher than under the '$x + y$' rules. The important issue is whether a given method is an adequate proxy for actual portfolio risk. In the case of the SFA/SIB approach there is good evidence that it does[15]. The question then becomes whether alternative methods, which are perhaps simpler, provide a good proxy to the SFA/SIB calculations. Figure 5 casts doubt on the ability of the '$x + y$' approach to satisfy this criterion.

The data given in Figure 5 provide a good illustration of the dangers of the ad-hoc theorising that sometimes seems to be a feature of financial regulation. Although we know that total portfolio risk can be decomposed into systematic and non-systematic components and although, in a very broad sense, the latter has more to do with the gross position than the net, the diagram shows that a linear formula does not capture the shape of the quadratic function in equation (4) at all precisely. Moreover, it is not at all clear what benefits the simple formula would bring in practice. All that is required to compute the SFA/SIB formula is a PC with a spreadsheet and this is surely not beyond the means of even the smallest financial institution today.

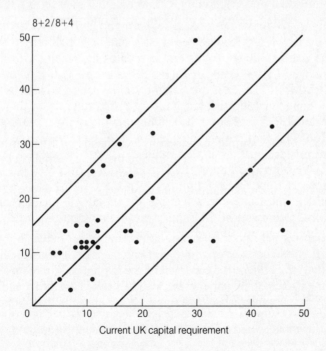

Fig. 5. Equity position risk requirement under current and '8+2/8+4' rules.

[15] See, e.g., E. Dimson and P. Marsh (1992), 'The Risks of UK Equity Market Makers' Books', Working Paper, London Business School.

**Table 1.   Estimated standard deviations of portfolios that
have the same Bank of England risk score**

Portfolio	Estimated standard deviation of portfolio returns
1	26.3
2	57.6
3	61.0
4	32.0
5	41.5
6	56.0
7	65.5
8	70.0
9	82.0
10	7.8
11	14.0

Source: R A Brealey and I D Rowley, 1989, 'Monitoring the Risk of Gilt-Edged Market,' Working Paper, London Business School.

A second example of the dangers of the *ad-hoc* approach is provided by work carried out by Rowley[16]. Rowley looks at a number of different ways of assessing the risk of gilt portfolios and compares his results with the risk measure produced by the Bank of England's rules for Gilt Edged Market Makers ('GEMM's). The latter are based on some sound good sense about the nature of bond portfolio risk but, as Rowley's results show, they are let down by the detail. Table 1 shows the actual volatility of the rate of return on eleven portfolios each of which has the same risk score under the GEMM rules. The results are striking in that, with the same risk score, the actual volatilities range from a minimum of 7% per annum to over 80% per annum. Figure 6 shows the poor association between the GEMM risk scores and actual volatility, this time for a sample of actual gilt market makers' positions. Table 2 shows, for the same data, the rank correlation between actual volatility, a duration based risk measure and the Bank of England measure.

The data on both equities and gilts illustrate the dangers of relying on what are, in both cases, *ad-hoc* approximations to portfolio risk. At a minimum the regulator needs to be aware of the extent of the approximation by testing a proposed risk measure using actual price data and actual position data. Obvious as this point sounds it would not appear to be the norm in practice.

---

[16] I D Rowley (1988), 'Measurements of the Risk of UK Government Stocks', PhD dissertation, London Business School. See also R A Brealey and I.D. Rowley (1989) 'Monitoring the Risk of the Gilt-Edged Market', Working Paper, London Business School.

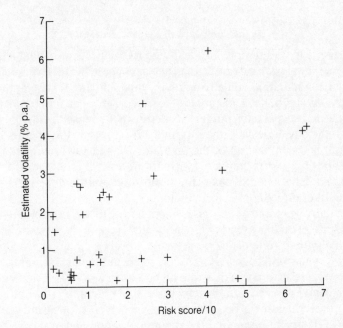

Fig. 6. GEMM risk score versus estimated portfolio risk.

Table 2.   Correlation Between Alternative Bond Risk Measures

Risk Measures	Rank Correlation
Duration Based Risk Score/ GEMM Risk Score	0.45
Actual Portfolio Volatility/ GEMM Risk Score	0.39
Duration Based Risk Score/ Actual Portfolio Volatility	0.84

Source: I D Rowley (1988), 'Measurements of the Risk of UK Government Stocks', PhD dissertation, London Business School.

7.4 CONCLUSIONS

In this paper I have attempted to deal with two aspects of capital adequacy regulation. First, I have set out a simplified account of the motivation for capital adequacy regulation and attempted to show that the 'level playing field' approach may not be consistent with the objectives of capital regulation. In the short term I suspect this point is academic in the sense that the 'levellers' have won the day, at least in the EC, and at least for the time being. Having said that, it is doubtful if all of the regulatory baggage with which we shall pass the starting post in January 1993 will necessarily be with us for ever. These issues have been debated for some time and doubtless the policy-makers will return to them before too long.

On the narrower topic of risk assessment it is difficult not to be pessimistic about the prospects of a greater rationality creeping into the system. In fact, it is quite likely that some of the progress that has been made in London over the past few years will be lost. If this were to occur it would be regrettable for at least two reasons. First, in insisting on home-brew solutions the regulators move themselves away from 'best practice' and practitioners will be unable to look to the rules for a benchmark against which to measure their own procedures. If practitioners find the regulator's approach to the assessment of risk inadequate for practical purposes then this is surely a disturbing sign. Secondly, I believe that there are real dangers that some of the *ad-hoc* approaches are inadequate in the sense that they are incapable of detecting positions which are subject to excessive risk. Thus, if capital regulation is of any importance at all, 'ad-hocery' is likely to lead to more accidents.

Chapter Eight

Comparing The Performance Of Stock Exchange Trading Systems*

AILSA RÖELL

8.1 INTRODUCTION

The past few years have seen an unprecedented increase in international competition for stock trading business among European stock exchanges. In particular, London's SEAQ International market has rapidly captured a large share of trading in blue-chip foreign equities. This has fuelled policymakers' interest in the organisation and regulation of stock exchange trading. Is it possible to recapture trading volume that has moved abroad? What determines the success or failure of a stock trading system? How do investors, listed companies and market professionals fare when rules and regulations are changed? These are some of the issues that are central to the policy debate.

In this chapter I would like to describe first a few stylised facts concerning the liquidity of the markets in French cross-listed equities. This will set the stage for a more theoretical discussion of the relative merits of the market institutions used for trading in Paris (and many other European centres) and in London. This includes some comments about market transparency, a very contentious issue in the EC at present.

* I am grateful to the ESRC 'Functioning of Markets Initiative' for funding this research; to officials at both the Paris Bourse and the London Stock Exchange for their generous input of time and trouble in providing data and accompanying information; to ECARE and the Université Libre de Bruxelles for providing facilities, and to Patrick Bolton, Marco Pagano and my colleagues at ECARE and the Financial Markets Group for valuable comments. Any errors, of course, remain mine alone.

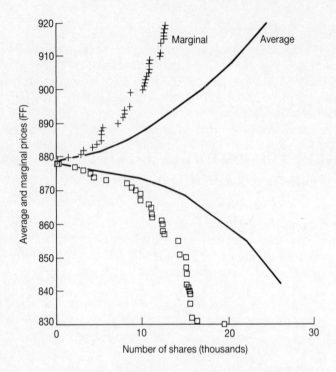

Fig. 1. Paris Limit orders, BSN, 24 June 1991.

8.2 THE MARKETS IN CROSS-LISTED FRENCH EQUITIES

It is not easy to compare the liquidity of the Paris Bourse and London's SEAQ International. The reason is that the trading systems are so different that one invariably finds oneself comparing apples with pears.

Measuring liquidity in Paris is relatively easy. The CAC (Cotation Assistée en Continu) electronic auction system provides a continuous picture of the reigning limit order book. Any trader who requires *immediacy* (trading without any delay to search for, or simply hope for, better terms of trade) need only hit these limit orders to obtain a deal. Thus, with a picture of the limit order book in hand, it is simple to compute the cost of trading for any given deal size.

Figures 1 and 2 show typical examples of the Paris limit order book. Figure 1 plots the average price a broker looking at the limit order book knows that he can obtain (pay) for sell (buy) orders of different size, for shares in a major French company (BSN). Note that the market is very *tight*: the 'fourchette', or bid-ask spread for minimal size deals, is very small indeed (less than 0.5%). On the other hand the market is not very *deep*. For larger deals, say of size 20,000 shares or more (about FF 20 million or more in value), the effective spread is quite wide: the average price obtained when selling a block this size would be more than 5% below the price paid when buying it. And beyond this size the limit order book soon runs out altogether. Figure 2 rounds out the picture by giving an impression of the extra liquidity supplied to the market by 'hidden orders': that is, portions of limit orders that are there to be executed against but invisible to the users of the system. Agents like to hide part of their larger orders in this way so as not to alarm market participants. In any case these 'hidden orders' do not seem to be overwhelming in relative size: in Figure 2, a typical case, they enhance the depth of the market by increasing the size one can trade at any given bid-ask spread by roughly 1/3 to 1/2.[1]

If you are contemplating a trade in Paris, what you see is what you get (apart from the hidden orders). Measuring the liquidity of the London market is more difficult, because prices are often negotiated to yield a better deal than is quoted onscreen. Market makers display bid and ask prices onscreen,

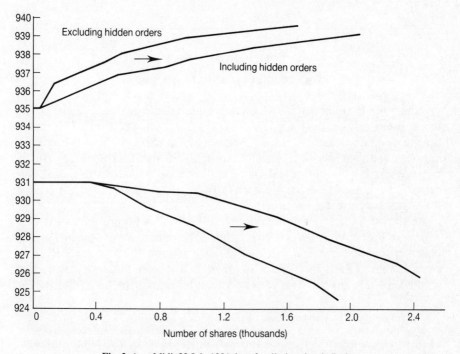

Fig. 2. Axa–Midi, 22 July 1991, best few limit orders in Paris.

---

[1] Market liquidity has other dimensions. One is *resiliency*: how long does it take the market to readjust back after absorbing a large order; and how good are the terms one can obtain by trickling in an order over time and waiting for new limit orders to appear over time, rather than by insisting on immediacy. On this issue I have no empirical information to offer.

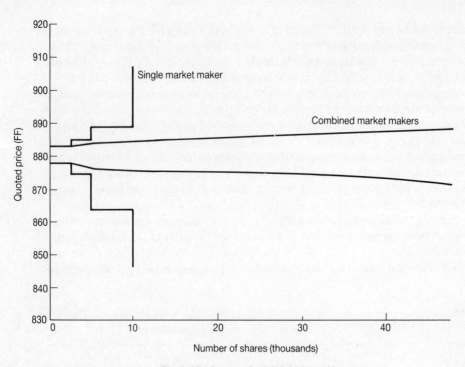

Fig. 3. SEAQ quotes for BSN, 24 June 1991.

together with the quantity for which they undertake to guarantee these prices to all customers (i.e. the trade size for which their price is 'firm'. This quantity must equal at least the NMS — Normal Market Size — for the security in question, set by the Stock Exchange at roughly the median trade size). But in practice customers who telephone a market maker to execute a deal can generally negotiate a better price or a larger quantity than quoted, especially if the deal is of substantial size.

As shown by the 'single market maker' prices in Figure 3, the London market in French equities is not very tight. The market touch (the difference between the best bid and ask quotes) at minimum trade sizes generally exceeds that in Paris by a factor of about 2. If it were the case that traders could only rely on the firm quotes of single[2] market makers, the market

---

[2] Figure 3 also shows a 'combined' measure of liquidity: the best average price obtainable for a deal of given size by splitting it and simultaneously trading with several market makers at their firm-quote prices and sizes. On this 'combined' measure of quoted liquidity, the London market is considerably deeper than the Paris market.

In theory this strategy is feasible, and the liquidity obtained can thus be regarded as a minimal measure of the quality of the market. But in practice there are serious problems with such a strategy. Firstly, it requires an inordinate amount of brokers' time as multiple deals must be struck. Secondly, market makers protect themselves by enquiring if there is 'more to go' on a deal. A broker who is known to split his orders without informing the market makers involved will find himself blacklisted by the market making community, and unable to negotiate within-the-quotes prices on his future transactions.

would not be very deep either. Figures 1 and 3 concern the same security (BSN) at the same moment of time, and are drawn to the same scale. Based on these figures one would conclude that the cost of immediacy in French equities is lower in Paris over the entire range of trade sizes.

Realised transaction prices present a rather different picture from market makers' quotes. Table 1 displays the average deviation between the transaction price and the quoted market mid-price for a selection of French equities on SEAQ International. This measure roughly represents half the realised bid-ask spread (but note that inaccurate reporting of deal times leads the transaction price to stray away from the presumed contemporaneous mid-price, so that this measure may be an overestimate). In Table 1, average realised spreads *decrease* with transaction size. Moreover, trade sizes far exceeding NMS and market makers' quoted sizes are commonplace. Thus the market is rather deeper than one would infer by looking at market makers' quotes.

It is not clear, however, whether Table 1 really represents the price of im-

Table 1   Average percentage deviation of transaction price from market mid-price on SEAQ International, May-July 1991, for selected French equities

Stock	Normal market size (NMS)	Median trade size	Price deviation for trade size ranges:			
			All	$^1/_{10}$ NMS and below	$^1/_{10}$ NMS to NMS	Above NMS
Axa-Midi	1000	1000	0.823	1.522 (30)	0.736 (183)	0.794 (177)
B.S.N.	2500	1000	0.565	0.693 (202)	0.498 (659)	0.652 (214)
Carrefour	500	500	0.690	0.939 (73)	0.704 (428)	0.611 (456)
Elf Aquitaine	5000	4800	0.670	0.860 (138)	0.659 (703)	0.639 (588)
Gen. des Eaux	500	500	0.572	0.726 (102)	0.549 (497)	0.563 (505)
L'Oreal	2500	1500	0.687	1.031 (52)	0.638 (353)	0.686 (198)
Pernod-Ricard	1000	615	0.673	1.084 (37)	0.597 (152)	0.685 (106)
Schneider	2000	1500	0.852	1.291 (37)	0.872 (157)	0.640 (91)
Un Ass Paris	2000	3000	0.659	0.824 (19)	0.600 (264)	0.693 (369)

Number of transactions in parentheses.

mediacy. Did the larger deals require extensive negotiation or delay before the price could be agreed? The data do not provide this information.

To summarise the facts: there has been considerable migration of trading volume, and in particular of larger deals, towards SEAQ International. Indeed, on occasion the day's trading volume in a blue-chip continental European equity on SEAQ international can exceed that on the domestic market, though on average the domestic market trading volume remains considerably higher (by a factor of about 3 in the case of France). The data on trading costs and liquidity suggest that Paris's electronic auction market provides tighter spreads for small deals but that the limit order book is not deep enough to accommodate large deals at prices that are competitive with those obtained from London's market makers. The London market makers' firm quotes are not particularly tight or deep; but the transaction data suggest that when asked to improve upon their firm quotes, they routinely do so; especially for large deals.

8.3 DISCUSSION OF TRADING STRUCTURE AND POLICY ISSUES

It is not just for French equities that large deals have migrated to London following their introduction onto the SEAQ International system. There is the same pattern in the trading of blue-chip equities from many other European countries such as Spain, Italy and Sweden. One can think of a number of different reasons why this might be so. Some are inherent in the trading systems used. Some concern additional specifications not inextricably tied to the trading system used. And some have nothing to do with the methods and regulation of trading at all.

In Paris, Madrid, Stockholm and now Milan also, shares are traded on a continuous electronic auction, using variants of a system developed by the Toronto stock exchange. This system differs from London's SEAQ system along a number of different dimensions.

Public limit order exposure

One important difference lies in the way entry into market making is regulated. In Paris, any member of the general public is free to 'make' the market by instructing a broker to input limit orders into the system on his behalf. Thus in theory everyone can come in and provide liquidity on the spur of the moment. In London, only registered market makers can display their limit orders on the screen: there is no 'public limit order exposure' (PLOE). While there is no great barrier to entry into market making (any stock exchange member who passes minimum competence and capital adequacy standards qualifies), day-to-day liquidity provision by members of the public is ruled out. Thus ordinary members of the public cannot trade directly with each other as in Paris; all trading must go via the market makers (unless one has access to a network of potential counterparties to trade with, and that is not worth building up except for large institutional investors who trade regularly and in size).

It is a common perception that this lack of PLOE alone increases transaction costs in London because ordinary traders cannot avoid giving a cut to the intermediary, namely the market maker's spread ('jobber's turn'), even when willing counterparties are available. But would not competition among market makers eliminate such an opportunity for excessive profit? Figure 4 shows the number of market makers per share for the French equities traded on SEAQ International. Securities with less than 10 registered market makers are rare. It seems unlikely that there are substantial opportunities for oligopoly profit.

More prosaically, the high spread in London for smaller deals may simply reflect the order processing costs involved. The process of trading by telephoning a market maker and the paperwork involved are costly in terms of time and trouble. Paris's automatic system, where trades are executed directly and electronically at the touch of a button, is simply less costly. And even with automatic execution of small orders in London, a trade between two final customers would still tend to be more costly as it necessarily

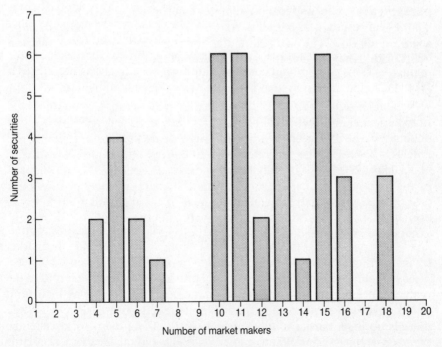

Fig. 4. SEAQ market makers per security.

involves intervention of a market maker, i.e. two separate transactions. Such order processing cost differentials clearly loom larger for smaller deals, explaining why London is less competitive in that category of trades.

Transparency and last trade publication

A second important difference, and the focus of the current debate about EC regulatory policy, is the *transparency* of the two types of market. Can all participants see the order flow promptly and simultaneously? On the electronic auction markets, all trades are necessarily inputted into the system at the moment they are executed. It is thus relatively simple for the exchange authorities to publish a wide range of information about recent deals: their size and price, and even the identities of the brokers involved. On a telephone dealing market accurate and prompt publication of trading information is harder to achieve. Traders have to be explicitly required to report their trades promptly and accurately. And traders who do not wish to reveal information about their current deals can easily evade such requirements and delay their trade reports, for instance by entering into provisional agreements to trade that are not officially finalised until some time later.[3] In short, the London system is inherently less transparent.

In addition, the exchange authorities in London have deliberately chosen not to try to enforce immediate trade reporting and publication. In the international equity section of the market exchange the authorities have not imposed any trade publication requirements at all, while for domestic equities (in response to pressure from market makers) publication of large deals is quite slow. The justification for this is that market makers can quote a better price if they are able to lay off a position they take on before it becomes publicly known that the deal is overhanging the market, moving the market price adversely.

It should be emphasised that there is a pure redistribution of trading costs from large and informed traders to small traders at work here. Why would a market maker offer a better price for large deals that are not published? Precisely because large deals in particular convey information; the market maker can take advantage of the fact that others do not have this information by trading at a price that does not reflect it yet, after completing the initial deal. So the initial trader's gain is the rest of the market's loss. In equilibrium, market spreads for all deals (in particular those that are too small to convey much information) will widen, as market makers need to protect

---

[3] See J Franks and S Schaefer, (November 1990), 'Large Trade Publication on the International Stock Exchange', report to the Department of Trade and Industry, for a discussion of this point. They describe the situation on America's NASDAQ market, where the imposition of immediate trade publication has led to this practice.

themselves against competitors who have superior order flow information, as well as against traders with superior information.[4]

Clearly, a market maker who is not subject to immediate trade publication can outcompete those who are, who have no window of time before everyone else knows about a trade. Thus it is not surprising that large trades gravitate towards the market with the slowest publication of trades: large institutional traders, and the market makers who vie for their business, prefer a market with slower trade publication. This point has been recognised by policy-makers. Thus in the debate about EC regulations, continental exchange authorities have tended to push for the imposition of greater transparency across the board, and in particular, for faster trade publication in London. Meanwhile London authorities argue that the current system is very successful and that prompt trade publication would drive away business (not just back to continental Europe, but also back to the USA and other countries whose shares are traded on SEAQ International). If it ain't broke, why fix it?

In this context it is interesting to note the new Paris proposals for reporting of block trades. Up to now, stock exchange member firms who arrange negotiated block deals have been required to report them promptly as a 'cross transaction' on the CAC system, where the information is displayed to all participants. The new proposals delay the publication of this information. It is hoped that this will increase the volume of block deals done in Paris and within exchange trading hours.

This tendency towards reduced market transparency as a result of competition among exchanges has a beggar-thy-neighbour ring to it. Why not have the EC impose greater transparency, a principle that has long guided US policy-making.[5] Or would the damage to London's position as an international marketplace for large transactions be too great?

Negotiating deals

Both the limit order book in Paris and the firm quotes of the market makers in London are generally not deep enough to accommodate most of the transactions exceeding the median trade size in London. This is not surprising. Any agent who places a limit order (or displays a firm quote) is in effect giving an option to trade at a fixed price to counterparties. If a counterparty trades just as the market price moves through the limit order, or if he trades on superior information, the placer of the limit order loses out.

Thus it is not surprising to see a reluctance to provide continuous liquidity. Telephone negotiation of large deals (for smaller deals, negotiation is not worth the time and trouble) allows the market maker to check whether there

---

[4] See Ailsa A Röell (October 1988), 'Regulating Information Disclosure among Stock Exchange Market Makers', L.S.E. Financial Markets Group Discussion Paper, for a more detailed analysis.

[5] See Merton H Miller and Charles W. Upton (1991), 'Strategies for Capital Market Structure and Regulation', chapter 8 of Merton H Miller, *Financial Innovations and Market Volatility*, Blackwell, for a discussion.

**Table 2.   Market makers in French sector of SEAQ
International, June 1991.**

BZW	Barclays de Zoete Wedd	41
CCF	CCF	9
CSFB	Credit Suisse First Boston	3
CNW	County NatWest	31
LYON	Credit Lyonnais	41
ENSK	Enskilda Sec	33
GOL	Goldman Sachs	31
JCAP	James Capel	32
KLWT	Kleinwort Benson	19
LEHM	Lehman Brothers	14
MER	Merrill Lynch	17
MSI	Morgan Stanley	28
NOR	Nomura International	9
UBS	Phillips & Drew	41
RFS	Robert Fleming	28
WBG	SG Warburg	41
SAL	Salomon Brothers International	6
SNC	Smith New Court	17
SGDA	Soc Gen S.T.	27

The last column gives the number of French SEAQ International
equities in which the market maker is registered.

is anything untoward going on at the instant of trading, and also to form an
opinion about the possible trading motives of the counterparty: (Can he give
a convincing reason for needing to trade that is not based on superior information? Is he a trusted repeat customer with a good reputation? etc.) This
means that the transaction prices that can be obtained through negotiation are
typically better than the electronically displayed quotes or limit orders. And
in equilibrium, the latter are likely to be wider apart than they would be in a
market where there is no scope for negotiation.

This explains why even in Paris, very large deals must be arranged outside
the electronic limit order book. It does not explain why large deals gravitate
to London. There is no fundamental reason for there not to be well-known
large institutions in the home markets, who are prepared to trade blocks upon
inquiry, effectively acting as market makers for large deals.

Other factors

Finally, there are a number of other factors, unrelated to stock exchange
trading systems, that may explain London's advantage in large-scale dealing
even though company information and customers tend to be concentrated in
the home countries.

One contributing factor is high home-country turnover taxes, which drive
business abroad. This explains some but not all of the migration of trading
business to London. Over time, European countries have competitively

reduced or eliminated their turnover taxes. There is again a beggar-thy-neighbour element to this which could be remedied by supranational policies. For reasons that are not entirely clear to me, the relevant EC directive is aimed at harmonising these taxes down to zero. There has been no discussion of whether a turnover tax might not be a relatively attractive source of government revenue.

Some have argued that in London there is a 'culture' of taking risks and making markets, while continental financial market participants are cautious and not used to large-scale speculation. But Table 2 lists the market makers involved in French equity market making on SEAQ International: hardly an all-British collection! And similarly, in the Italian sector of SEAQ International the largest market maker is Italian (IMI). Even so, most of the skilled individuals employed in market making may well be Anglophone and unwilling to move to the Continent.

Others have argued that it is the presence of a large concentration of large financial players in London that keeps the trading business there. Still, the explosive growth of European equity trading in London is a fairly recent phenomenon. Moreover, many trades involve home-country institutions trading with home-country market makers on SEAQ International. Why go to London?

8.4 CONCLUDING COMMENTS

How and why has London's SEAQ International been able to capture such a large share of trading volume in European equities? The data on dealing spreads in this paper agree with the actual patterns of trading volume: London's advantage is confined to larger sized deals. Why is this so? Apart from London's pre-eminent position as an international centre, there are a number of innate features of the market maker based dealing system which makes it suitable for large scale deals. Amongst these, slower trade reporting seems to be a significant factor in its attractiveness to large-scale dealers. One would expect harmonisation of trade publication speeds — either through stricter EC rules or through laxer rules on the Continent — to lead to some repatriation of trading activity to the domestic stock exchanges.

Discussion

JOEL HASBROUCK

Ailsa Röell's paper is an admirable analysis of a situation neglected by conventional economic wisdom. It was long thought that securities markets were natural monopolies. This followed from the joint principles that orders would flow to the exchange with the greatest liquidity, and that the most liquid exchange would be the exchange with the most orders. While few observers would deny the existence of these forces for consolidation, it is now generally recognised that a market architecture distinct from that of the primary market may enable a competing exchange to survive by attracting a particular subset of traders. This paper characterises the London and Paris markets in French equities, and discusses their coexistence.

The paper raises some interesting points about market organisation. A distinctive feature of the London market is the absence of a public limit order mechanism, i.e., a role for the direct provision of liquidity by the trading public. The paper takes the view that the number of dealers is sufficiently large that one would not expect abnormal dealer profits due to market power. Whatever the truth of this conclusion, it is not an argument against public limit orders. Users of limit orders are generally not trying to act as dealers. They have little intention of maintaining an ongoing market presence. They are simply trying to minimise the cost of an intended sale or purchase. In contrast with dealers, there is no need for public limit order traders to make a profit on their short-term trading activity. One would therefore expect the quotes of such traders to better those of the dealers.

On the controversial issue of transparency, this paper notes that reduced transparency is privately optimal: full and immediate disclosure of the terms works to the detriment of the traders. Markets therefore have an incentive to compete by curtailing transparency. The paper's comparison to beggar-thy-neighbor tariffs, however, is particularly apt. The larger question is, supposing transparency rules to be verifiable and enforceable, what is the socially optimal level of transparency?

To take a specific example, is immediate last-trade publication optimal? For reasons already noted, the observation that trading gravitates to the market with delayed publication merely confirms the private optimality of delayed publication, while saying nothing about its social desirability. In searching for a socially optimal publication strategy, one might first ask if a unanimous consensus among traders might exist. The theoretical and practical conditions for this are not known. There is, however, some relevant historical evidence. Immediate last trade publication has long been the standard in US equity and futures markets. On all exchanges, this practice seems to have arisen endogenously, by agreement of most exchange members. Last trade publication precedes the establishment of any official regulatory bodies capable of compelling the practice. The principal US market that does not exhibit last-trade publication is the government debt market. This absence may not reflect the preferences of the participants, but may instead arise from the difficulties in imposing the requirement on a market that has been decentralised from its inception. One might draw the qualified conclusion that if it is enforceable, most market participants would prefer immediate last trade publication.

In comparing the London and Paris markets, a significant question remains unanswered. The most important public good that a market produces is the price. While the measurement of the value of this information good is not obvious, it may be easier to assess the relative value of the prices produced in two different markets. Put simply, to what extent do transaction prices (or quotes) in one market lead or follow those in another market? The relative amounts of trade information that actually get incorporated into future prices would give a good indication of which market is producing the larger public good.

Part V

The Limits Of
International Regulatory
Coordination

Chapter Nine

The Market for Markets: Competition between Investment Exchanges

CAROLINE BRADLEY

9.1 INTRODUCTION: INTERNATIONALISATION — FOCUS ON EXCHANGES

The internationalisation of financial markets has dramatically increased opportunities for competition between investment exchanges, including stock exchanges and futures exchanges and between investment exchanges and non-exchange trading facilities, such as those provided by the Association of International Bond Dealers ('AIBD') for the eurobond market, or those of the London Stock Exchange's automated quotation system, SEAQ, and SEAQ International. This paper considers the advantages and disadvantages of this increased competition, and suggests that regional and international harmonisation of the regulation of securities and futures activity should preserve these advantages, enhancing efficiency,[1] while dealing adequately with the disadvantages, ensuring that the interests of investors are not harmed.

Politicians and regulators assume that significant benefits are produced by the attraction of financial services business, and often express concern that the imposition of rules which are too restrictive will drive business away to

---

[1] Although, for arguments that capital markets tend to be speculatively efficient, rather than allocatively efficient, see, e.g., Stout, 'The Unimportance of Being Efficient: An Economic Analysis of Stock Market Pricing and Securities Regulation', 87 *Michigan Law Review* 613 (1988).

other jurisdictions where the rules are less severe.[2] Financial services activity tends to be concentrated in locations where there are active investment exchanges, and so it is likely that governments which wish to attract financial services activity to their territory will wish to encourage the development of investment exchanges there. The most obvious gains which accrue from financial services activity are invisible earnings but because it is difficult to quantify these gains, they may not be as significant as politicians like to claim. In addition, not all of the apparent gains increase welfare, for example, waste occurs when financial services firms expend resources to persuade regulators to act in their interests.[3] Rent-seeking activity is generally wasteful.[4]

9.2 COMPETITION BETWEEN EXCHANGES — BARRIERS TO ENTRY

Investment exchanges are a type of firm involved in the business of matching up prospective buyers and sellers of investments, and providing clearing and settlement systems to facilitate these deals. However, the business of investment exchanges is unusual, because part of it is to regulate. Exchanges are involved in the regulation of those who are involved in business on the exchange as market-makers or brokers, and the regulation of issuers and selling documents. Investment exchanges also usually benefit from a lack of competition from other domestic exchanges, because of barriers which prevent others from setting up competing exchanges. These barriers derive from the need for significant investment in technology, and from regulation which may require exchanges to obtain authorisation to carry on business. These barriers are arguably undesirable, because they interfere with the pursuit of efficiency,[5] but many of them are justified by those who support them on the grounds that it is necessary to protect those who deal through investment exchanges.[6] For example, the over-the-counter market for securities in the UK, a non-exchange market which was not really affected by regulation

[2] See, e.g., 'The Single European Market: Survey of the UK Financial Services Industry' *Bank of England Quarterly Bulletin*, August 1989, 407, at 409; *Review of Investor Protection* Report : Part I. Cmnd 9125, 1984, Chapter 6, para 6.11.

[3] See, e.g., Mueller, *Public Choice II*, Cambridge University Press, Cambridge, 1989, at 237: 'Both consumers and producer interests devote resources trying to convince the regulator-bureaucrats to set prices in a manner favorable to them.'

[4] On rent-seeking see idem at 229-246.

[5] See, e.g., idem at 311: 'each restriction on entry, each quota, each regulation creates an efficiency loss...' But cf. Neave, *The Economic Organisation of a Financial System*, Routledge, London, 1991 at 157: 'Market power is sometimes thought to arise from regulatory barriers to entry, but these barriers do not seem to be a very important source. History shows that regulations are usually ineffective in preventing profitable economic activity, particularly over longer time periods.'

[6] Generally, on market failure justifications for regulation, see, e.g., Neave, op. cit., pages 154-159.

until the Financial Services Act 1986 came into force, has been characterised as a market involving high risks to private investors because of the limited amount of information on some stocks, the nature of the companies involved, and the spread between bid and offer prices. It has been suggested that these difficulties were 'inevitable in an unregulated market which, for many stocks, lacks liquidity and competition.'[7]

In the UK carrying on business as an investment exchange or clearing house would require authorisation under the Financial Services Act 1986 except that recognised investment exchanges and clearing houses are exempted from the requirement of authorisation.[8] In order for an exchange or clearing house to be recognised it must satisfy certain requirements. For example, an exchange must have financial resources sufficient for the proper performance of its functions.[9] This is an example of a regulatory provision which would act as a significant barrier to entry, were the financial resources required fixed at too high a level. Other requirements which must be satisfied are that:

> The rules and practices of the exchange must ensure that business conducted by means of its facilities is conducted in an orderly manner and so as to afford proper protection to investors.[10]

In addition, the exchange must only allow dealings in investments in which there is 'a proper market', and require the provision of the proper information for determining the current value of investments;[11] there must be arrangements for clearing and recording transactions, and systems for monitoring and enforcement of compliance with the exchange's rules and for the investigation of complaints.[12] The exchange must also be 'able and willing to promote and maintain high standards of integrity and fair dealing' and to co-operate with regulators.[13] The terms in which these requirements are expressed allow to the Securities and Investments Board a significant degree of discretion in relation to the recognition of investment exchanges, and similar discretion applies to the recognition of clearing houses.[14]

Overseas investment exchanges and clearing houses may be recognised if there is:
— supervision in the country where the exchange or clearing house is situated which affords to investors in the UK protection which is 'at least equivalent' to the protection given by the Financial Services Act's

---

[7] See Bannock & Doran, *Going Public*, Harper & Row Publishers, London, 1987, at 43. See also Buckland & Davis, *The Unlisted Securities Market*, Clarendon Press, Oxford, 1989, at 123-131.

[8] See Financial Services Act 1986, sections 36-39.

[9] See Financial Services Act 1986, Schedule 4, paragraph 1.

[10] Idem at paragraph 2(1).

[11] Idem at paragraph 2(2).

[12] Idem at paragraphs 2(4),2(5), 3 and 4.

[13] Idem at paragraph 5.

[14] See Financial Services Act 1986, section 39(4).

provisions dealing with recognised investment exchanges and clearing houses;[15]

— capacity and willingness to co-operate with the supervisory authorities in the UK;[16]

— adequate arrangements for co-operation between the supervisory authorities in the country where the exchange or clearing house has its head office and the UK;[17] and

— equal access to the financial markets in the foreign country concerned for people from the UK and people from that other country.[18]

Overseas investment exchanges and clearing houses are subject to a range of obligations to provide information to regulators in the UK,[19] and they must pay an annual fee.[20] A recognition order may be revoked, and the grounds for revocation include the ground that it appears that revocation is desirable in the interests of investors and potential investors in the UK.[21] The Chicago Mercantile Exchange was recognised as an overseas investment exchange in August 1989, and other recognised overseas investment exchanges include the Sydney Futures Exchange and National Association of Securities Dealers Automated Quotations (NASDAQ), but the criteria for recognition allow to the regulators much discretion, and may disguise real barriers to entry.[22]

Recent developments in the process of negotiation of the proposed EC Investment Services Directive[23] suggest that some Member States are keen to protect their investment exchanges from competition. This proposed Directive was intended to affect the way in which national stock exchanges operate in future, and contains provisions designed to allow firms which are authorised to provide broking, dealing or market-making services in their home Member State to join stock exchanges and financial futures and options exchanges in other Member States, although these provisions are currently controversial. However, although the proposed Directive was intended to prevent restrictions on access to exchanges from creating

[15] See Financial Services Act 1986, section 40(2)(a).

[16] See Financial Services Act 1986, section 40(2)(b).

[17] See Financial Services Act 1986, section 40(2)(c).

[18] See Financial Services Act 1986, section 40(3). This section provides that account may be taken of this factor.

[19] See Financial Services Act 1986 (Overseas Investment Exchanges and Overseas Clearing Houses) (Notification) Regulations 1987 S.I. 1987 No.2142.

[20] See Financial Services Act 1986 (Overseas Investment Exchanges and Overseas Clearing Houses) (Periodical Fees) Regulations 1987 S.I. 1987 No. 2143.

[21] See Financial Services Act 1986, sections 40(4), 37(7), 39(7) and 11.

[22] Cf. Commission of the European Communities, Research on the 'Cost of Non-Europe', Basic Findings. Volume 9., *The Cost of Non-Europe in Financial Services*, 1988 at 63.

[23] For comments on the original proposal see Explanatory Memorandum to the Proposal for a Council Directive on investment services in the securities field, COM(88) 778- SYN 176, *OJ No. C*. 43/7, 22.2.89. See also Amended proposal for a Council Directive on investment services in the securities field (90/C 42/06), *OJ No. C*. 42/7, 22.2.90 (the proposed 'Investment Services Directive'); *EC Investment Services Directive. A Consultative Document*, DTI, July 1990.

barriers to the carrying on of investment business, as the chairman of the London Stock Exchange has recently written:

A directive intended simply to extend to non-banks the rights of establishment and cross-border provision of services, as was accorded to banks in the Second Banking Coordination Directive, may be transformed by late French proposals for amendments which attempt to reinforce national bourses and push all trading onto 'organised' markets, defined in a way which could exclude SEAQ International.[24]

This suggestion that trading should be concentrated in 'organised' markets has been justified as a way of ensuring investor protection,[25] although it is clear that it can also be seen as a mechanism for reducing the amount of competition to which 'organised' exchanges are subject. The new legislation, for example, in both Belgium and Italy includes requirements designed to concentrate securities business on existing stock exchanges and diminish the trading which currently takes place involving banks away from the exchanges (in Italy around 70% of securities trading is estimated to be off-exchange).[26] A related development is the failure of European stock exchanges to agree on the implementation of a joint trading system.[27] Although investment exchanges have often been protected from competition in the past, [28] policy makers often claim that increasing the competitiveness of financial markets is an important policy goal.[29]

Although exchanges have traditionally been protected from competition, and still retain some of this protection, there has been a recent trend towards deregulation, which has included the removal of controls on commissions

[24] London Stock Exchange, *Annual Report 1991*, at 7. See also the Second Banking Directive: Second Council Directive on the co-ordination of laws, regulations and administrative provisions relating to the taking up and pursuit of the business of credit institutions and amending Directive 77/780/EEC, (89/646/EEC) *OJ No. L.* 386/1, 30.12.89. For the background to the Second Banking Directive see Zavvos, 'The Integration of Banking Markets in the EEC: The Second Banking Directive', [1988] 2 *Journal of International Banking Law* 53. See also Zavvos, 'Towards a European Banking Act' 25 *Common Market Law Review* 263 (1988).

[25] For example, comments of Jean-Claude Delespaul, Secretary-General of the Commission des Opérations de Bourse, at a conference organised by IIR Limited at the Regents Park Hilton on 24th October, 1991.

[26] Cf. 'Some recent reforms and modernisation in Italian and Belgian financial markets', *Bank of England Quarterly Bulletin*, May 1991 at 218.

[27] See, Waters, 'Bourses Build up Defences', *Financial Times*, 24.9.91, p. 25, col. 2.

[28] 'Big Bang', which occurred in London in 1986 was the result of a compromise of proceedings against the Stock Exchange for breach of rules against restrictive trade practices. See, e.g., Lomax, *London Markets After The Financial Services Act*, London: Butterworths, 1987, at 1-2; 'The Economics of 'Big Bang', *Midland Bank Review*, Summer 1987, 6.

[29] See, e.g., *Financial Services in the UK: A New Framework for Investor Protection*, Cmnd 9432, 1985, at Chapter 3, [F2]+[10]3,1,ii : 'the industry must be competitive both domestically and internationally. Regulation must stimulate competition and encourage innovation; it must be responsive to international developments and not a cover for protectionism.'

which has facilitated competition between exchange participants.[30] Until recently, the London Stock Exchange had a monopoly on company news, but
this has been removed because of the Department of Trade and Industry's
concern that this monopoly contravened the provisions of Article 86 of the
Treaty of Rome, regulating abuse of dominant positions. The Stock
Exchange has since warned listed companies that disclosures of information
to other company news agencies could result in incomplete information
reaching the market, which would entitle the Stock Exchange to declare a
period of inactive trading.[31]

Deregulation, combined with the process of internationalisation of financial markets, has provided opportunities for increased competition, but the
increasing need for exchanges to have sophisticated technology means that
there are significant economies of scale involved in the business of investment exchanges, so that the existence of a small number of exchanges is the
efficient outcome:

> In domestic terms the almost total location of physical markets in London and their non-
> replication in other regional centres is accounted for by the fact that to prosper a finan-
> cial market must exhibit sufficient critical mass. Size in turn permits scale economies to
> be enjoyed, improves market liquidity and enhances the efficiency of operations in the
> market. Furthermore different groups of markets and market participants tend to locate
> in close proximity which enables them to feed off each other and in so doing minimise
> information costs.[32]

Exchanges can improve their competitiveness and produce economies of
scale by merging with other exchanges. For example, the Chief Executive of
the London Stock Exchange has recently commented on the proposed
merger between London Traded Options Market (LTOM) and London International Financial Futures Exchange (LIFFE) in the following terms:

> The negotiations have unearthed many difficult issues, and have taken longer than we
> expected. But there is a very clear determination on the part of everyone involved to se-
> cure a thriving and profitable single financial derivatives exchange and thus strengthen
> the attractiveness of London's securities markets.[33]

Similarly, trading and information links between different exchanges may
reduce uncertainty and unfamiliarity and provide competitive advantages.[34]

---

[30] On the removal of controls on commissions, see Lorie, Dodd & Kimpton, *The Stock Market. Theories and Evidence* (2d ed. 1985); Jarrell, 'Change at the Exchange: The Causes and Effects of Deregulation, 27 *Journal of Law and Economics* 273 (1984); Miller, 'Regulating Financial Services in the UK-
An American Perspective', 44 *Business Lawyer* 323 (1989); Gower, 'Big Bang and City Regulation', 51
Modern Law Review 1 (1988); Terry, 'The 'Big Bang' at the Stock Exchange', 156 *Lloyds Bank Review*
16 (April 1985).

[31] See Waters, 'SE Warns Companies On Price-Sensitive Data', *Financial Times*, 10.12.91, p. 8, col. 1.

[32] See, McKillop & Hutchinson, *Regional Financial Sectors in the British Isles*, Avebury, Aldershot,
1990 at 44; See also, Buckland & Davis, *The Unlisted Securities Market*, note above, at 115-117.

[33] London Stock Exchange, *Annual Report 1991*, at 12.

[34] See, e.g., Cox & Michael, 'The Market for Markets: Development of International Securities and
Commodities Trading', 36 *Catholic University Law Review* 833, 862 (1987): 'Exchanges compete for
listings and for trades.'

However, such mergers and linkages involve the risk that an exchange or group of exchanges might obtain a dominant position and abuse it. The existence of real competition should benefit issuers and investors, ensuring improved services and reduced costs. However, excessive competition could cause too much volatility, which would be undesirable.[35] In addition, where competition is international, there is an increased risk that investors will encounter informational asymmetries, so governments have an interest in trying to protect their own nationals by restricting the activities of foreign exchanges and non-exchange trading systems.[36] For example, differences in accounting practices in different jurisdictions may make it difficult for prospective investors to understand and çompare information provided to them to enable them to make investment decisions.[37] Governments also see advantages in ensuring the existence of exchanges within their own territory, perhaps as the basis for a local financial centre, or in order to facilitate the raising of capital by businesses based in their territory.

9.3 COMPETITION BETWEEN EXCHANGES — REGULATION

Investment exchanges have begun to react to increased competition from other exchanges in the level of regulation which applies to activity on those exchanges. This type of competition has various elements, such as persuading governments to reduce the incidence of taxation on exchange transactions, cutting charges, and reducing transaction-reporting and disclosure requirements. Within Europe many of these tactics have recently been employed: the Netherlands abolished fixed commissions and equity turnover taxes in July 1990, Germany abolished turnover taxes at the beginning of 1991, the Paris Bourse introduced a new rolling settlement system in November 1990, and the Swedish Bourse introduced an electronic trading system in June 1990.[38] The London Stock Exchange has been particularly successful in attracting business, in particular secondary market trading of foreign equities. It has been suggested that this is because trading

[35] For a suggestion that not all types of volatility in investment markets are harmful, see, e.g., Harris, 'The Dangers of Regulatory Overreaction to the October 1987 Crash' 74 *Cornell Law Review* 927, 928 (1989).

[36] On information asymmetry see, e.g., Neave, *The Economic Organisation of a Financial System*, note above, at 135-141; Cooper & Fraser, *Banking Deregulation and the New Competition in Financial Services*, Ballinger Publishing Company, Cambridge, Massachusetts 1984, at 37.

[37] See Choi & Levich, *The Capital Market Effects of International Accounting Diversity* (1990). On the harmonisation of accounting standards see, e.g., Hopwood (ed.), *International Pressures for Accounting Change* (1989); Blanchet, 'IASC E32 and the Future of International Harmonisation of Accounting', 6 *Journal of International Banking Law* 257 (1989).

[38] Worthington, 'Global Equity Turnover: Market Comparisons', *Bank of England Quarterly Bulletin*, May 1991, pp 246-249, at 248.

costs are low in London, due to low transactions costs, and a high level of liquidity, and because of the intermediation function of market makers.[39]

The introduction of relaxed listing requirements may be an important element in this competition. For example, the American Stock Exchange has announced plans for a new market for small companies with lower listing standards to compete with NASDAQ.[40] The London Stock Exchange has produced marketing literature for a listing in London as a product which can ensure investor confidence,[41] although at the same time relaxing its rules.[42] In part, these apparently conflicting actions derive from the tension between the exchange's role as a business, and its role as a regulator. The conflict between these roles may not matter, as it is possible that the net result will be the development of rules which impose the lowest costs on issuers consistent with investor protection, which would, of course, be the ideal solution. However, competition may also be wasteful:

> When competition uses up resources, as in all non-price modes of competition, more competition need not improve social welfare on net, even when the advertising or research and development does generate useful information and improved products, since the costs of this competition can exceed the benefits it creates. When no benefits are created, as in distributional struggles or pure rent-seeking, the costs of competition are all waste, and the more competition there is, the greater the social waste there will be. This fundamental insight from the rent-seeking literature has yet to penetrate fully the Weltanschauungen of those who see competitive markets as the solutions to most social problems.[43]

Although exchanges do appear to be competing amongst themselves on the level of costs imposed by regulation on issuers and on those who deal on the exchanges, there are limits on their ability to compete in this way. The major limitation on this type of competition derives and will derive from the international harmonisation of regulation. However, the way in which harmonised standards are phrased varies, and may allow for much freedom

---

[39] See idem at 249: 'In the current liberal capital environment trading will tend to move to where market conditions are favourable. Future trends in London's market share will be an important test of the City's practitioner-guided approach to the provision of market facilities.'

[40] See Harverson, 'ASE seeks to win Nasdaq business', *Financial Times*, 13.9.1991, p. 28, col. 8.

[41] The International Stock Exchange, *A Listing in London*. See also advertisements for NASDAQ, for example: NASDAQ 'offers...the proven efficiency, liquidity and regulatory standards of a screen- based electronic market', *Financial Times*, 15 February, 1990, at 3 col 4.

[42] The Stock Exchange relaxed its rules for euro-currency securities in April 1989, and announced further relaxations to its rules, including a reduction in the length of the trading record required of companies admitted to the Official List and the Unlisted Securities Market, in February 1990. See FitzSimons, 'EC Directives change securities markets', *Financial Times* 15.2.90, p 37, col 1. The Bank of England has stated that: 'The need to maintain and enhance London's competitiveness as an international financial centre continues to be an object of the Bank's supervision.' See *Bank of England Banking Report for 1989/90*, 13, (1990).

[43] See, Mueller, *Public Choice II*, note above, at 244.

which can result in a 'race to the bottom'.[44] Within the EC, harmonised rules have been developed in many areas, including the control of insider dealing[45] and the listing of securities on European stock exchanges.[46] These directives provide for minimum standards which must be applied within the Member States, so that, if these minimum standards are adequate, investors should be adequately protected. The listing particulars directive contains a general provision that:

> The listing particulars shall contain the information which, according to the particular nature of the issuer and of the securities for the admission of which application is being made, is necessary to enable investors and their investment advisers to make an informed assessment of the assets and liabilities, financial position, profits and losses, and prospects of the issuer and of the rights attaching to such securities.[47]

In addition, this directive contains in Schedules detailed lists of information which must be required. Other directives and proposed directives allow more freedom to the Member States in determining the appropriate content of national implementing measures. For example, a provision in the amended proposal for a Directive on investment services[48] states that the home Member State's prudential rules must require sound administrative and accounting procedures and internal control mechanisms, the separation of clients' and firm's money and securities, membership of compensation schemes to protect investors, the provision of information to the competent authorities, the keeping of adequate records, and that firms are organised in such a way that conflicts of interest between the firm and its clients or between one of its clients and another do not result in clients' interests being prejudiced. This is a minimum standard which does nothing to suggest appropriate contents for these types of prudential rule. The EC is not the only

[44] On the 'race to the bottom' see, e.g., Cary, 'Federalism and Corporate Law: Reflections Upon Delaware', 83 *Yale Law Journal* 663 (1974) ; Weiss & White, 'Of Econometrics and Indeterminacy: A Study of Investors' Reactions to 'Changes' in Corporate Law', 75 *California Law Review* 551, 554-59 (1987); Fox, 'The Role of the Market Model in Corporate Law Analysis: A Comment on Weiss and White', 76 *California Law Review* 1015 (1988) at 1042-45. See also Bryant, *International Financial Intermediation*, The Brookings Institution, Washington D.C., 1987, at 129.

[45] Council Directive coordinating regulations on insider trading (89/592/EEC) *OJ No. L.* 334/30, 18.11.89; and see *The Law on Insider Dealing. A Consultative Document*. DTI.

[46] See the Council Directive co-ordinating the conditions for the admission of securities to official stock exchange listing (79/279/EEC) *OJ No. L.* 66/21, 16.3.79 (the 'Admissions Directive'); the Council Directive co-ordinating the requirements for the drawing up, scrutiny and distribution of the listing particulars to be published for the admission of securities to official stock exchange listing (80/390/EEC) *OJ No. L.* 100/1, 17.4.80 as amended by Directive 87/345/EEC *OJ No. L.* 185/81, 4.7.87, and Directive 90/211/EEC *OJ No. L.* 112/24, 3.5.90 (the 'Listing Particulars Directive', which now provides for mutual recognition of listing particulars within the EC); and the Council Directive on information to be published on a regular basis by companies the shares of which have been admitted to official stock exchange listing (82/121/EEC) *OJ No. L.* 48/26, 20.2.82.

[47] See the Listing Particulars Directive, Article 4(1).

[48] See, Amended proposal for a Council Directive on investment services in the securities field (90/C 42/06), *OJ No. C.* 42/7, 22.2.90, Article 11(1).

forum for the harmonisation of financial regulation, although it is unusual in its institutional structures which should enhance the effectiveness of its harmonisation programme. The activities of IOSCO also limit the possibilities of competition, for example, it has recently promulgated a Resolution on International Conduct of Business Principles.[49] However, IOSCO is not nearly as developed a harmonising body as the Basle Committee in the context of bank regulation.

> IOSCO has been making appreciable progress in the last few years in creating a forum for international discussion between securities regulators but has not yet proved itself as a vehicle for securing international commitment to common action. This partly reflects the diverse composition of its membership which follows from the diversity of national supervisory regimes . . .[50]

9.4 COMPETITION BETWEEN EXCHANGES — TECHNOLOGY

Much competition between investment exchanges and non-exchange trading systems focuses on the technology used by these systems, rather than on the rules they promulgate, and it is clear that this competition is generally efficiency-enhancing.[51] The provision of better clearing and settlement systems, and better information networks benefits all those who deal through an exchange, and perform an important function in reducing the systemic risks associated with securities market activity:

> The two main objectives in recent reviews of settlement systems have been: to increase efficiency and lower costs, mainly by exploiting technological advances (especially by substituting book-entry transfer systems for systems based on the movement of paper); and to identify, and then either reduce or manage more efficiently, the risks inherent in the settlement process.[52]

Moreover, it is likely that within Europe the exchanges which have the most efficient clearing and settlement systems will attract most business:

> Information technology. . .opens up opportunities for 24-hour trading on exchanges.

---

[49] Published in IOSCO News, January 1991, Vol.12, No.I, pp 9-11, reproduced in Blair, *Financial Services. The New Core Rules*, Blackstone Press Limited, 1991, at 193-196.

[50] See, OECD, *Systemic Risks in Securities Markets*, Paris, 1991, at 43.

[51] See, McGahey, Malloy, Kazanas, & Jacobs, *Financial Services, Financial Centres*, Westview Press, 1990, at 2-3: 'New technology, for example, now makes it possible to trade stocks, bonds, currency, futures, options, and other financial instruments 24 hours a day, tying together national and global financial markets more closely than ever before. Computer-based technology, deregulation, and increasing global competition are encouraging the pace of innovation in the financial industry, making new financial instruments, markets and products far more common. As a result, financial services markets and the jobs that they provide are being challenged by new forces. Routine jobs in financial services firms are less tied to any particular location, even to historically dominant centres of financial activity.'

[52] See, OECD, *Systemic Risks in Securities Markets*, note above, at 29.

This then, for example, reduces the need for so many exchanges in each time zone and will increase market turnover in those markets which remain. The freeing of capital movements within Europe may also lead to increased financial market concentration. The financial centres which most benefit from this concentration will be those which, through the successful adoption of information technology, have in place the lowest cost and most efficient markets and payments mechanisms.[53]

The Stock Exchange in London has for some time been working on a new settlement system called Taurus, which is 'thought by many to be the most important single development in London's attempts to remain Europe's leading financial centre'.[54] However, although the introduction of Taurus should improve efficiency, and offers opportunities 'to consolidate and extend London's leading position in the global securities market',[55] concern has arisen in relation to the rules which have been proposed to protect investors. Dematerialisation of shares will introduce new opportunities for fraud, which could harm investors, unless new protective mechanisms are introduced.[56]

9.5 BENEFITS FROM THE COMPETITION

The gains which financial services activity may produce for an economy have been described in the following terms:

> The financial services industry ...provides not only necessary financial services to businesses and households, but jobs, tax revenues, and economic development in its own right...Financial services jobs are especially attractive for economic development reasons, as they are environmentally benign, are more likely to provide full-year/full-time employment, and offer above average wages and salaries.[57]

Although many of these gains are gains from the financial services industry, rather than from the existence of investment exchanges, the existence of such exchanges is a central element of a financial services industry. The gains which investment exchanges produce directly include employment, on

---

[53] See, McKillop & Hutchinson, *Regional Financial Sectors in the British Isles*, note above, at 61.

[54] Waters, 'Taurus Settlement System' Likely To Miss Target Date'', *Financial Times*, 16.9.91, p 1, col 3, at col 5.

[55] See *The Uncertificated Securities Regulations. A Consultative Document*, Department of Trade and Industry, May 1991, Foreword.

[56] See idem, setting out a proposed scheme for Taurus, including provisions relating to protection of investors.

[57] McGahey, Malloy, Kazanas, & Jacobs, *Financial Services, Financial Centres*, note above, at 1.

the exchange and in firms of market makers and brokers,[58] although technology is likely to reduce employment gains in future.[59] Other direct gains accrue from listing fees required by the exchange, from charges imposed on members of the exchange and from percentage fees charged on all transactions through the exchange. In the year ended 24th March 1991, however, because of 'depressed activity levels and exceptionally high investment in new systems' the London Stock Exchange reported a deficit after tax of £5.1 million.[60] Much of the trading activity in London is in international equities which are listed elsewhere; for example, over 60% of all cross-border trading in the world passes through London.[61] The direct gains which accrue to the UK from this activity derive from income to the Exchange, although there may also be some indirect gains.

Where taxes are charged on transactions in investments these taxes benefit an economy, although, as we have seen, there is a growing tendency for these gains to be sacrificed in order to produce more activity on exchanges, and, therefore, other gains. Gains produced by increased levels of employment, and by fees charged by exchanges and taxes are easily quantifiable, but there are other gains which are less easily quantifiable, such as those which accrue to an economy from the availability to firms of sources of capital. It may be that it is easier for firms to raise capital if they are established in a jurisdiction with an active investment exchange than for firms established in jurisdictions without such exchanges. Other indirect gains accrue. On the other hand, it is arguable that where exchanges exist resources are wasted on transactions which do not contribute to the efficient allocation of resources.[62] In addition, there is much rent-seeking activity. For example, lawyers and other professionals have incentives to ensure that rules which are promulgated provide more work for them.

---

[58] See, e.g., idem at 263: 'Competition among locations for financial services jobs. . .is likely to grow in coming years. These jobs are relatively high-paying, and non-polluting. They can provide steady employment, real estate development, taxes and income to an area. As manufacturing and other traditional industries in the USA continue to show slow or negative economic and employment growth, the relative attractiveness of financial services will grow.'

[59] But see McKillop & Hutchinson, *Regional Financial Sectors in the British Isles*, note above, at 59: 'Over the last ten years UK financial institutions have generated almost nine hundred thousand new jobs and currently employ nearly 2.7 million people.'

[60] London Stock Exchange, *Annual Report 1991*, at 13.

[61] London Stock Exchange, *Annual Report 1991*, at 26. London also has 93% of cross-border trading within Europe.

[62] See, e.g., OECD, *Systemic Risks in Securities Markets*, note above, at 9 : 'it does not necessarily follow that every new financial instrument increases the efficiency of capital markets and the real economy'. Cf. Plenderleith, 'Current Issues in Securities Lending', 1991 *Bank of England Quarterly Bulletin* 225: 'London has pre-eminent strengths in a whole variety of areas which taken together underlie its role as a major financial centre. But one of its distinctive strengths has always been skill and versatility in intermediation. . .The distinctive skills which these players have demonstrated in securities lending in the London markets has made London the indisputable international centre for securities lending and borrowing, and this is a not insignificant contribution to the City's international role and its overseas earnings.'

9.6 UNILATERAL/MULTILATERAL HARMONISATION/ RECOGNITION AND COMPETITION

Within the EC it appears that investment exchanges and Member States perceive that the development of the single internal market in financial services and harmonisation of regulation of financial services activity provide an opportunity to capture business and economic gains. The Directives and proposed directives seek to eliminate barriers to entry, and to ensure that investment businesses may carry on business throughout the Community on the basis of a single authorisation. It has been argued that the achievement of the single market will produce gains which will probably exceed 200 billion ECU, which represents between 4.3% and 6.4% of the Community's gross domestic product in 1988.[63] As much as one sixth of this may be due to the creation of a single market in financial services. The prospect of such large gains to be shared out between the Member States has helped to overcome some of the collective action problems which often interfere with group decision-making.[64] However, as competition between the various exchanges develops, the situation will change, and it is likely that it will be more difficult to deal with any weaknesses in the existing rules. Regulation of activity on investment exchanges is necessary to protect investors and depositors, and it is not clear that the EC's rules are really strong enough to provide this protection.[65]

9.7 CONCLUSION

Internationalisation of financial markets creates new opportunities for competition between investment exchanges. This increased competition is desirable if it has the effect of improving the allocative, rather than speculative, efficiency of investment markets. However, competition may involve disadvantages, such as increases in volatility of the markets,[66] the lowering of standards and the reduction of protection provided to investors. Competition may also be socially wasteful, and may result in the loss by businesses of opportunities for the raising of capital. Harmonisation of rules should aim to provide for an appropriate level of competition, for example, by removing those barriers to entry which are not justified by the need to ensure an adequate level of investor protection. However, although this

[63] Cecchini, *The European Challenge: 1992 The Benefits of a Single Market*, Wildwood House, Aldershot, 1988 at 83.

[64] Although some of the proposed directives, such as the proposed Investment Services Directive, have been held up for long periods of time because of disputes about their contents.

[65] See, e.g., Bradley, 'Competitive Deregulation of Financial Services Activity in Europe after 1992', 11 *Oxford Journal of Legal Studies* 545 (1991).

[66] Cf. Smith Jr., 'Market Volatility: Causes and Consequences', 74 *Cornell Law Review* 953 (1989) at 956: 'increased volatility gives people in Washington an excuse to "fix" the markets.'

should be the aim of harmonisation, the desire of those involved in the negotiation of harmonised rules to protect their own interests tends to result in harmonised rules which achieve neither of these objectives, allowing for the maintenance of barriers to entry, without providing for an adequate level of investor protection.

Chapter Ten

International Regulatory Coordination of Banking*

GEORGE J. BENSTON

10.1 BANKING HAS BECOME INCREASINGLY INTERNATIONAL

As international trade and transactions have increased since the Second World War, so too, inevitably, has international banking. Indeed, international financial transactions have increased more than proportionately to the substantial increases in international trade. Furthermore, improvements in informational technology have made it possible for borrowers to obtain funds world wide, and funds traverse national boundaries rapidly and with few impediments.[1] These developments and their likely continuation and growth have raised concerns about the need for additional or new regulation and coordination among national bank regulators.

These concerns are addressed by considering, first, the basic theoretical reasons that might support international regulation of banking. These reasons have also been put forth to support national banking regulation. The seven reasons delineated are listed in the following section and then each is analysed and conclusions are drawn in succeeding sections. Overall conclusions are presented in the final section.

* I am indebted to Edward Kane for helpful comments.

[1] For supporting evidence, see George J. Benston, 'US Banking in an Increasingly Integrated and Competitive World Economy', *Journal of Financial Services Research*, 4 December, 1990, 331-339.

10.2 REASONS FOR DOMESTIC AND INTERNATIONAL REGULATION OF BANKING

Economic and political theory support or explain regulation in general in terms of enhancing the public interest or the self-interest of people who might privately benefit from regulation. The 'public interest' theory of regulation is based on the belief that individuals acting in their own self-interest, without regulation by government, would tend to take actions that, on balance or as a matter of public policy, would be more damaging than beneficial to society as a whole. Those who support regulation from a public interest perspective usually recognise that it is not possible to make objective interpersonal comparisons of utility that would allow one to determine when the total benefits to some people from a regulation exceeds the total cost to others. Consequently, they look to the existence of externalities (neighborhood effects), economies from government compared to individual actions, and potential damage to members of society who cannot adequately protect themselves as necessary though not sufficient justifications for government regulation. A sufficient justification could be obtained when the costs of regulation did not exceed the perceived benefits.

Public policy theory, then, would support regulation, at least initially before consideration of costs, to reduce externalities that might be derived from supporting monetary (macroeconomic) policy or result from financial collapse (often called systemic risk) and disruption of the check clearance (payments) system. Assuring the safety and soundness of individual banks also might be considered to be a reduction of an externality on the assumption that the failure of individual banks lessens public confidence in the banking system, thereby increasing systemic risk. Assurance of individual bank soundness also is justified as an efficient governmental function or to protect sound banks from runs and government supported *de facto* or *de jure* deposit insurance from losses. Finally, bank regulation might be employed to protect consumers from fraud and invidious discrimination.

The 'private interest' theory explains rather than justifies regulation. Private interests includes protection of some suppliers from competition by others, subsidies to some consumers through government actions supported by taxpayers generally, and increases in government or government officials' revenues.

Thus, seven reasons that might support domestic or international regulation derived from consideration of public and private interest theories have been delineated:

— Monetary (macroeconomic) policy considerations;
— Prevention of financial collapse — systemic risk;
— Payments system protection;
— Safety and soundness of individual banks;

— Promotion of competitive markets or constraints on competition for the benefit of some suppliers;
— Enhancement of consumer welfare, including protection from fraud and invidious discrimination; and,
— Increase in government or government officials' revenues.

I will discuss each of these reasons, with emphasis on international banking activities and the role of international regulatory coordination. Domestic bank regulation generally is considered first, because if there is no theoretical justification for domestic regulation, the case for international regulation is unlikely to be supported.

10.3 MONETARY (MACROECONOMIC) POLICY

Monetary policy might be defined as control over the money supply, control of interest rates, or allocation of credit by the central bank. Only the goal of credit allocation, if it could be achieved, would be affected by domestic bank regulation. International regulation of banks has almost no role to play for any aspect of monetary policy.

Central banks can control the money supply with open market operations, changes in required reserve ratios, and by allowing or preventing banks from borrowing reserves. Open market operations is the most prevalent method of changing the amount of high powered money in the economy. By this means the central banks can offset any action that individual banks or depositors might take. For example, consider the effects of a bank run should depositors fear that a bank or group of banks might fail. In this event, depositors are likely to shift their funds to safer banks. But total bank reserves will not be affected except when the receiving banks have different preferred or required reserve ratios than the banks from which funds are withdrawn. If depositors have lost confidence in all banks and consequently put their funds into securities the situation is unchanged because the seller of the securities will put the funds received from the sale into a bank account since it would not make sense for someone to sell an interest-bearing safe security in order to hold non-interest-bearing currency. However, even if depositors move from deposits to currency, the central bank can offset the resulting lower money multiplier with open market operations. But it is unlikely that this action would be necessary in countries with *de facto* or *de jure* deposit insurance, as depositors who believed their funds were not at risk of loss would have no reason to hold their funds in currency or run from a bank even though it might fail.

A foreign presence does not make prediction of individual bank actions more difficult. Deposits transferred from domestic to foreign banks do not affect the domestic money supply except when the foreign and domestic banks have different reserve ratios. As just noted, the central bank can offset changes in total reserves with open market operations. Frequent reporting to the central banks by banks, domestically or foreign owned, would be helpful for this purpose.

The conclusion is not changed even when the central bank chooses changes in required reserves or discount window borrowings as its preferred means of affecting the money supply. This result obtains even if the central bank does not permit foreign banks to borrow from it. Total reserves still can be changed by allowing domestic banks from borrow or requiring them to repay central bank loans.

Foreign banks' operations also have little effect on monetary policy defined as control over interest rates. The central bank may be able to control nominal domestic interest rates in the short run and real (price-level adjusted) interest rates in the very short run through open market operations. But, as just discussed, these operations are not affected by bank regulation or the presence of foreign banks. However, the effectiveness of even short-run government control over interest rates is diminished by lower transactions costs in transferring and borrowing funds worldwide. The presence of foreign banks and the international operations of domestic banks make it less costly for people to take advantage of disparities between real *ex ante* interest rates in different countries.

Credit allocation, which rarely is effective except in the very short run, becomes even more difficult to achieve when foreign banks are present, for three reasons. First, assuming that the foreign banks do not force domestic bank exits, there are more banks and thus government control of banks' investments may be more difficult to achieve. Second, investments by foreign banks may be more difficult for government officials to control, particularly when these banks operate through branches rather than through domestically chartered subsidiaries. Third, foreign banks may be somewhat better positioned than are domestic banks to avoid regulatory control over investments with out-of-country contracting. (Domestic banks, though, can effect such contracts through their overseas branches or foreign correspondent banks.)

But banks are only one of many possible channels for funds to flow among countries. Hence, if control over domestic interest rates and credit allocation are goals that governments want to pursue (however fruitlessly), they would have to exercise control over a much wider range of institutions. These credit granting entities include nonchartered lenders such as the financing subsidiaries of manufacturers and distributors (e.g., General Electric Credit Corporation), business and consumer lenders (e.g., factors and consumer finance companies), mortgage bankers, and investment bankers. Companies that sell on credit also are major lenders. Foreign banks are likely to grant relatively little of the credit offered in most countries; hence, control over them is unlikely to be of much importance for this macroeconomic goal. In any event, should a government attempt to allocate credit, it could require foreign banking organisations to conform to credit allocation regulations and reporting requirements that apply to domestic banks. International coordination would not be useful for this purpose.

10.4 PREVENTION OF FINANCIAL COLLAPSE — SYSTEM RISK

In the past, domestic financial systems have collapsed when a major bank or a group of banks failed. The primary reason for systemic collapse is fractional reserve banking rather than faulty or insufficient regulation. When a bank was thought to be insolvent, people withdrew their funds and held currency and gold, which resulted in a multiple collapse of the money supply, a liquidity crisis, additional failures, and economic distress. Runs exacerbated the situation when funds were withdrawn from solvent banks. If regulation could make banks failure proof, this situation could be avoided. To this end, banks might be required to hold only securities that could be sold in the market for a close-to-certain price and have equity capital sufficient to absorb almost all expected declines in the price of these securities. This 'narrow' bank would have to have a duration-balanced portfolio of securities and deposits such that changes in interest rates would not affect the net value of the equity.[2] Note that banks would no longer make business loans, a change that would profoundly alter the business of banking. If a country wanted to change to this form of banking, it could similarly restrict the domestic operations of foreign banks. Although few foreign banks are likely to change their operations so radically to gain the advantage of operating in another country, they could establish separately chartered subsidiaries in a country that required narrow banking. In this event, there would be no advantage to international regulation or coordination.

However, narrow banking or bank regulation of any kind is not necessary and certainly not for preventing domestic systemic collapse. A multiple collapse of the money supply cannot happen now unless the central banks allows or causes it. Gold is no longer the basis for the money supply and people cannot and need not hold currency out of the banking system. As noted above, depositors who fear a bank's collapse can withdraw funds, but these would be redeposited in another bank — there is no depletion of deposit reserves, hence no contraction of the money supply. In any event, the central bank can offset any 'run to currency' with open market operations. Thus, the domestic situation is not affected by depositors' confidence in individual banks or the banking system.

---

[2] For a description of the narrow bank and a related alternative, collaterized deposits, see George J. Benston, R. Dan Brumbaugh, Jr., Jack M. Guttenag, Richard J. Herring, George G. Kaufman, Robert E. Litan, and Kenneth E. Scott, *Restructuring America's Financial Institutions*, Washington, DC, The Brookings Institution, 1989.

International banking and fund flows do not alter this conclusion. The collapse of a foreign bank with an office or subsidiary in another country is no different from the collapse of a domestic bank — to customers, it is just another bank. Transfers of funds to foreign branches or subsidiaries are the same as transfers to domestic banks. The funds stay in the banking system because transfers to banks in other countries result in the funds returning to the domestic system directly or through central banks. Furthermore, the central bank can offset any shortfall caused by delays or runs to currency. Finally, the international financial markets cannot collapse as a result of bank failures, as there is no international currency and there cannot be a multiple collapse of the money supply. Should the European Community adopt a common currency, there could be a community-wide collapse should the EC central bank permit this to occur. But this is no different than a domestic systemic collapse as the EC would have become simply a domestic economy much as the USA is a single economy.

10.5 PAYMENTS SYSTEM PROTECTION

A negative externality could result from the disruption of the payments system which could be triggered by the collapse of a participating bank. Banks with uncleared funds in the process of transmittal to the failed bank would be unable to collect and, in turn, possibly be unable to pay banks with claims on it. Although not externalities, there is concern that the central bank and other banks could incur losses on the failed bank's uncollateralised overdrafts on its accounts with them.

International regulation is not required to deal with this situation. Rather, four actions could be taken that would substantially if not entirely alleviate the situation. First, banks that participate in the payments system should be required to have adequate capital and controls. The Bank for International Settlements (BIS) standards for controls are one means of achieving this, although the BIS supported Basle capital standard is not sufficient for this purpose.[3] Second, legal obligations should be spelled out clearly in advance. Third, government systems can charge for overdrafts, thus reducing the amounts banks allow to accrue, and insist that capital and collateral requirements apply equally to all banks, foreign and domestic. Fourth, individual

[3] A complete discussion of the inadequacies of the Basle risk-based capital standard is not appropriate here. Among the standard's major shortcomings are the lack of support for imposing half the capital requirement for home mortgages as for other private loans and the same requirement for all other commercial loans, the failure to recognize that the total variance of net cash flows rather than of individual assets is the appropriate measure of risk, and the nonrecognition of interest-rate risk. For a more complete discussion see George J Benston, 'International Bank Capital Standards,' in *Emerging Challenges for the International Financial Services Industry*, James R Barth and Phillip F Bartholomew, (eds), Greenwich, CT, JAI Press, 1991.

banks can protect themselves in private systems, much as they protect themselves from defaults by their other customers and correspondents or respondents, by refusing to deal with banks that are undercapitalised and/or insisting on adequate collateral and other means of reducing the likelihood and magnitude of loss.

International cooperation might be useful only for the managers (government or private) of a domestic payments system to be assured that foreign banks are sufficiently well run and well capitalised to be trusted. But coordination of regulation among domestic regulatory agencies would be of little value because each country's authorities are not affected by the regulations imposed on banks in other countries, except as such activities might enhance the welfare of government agencies or officials.

10.6 SAFETY AND SOUNDNESS OF INDIVIDUAL BANKS

Four reasons may be delineated for public concern about the condition and operations of both domestic and foreign banks that serve the domestic public:

— protection of depositors;
— protection of borrowers and users of other bank services;
— employee welfare; and
— protection of shareholders and debtholders (other than depositors).

An analysis of each of these concerns yields the conclusion that international regulation or coordination is not useful. After each reason for concern is discussed from a domestic viewpoint, international considerations are considered.

Protection of Depositors

In most (if not all) countries protection of depositors from losses resulting from bank failures is almost always taken to be a function of government, even though most depositors could protect themselves much as they protect themselves from losses in other investments (such as real estate, stocks, and bonds). For example, banks could offer depositors privately purchased insurance, could hold sufficient capital to make losses very unlikely, or could pay depositors amounts sufficient to compensate them for expected losses. However because governments tend to bail out depositors (in whole or in part) when banks fail, government has reason to be concerned about bank safety and soundness.

In countries such as the USA and Canada, and to a more limited extent the UK and, shortly, the European Community, governments provide mandatory deposit insurance. For depositors whose accounts are insured, the condition of the banks they use is of little concern. The deposit insurance agency and banks that pay higher deposit insurance premiums, though, have reason for concern.

A number of methods have been employed by governments and their agents to control risk taking by banks. These methods include restraints on or regulation of assets (e.g., securities and insurance in the USA, limitations on participation loans, collateral and maturity requirements) and on liabilities (such as ceilings on deposit interest rates). Some products and activities have been denied to banks (e.g., in the US commercial securities underwriting and full service transactions, travel services, insurance underwriting and some forms of sales, and direct investments). Constraints have been imposed on entry, including examining and passing on the probity of potential bank owners and prohibitions against branch banking. Banks are field examined and extensively supervised, and are required to report periodically to the supervisory agency and the public. The amount and type of capital is speci- fied, including limitations on loans to one borrower tied to capital.

It is important to note that controls on assets, liabilities, activities, and entry have often been used to reduce competition among banks and between banks and other suppliers of products and services. Furthermore, these con- trols have more often reduced rather than increased bank safety and sound- ness, as they reduce banks' opportunities for diversification, cost reduction, and revenue.[4] But, capital requirements with structured early intervention and closure rules do not have dysfunctional effects with respect to consumer welfare and are effective in reducing if not completely eliminating the cost of bank failures to depositors and deposit insurers. These requirements do not impose costs on banks (other than withdrawal of a deposit insurance subsidy if, as usually is the case, the insurance is underpriced) if nondeposit, expli- citly and implicitly insured debt that cannot be withdrawn before the bank is closed is counted fully as capital. This debt fully protects depositors. Interest on the debt is as deductible an expense as is deposit interest and depends on the risk that the debt holders face.[5]

Protection of Borrowers and Other Users of Bank Services

If entry is not constrained, the failure of an individual bank usually is less im- portant than the failure of other firms. Banks offer relatively homogeneous products. Checking and deposit accounts are almost the same at any bank.

---

[4] For a more complete discussion including examples from the USA's experience see George J Ben- ston, 'Does Bank Regulation Produce Stability? Lessons from the USA,' in *Unregulated Banking: Order or Chaos?*, Forrest Capie and Geoffrey E. Wood, (eds), MacMillan, London, 1991, pp. 207-232.

[5] For a more complete elaboration see George J. Benston and George G Kaufman, *Risk and Solvency Regulation of Depository Institutions: Past Policies and Current Options*, New York, New York Uni- versity Graduate School of Business Administration, Salomon Center Monograph Series in Finance and Economics, Monograph 1988-1, 1988. Also published in a shortened version as 'Regulating Bank Safety and Performance,' in *Restructuring Banking and Financial Services in America*, William S Haraf and Rose Marie Kushmeider, (eds), Washington, DC, American Enterprise Institute, 1988, pp. 63-99.

One bank or another may give better loan, note collection, trust, or foreign exchange services than other, but the differences are unlikely to be great and most customers do business with several banks. In contrast, the failure of the manufacturer of machines may result in the unavailability of spare parts and servicing. Many products and services have no close substitutes.

Furthermore, banks that fail or are in danger of failing often are acquired by or merged with another bank. Hence, customer relationships need not be severed. Should a failed bank be closed, its customers and employees would incur costs. But, most of these customers would be served readily by other banks or credit providers. As long as entry (particularly branching) were not constrained, most people in most communities would have other banks who were able and eager to take their business or to purchase and continue operations of the failed bank. Thus, this concern has little validity.

Employees and Shareholders

Bank employees usually have readily transferrable skills; more so than the employees of most other types of firms. Shareholders in banks have no special need for government protection. Indeed, it generally is easier for shareholders to determine what banks do and they can choose to invest elsewhere. Furthermore, government should want bank shareholders (and nondeposit debt holders) to be concerned about the failure of their bank.

International Considerations

Foreign subsidiaries can be treated the same as domestic banks (indeed, they actually are only domestic banks that are owned by foreign banks). As noted above, the Basle standards are of limited value for bank safety and soundness, except as they give domestic regulators political power to enforce higher requirements on *their* banks.

However, the branches of foreign banks pose a more difficult problem because a bank's capital is not clearly restricted to branches and assets and liabilities often are or can be shifted among branches in different countries. In this situation, a country would have to rely on the supervisor of the bank in its headquarter country or insist on and be convinced that there would be sufficient assets held in the host country to protect depositors. The Bank for Credit and Commerce International (BCCI) provides an instructive example. If the owners or managers of BCCI were considered to be unlikely to operate the bank in a safe and sound manner, subsidiaries of the bank could have been denied entry or have been taken over, much as could a domestic bank. If, as appears to be the situation, there was no effective supervision of the bank by a responsible agency, branches of BCCI should not have been permitted. This was the procedure followed in the USA, and US depositors suffered no losses.

Thus, international banking does not affect safety and soundness concerns, except for branches. A country admitting branches of a foreign bank should either feel comfortable relying on supervision of the entire bank by a responsible country or be able to seize sufficient branch assets to protect depositors.

10.7   PROMOTION OF COMPETITIVE MARKETS OR CONSTRAINTS ON COMPETITION FOR THE BENEFIT OF SOME SUPPLIERS

It is well known that competitive markets are promoted when entry (including branching) is not constrained, except for considerations of owners' probity, and when banks' assets, liabilities, activities, products, and prices are not constrained. Although the 'infant industry' argument for protecting domestic and specialised producers is occasionally invoked as justification for limitations on entry, it has little justification for developed countries (as well as most, if not all, other countries). Rather, constraints on entry and banks' activities most often are imposed to reduce competition among banks and by banks for products offered by other suppliers. Of course, such constraints are usually justified by reference to some generally accepted goal, such as reductions in bank risk to protect depositors or the deposit insurance fund. This is the present justification for the Glass-Steagall Act's mandated separation of commercial and investment banking in the USA. However, a careful review of the record and of empirical evidence reveals that this separation tends to increase rather than decrease the risk of bank failure.[6]

In particular, entry by and activities of foreign banks should not be constrained unless the purpose is to protect domestic banks or other suppliers or enhance the welfare of government officials at the expense of domestic consumers. This conclusion holds even when foreign banks are subsidised by their taxpayers, and hence have an advantage over domestic banks. Domestic consumers benefit from these subsidies, much as they benefit from any subsidies paid for by others. Similarly, domestic consumers and taxpayers do not benefit when banks in other countries are forced to have higher capital requirements or are more rigorously regulated, as the cost of potential failures would no longer be borne by taxpayers in other countries.

A political argument for constraints on foreign banks should be considered. The concern is that if they are not constrained, foreign banks might dominate and (by implication) control domestic firms and markets. But foreign banks can be controlled and their stockholders expropriated by governments. Consequently, the foreign banks have more to fear from domestic governments than the reverse. However, it should be acknowledged that, at times and in some countries, foreign banks have been permitted to

---

[6] See George J. Benston, *The Separation of Commercial and Investment Banking*, Macmillan, London, 1990.

take advantage of domestic consumers and taxpayers as a result of favours granted by government officials who shared in or expropriated the gains. In these situations, though, if the public has the political power to control foreign banks, that power would be better employed to control domestic government officials, especially bank regulators.

10.8 ENHANCEMENT OF CONSUMER WELFARE

It is (or should be) well known that competitive markets are the most effective means of increasing consumer welfare, in the absence of significant externalities. When markets are competitive, consumers have many suppliers vying to serve them, price is likely to reflect marginal cost (monopoly pricing is not possible), and resources are likely to be allocated efficiently, given consumer wealth. The analysis presented above leads to the conclusion that externalities caused or exacerbated by banks can be dealt with effectively without banks being regulated as long as a bank's capital is sufficient to absorb losses that it might incur. However, possible societal goals of wealth redistribution and prevention of invidious discrimination also should be considered.

If wealth redistribution were a goal accepted by a nation, regulation of banks might be desirable if it could efficiently further the goal. But, individuals' demand for banking services is likely to be a positive function of their wealth. Furthermore, theory and a considerable body of evidence indicates that resources are not effectively reallocated to the poor by means of price, asset, liability, or activity regulation.[7]

Protection of individuals against invidious discrimination might be considered to be a societal goal. In general, competitive markets are the most effective means of preventing people from being hurt by bigots, as suppliers benefit from providing goods and services to consumers regardless of the consumers' financially irrelevant personal characteristics. However, if anti-discrimination laws applied to banking services are considered to be desirable, they can be imposed equally on domestic and foreign banks. International regulation or cooperation is of no value for this purpose.

However, a reduction of criminal activities such as money laundering, tax evasion, and the transfer of resources to more lenient jurisdictions, probably would be enhanced by international cooperation directed at these concerns.

[7] For a review of and references to much of this evidence, see George J. Benston, 'Federal Regulation of Banking: Analysis and Policy Recommendations,' *Journal of Bank Research*, 13 (Winter) 1983, pp. 216-244 or an updated version, 'Why Continue to Regulate Banks? An Historical Assessment of Federal Banking Regulation,' *Midland Corporate Finance Journal*, 5 (Fall) 1987, pp. 67-82.

10.9 INCREASE IN GOVERNMENT'S OR GOVERNMENT OFFICIALS' REVENUES

Banks may provide revenues to government in three ways. First, their net profits may be taxed. Second, they may be required to keep non-interest-bearing reserves with the central bank or hold government bonds, determined as a percentage of deposits. Third, they may be forced to make loans to government units at less than market rates. All three sources of revenue could be increased were only a single monopoly bank or a small banking cartel permitted and if alternative providers of banking services could be constrained effectively. However, if a profitable monopoly or cartel is not feasible, government revenue would be enhanced when entry and bank products and activities are not restrained. Total bank profits would be maximised in this situation, which in turn would maximise total income taxes imposed on banks. Taxes on bank money and services also would be maximised as the total quantity and value of these products results from competitive markets. However, loans by banks to government units would be more readily forthcoming where entry into banking is limited. Government officials then could offer prospective entrants charters if they agree to make such loans or threaten banks that balk at making loans with having their charters withdrawn.

Government officials' welfare similarly can be enhanced when entry is constrained and banks are regulated. International banks, though, are likely to be less susceptible to government officials' actions to transfer wealth to themselves or their supporters, particularly if the banks are supervised in their home countries by honest and competent officials.

However, international banks (and international corporations generally) might find it easier than national corporations to evade or avoid taxes and regulations of some types (such as exchange rate controls) by selectively booking transactions outside the country. International coordination might be helpful to reduce such activities.

10.10 CONCLUSIONS

The analysis presented above leads to the general conclusion that international regulation does help reduce negative externalities, in large measure because the relevant externalities (such as financial collapse and bank runs against solvent banks) can be dealt with effectively by measures that do not require regulation or control of financial institutions. Other public benefits, such as protection of depositors, enhancement of competition, avoidance of invidious discrimination, and increases in government revenues (other than with underpriced loans) are reduced rather than increased by government regulation. In any event, international regulation and cooperation add little to domestic regulation. Nor is there any reason to believe that, in general, such additions to bank regulation serve to counter harmful regulations (as is suggested by the theory of the second best).

To summarise, international regulatory coordination is *not* useful for:

— monetary (macroeconomic) policy;
— prevention of financial (systemic) collapse;
— payments system protection;
— safety and soundness of individual banks (not foreign branches);
— promotion of competitive markets;
— enhancement of consumer welfare; and
— increase in government or government officials' revenues.

But international regulatory coordination is useful for dealing with concerns about:

— the safety and soundness of domestic branches of foreign banks;
— tax and regulatory avoidance and evasion by banks; and
— illegal activities, such as money laundering and tax evasion by banks' customers.

Discussion

ALFRED STEINHERR

Professor Benston is a firm advocate of unregulated banking. Once this view is taken it seems quite obvious to take a further step and see no advantage in the international coordination of regulations. He finds international regulatory coordination only useful for (a) safety and soundness of branches of foreign banks; (b) reduction of tax avoidance and evasion of banks; and (c) control of illegal activities, such as money laundering.

This view is claimed to be backed up by theory and by empirical evidence. The theoretical support derives from the general result in the theory of value that a competitive equilibrium is Pareto optimal — more on this below. The empirical evidence is not totally conclusive as it can only demonstrate the problems associated with regulations, but not the benefits of the as yet unobservable free banking. Nobody would doubt that regulations can be sub-optimal, as amply demonstrated by the crisis in the US Savings and Loans industry.

We are, therefore, left with theoretical arguments. In markets such as banking, where problems of asymmetric information, incomplete markets, and hence of moral hazard and adverse selection, abound, it is somewhat intrepid to rely on general perfect competition results. This reviewer is reminded of the well-established presumption in favour of free trade, for a long time interpreting the differences between theoretical wisdom and the real world as being simply due to a lack of understanding. More recently the theory of international trade has successfully incorporated elements of imperfect competition and strategic behaviour, providing support for certain types of interventions and policies.[1]

Until a decade or two ago, the competitive equilibrium model and its derivative welfare theorems represented the core wisdom of economics. Then it was felt safe to claim that competitive equilibrium was best in a precise sense. In the meantime economists have tackled difficult but very real problems related to the distribution and acquisition of information, entry and exit, the degree of rationality and have analysed product differentiation.

[1] See, for example, P Krugmann, *Rethinking International Trade*, Cambridge, Mass, MIT Press, 1990.

The result is that the general case in favour of unregulated competition is less solid than once thought. Hence, Professor Benston's claim of a general support for his views is not obvious in the light of more recent theory.

Once informational problems are introduced the results of the general competition model break down. As shown by Rothschild and Stiglitz[2], even the existence of equilibrium is problematic and even if it exists it may not be a market-clearing one[3] but may involve credit rationing.

As for entry and exit, the absence of complete futures markets implies that agents must form expectations about the behaviour of other agents, and the optimality of atomised decision-making may vanish.[4] As for product differentiation, it is easy to construct examples in which market economies produce too many varieties.[5] These examples are comparable to some results of 'excessive volatility' correlated with a lowering of transaction costs.

We are, moreover, warned by the theory of second-best that in an imperfect world generalisations about gradual market liberalisation are hazardous. Let me just pursue one example. The Bundesbank has retarded financial innovation (e.g. development of money market instruments) with the concern about its ability to control monetary aggregates. And, indeed, the Bundesbank has been quite successful in pursuing its goal of price stability. Regulation may have been the necessary price to pay for price stability. Note that the other contenders for top prize for delivering price stability are Switzerland and Japan, who also regulate their financial industry quite strictly. Price stability may thus be an externality of the financial sector, captured by stern regulation. On what basis can we then be sure to advance the proposition of unregulated banking? I am convinced that other reasons discarded by Professor Benston, such as stability of the banking system, also justify some regulatory action.

It is also puzzling that the correlation between deregulation and economic performance is quite weak. For example, Japan did not pay the price of low economic growth for regulating its financial industry severely. Nor did depositors or tax payers pay the price of bank failures. I therefore remain unconvinced by the arguments in favour of free banking. Once one argues in favour of national regulation, it is of course easier to justify international harmonisation or cooperation of regulatory actions, be it only in favour of a levelled playing field.

A good example is provided by the European endeavour to create an integrated financial market for the Community. Without harmonisation of basic

[2] M Rothschild and J Stiglitz,' Equilibrium in Competitive Insurance Markets: An Essay on the Economics of Imperfect Information', *Quarterly Journal of Economics*, November 1976.

[3] J Stiglitz, 'The Causes and Consequences of the Dependence of Quality on Price', *Journal of Economic Literature*, March 1987.

[4] W Novshek and H Sonnenschein, 'General Equilibrium with Free Entry: A Synthetic Approach to the Theory of Perfect Competition', *Journal of Economic Literature*, September 1987.

[5] M Spence, 'Product Selection, Fixed Costs, and Monopolistic Competition', *Review of Economic Studies*, June 1976.

principles, as embodied in the Second Banking Directive, and specific accompanying coordinated regulations, as in the Solvency Ratio Directive, the whole enterprise would not have been possible.

Another example is provided by international cooperation in the area of payments systems. In diametric opposition to Professor Benston, Folkerts-Landau[6] concludes:

> Since many of the liquidity risks cannot be directly controlled by individual partici-
> pants, it is unlikely that market forces alone would produce international payment
> arrangements that would adequately manage the systemic risks. Private cooperative
> arrangements without central bank involvement are unlikely to reduce systemic risk to
> acceptable levels, because the power of private clearing houses to impose restrictions
> on members, as well as to provide liquidity occasionally required by members at
> closing time, is limited. Furthermore, the ability of private financial institutions to
> undertake regulatory arbitrage (i.e. relocate activities to a less regulated environment)
> suggests that cooperation between major central banks will have to be an important
> element in the management of payments system risks. Central bank cooperation in the
> strengthening of the international payments would complement the cooperation that
> has already been achieved in the area of bank supervision and monetary policy.

The debate is therefore certainly not a closed one and I am convinced that Professor Benston will remain one of the main contributors to the debate, forcing those too hastily inclined in favour of more regulatory cooperation to think more carefully about it.

---

[6] D Folkerts-Landau, 'Systemic Financial Risk in Payment Systems', International Monetary Fund, June 1990, page 26.